TODAY

Thomas S. Haggai

The contents of *Today* is a compilation of essays previously published in the
GROCERGRAM, a monthly magazine of IGA, Inc.

THOMAS NELSON PUBLISHERS
Nashville

Published in Nashville, Tennessee, by Thomas Nelson, Inc., and distributed in Canada by Lawson Falle, Ltd., Cambridge, Ontario.

Printed in the United States of America.

Scripture quotations are from the NEW KING JAMES VERSION of the Bible. Copyright © 1979, 1980, 1982, Thomas Nelson, Inc., Publishers.

1 2 3 4 5 6   92 91 90 89

THE READERS COMMENT

Tom Haggai is a bonus.

Several years ago our company, Federated Foods, Inc., was selected by the Board of Directors of the Independent Grocers' Alliance to be their official broker. It has proven to be mutually beneficial. As we've worked together, we've become better and better acquainted with the officers of IGA and especially their chairman.

We've found there was a dimension beyond business, for Tom Haggai has been gifted with an inspirational type of leadership that somehow can bring encouragement in a time of decision, calmness amidst complexity. He is a friend, and that's what you feel the first moments you hear him in a speech or reading his monthly editorials in the *IGA GROCERGRAM*.

As IGA prepared for its 60th Anniversary, we wanted to say "thank-you" for our relationship in a tangible and lasting way. Thus, we commissioned a collection of the editorials of Tom Haggai since the moment he assumed the mantle from IGA's founder, the late J. Frank Grimes, and present them to you as a "starter" for each business day.

> Richard H. Albrecht
> President and C.E.O.
> Federated Foods, Inc.

"A page from my dog-eared copy of Tom Haggai's *Today* cuts through a cluttered world each morning for one single but peaceful minute. It's a message of value, and I'm delighted that Tom has added Saturday and Sunday to the second edition."

> Russell L. Ray, Jr.
> Vice President-General Manager
> Commercial Marketing
> McDonnell Douglas

"Whether it be high school students, college graduation classes, business leaders, parents, or grandparents, I've never known another person who could inspire people of all ages and walks of life as Tom Haggai does. The pages of *Today* are filled with that inspiration, and his life is a personal example."

> Dr. Charles Runnels
> Chancellor
> Pepperdine University

"As Eastern entered the uncharted waters of deregulation, I reached out to Tom Haggai to help our people see life through his eyes—eyes that look at what others call disappointment and see instead God's appointment. Taking a few minutes each day to read a page from *Today*, you will discover the reason I consider Tom to be a valuable asset in our contemporary, competitive society."

> Col. Frank Borman

INTRODUCTION

Tom Haggai is gifted with the ability to be inspirational without being "preacherish." Have no doubt about it, he senses very keenly his calling by God to be a minister—and leaving the local pulpit in 1963 in no way diminished that commitment. Now, as an individual who is highly involved with commerce of every type in this country as well as other countries throughout the world, he effectively blends strong economic convictions with warm compassion.

In his leadership role as CEO of IGA, Inc., Tom works tirelessly to improve food industry business relationships and to harmonize the interests of manufacturers, wholesalers, retailers, and consumers. In the new era of the global village, Tom has positioned IGA to advance the entrepreneurial spirit worldwide. Already it has been established on both ends of the Pacific Rim in Japan and Australia. Now Tom is looking to Europe in 1992.

In these essays, Tom aptly illustrates that being humane does not mean being inefficient; that being ethical does not retard profits; that being pleasant is not a sign of softness. It greatly pleases me that these editorials, written for the IGA family of seventeen wholesale companies and approximately three thousand retail stores across the country, are now being shared with the rest of us.

Robert O. Aders
President
Food Marketing Institute
Washington, DC

PROLOGUE

Some years ago a prominent neurosurgeon told me he was convinced that what each of us thinks the first five minutes of every day determines the entire day. Viewing my own life, I agree with his conviction, since I work diligently to start the day and finish the day properly. Somehow, when the beginning and end are in synch, all parts in between seem to fit in place, including unexpected events.

In the hope of contributing to the start of your day, I have compiled this group of essays. It would be presumptuous to ask for all five of your important first minutes, but I offer a reading for a minute or two each day that might be beneficial.

These writings began in 1968 as editorials for the *Grocergram,* our monthly magazine at IGA, Inc. It was the tradition of J. Frank Grimes, who founded the Independent Grocers Alliance over six decades ago, to write the editorial page. He distinguished this corporation as "a movement for entrepreneurs" that was moved by inspiration. During his thirty years at the helm, he would periodically compile the editorials in book form. As we approached our sixtieth Anniversary in 1986, Rich Albrecht, chairman of Federated Foods, the designated broker of our owned brands, insisted he underwrite the first compilation of my essays since humbly accepting Mr. Grimes's mantle. Your response to the first edition published by the Ideals Division of Thomas Nelson overwhelmed me. With the prodding of Sam Moore, the head of Thomas Nelson, you now have this revised and enlarged second edition.

My gratitude continues for Rich Albrecht; Ron Humiston of Wetterau Communications Group who updated the early essays; Earle Ludgin, an old friend and master wordsmith; Mary Helen Batten, my executive secretary for over twenty years; and most especially, the lady of my life and my colleague, Buren.

Now, I thank you—the reader—for letting me spend a few moments with you each day, for sharing my thoughts and convictions. And I invite you to join me in my daily prayer of nearly forty years:

"Oh, God, don't let me die until I'm dead!"

Thomas S. Haggai
Chairman and President
IGA, Inc.

The beginning of a new year is traditionally the time for making resolutions. Such resolutions are worth making whether or not we are successful in keeping them. Our personal goals may prove too challenging to reach, but we are somehow better for making the attempt.

The following resolutions can serve as worthy aspirations for all of us, as we chart the course of our lives for this year and all the years ahead:

- I will live by the premise—if I expect increased productivity from others, I must expect the same from myself.
- I will realize that the most important resource in reaching my goal is my interrelationship with my fellow man. Therefore, I resolve to bridle my tongue from criticism, but give it loose rein in praise. What I say about others reflects how I think of myself.
- I will refuse to take advantage of any situation that gives me quick gains but reflects adversely on my long-term reputation. I will reject any situation that compromises my morals.
- I will strengthen my belief that the Creator has endowed me with creative powers. Therefore, I will strive to be positive, instructive and developmental in confronting problems; and I will retain my composure in the midst of crisis.
- I will not adopt morals merely to satisfy the law; nor will I tell half-truths that are more damaging than whole lies. For I believe that my intentions, though unseen, are more important than the act that is seen.
- I will make it my intention to be candid, yet warm; understanding, though forceful; objective, yet personal.
- I will underline the word "united" in the United States, believing it is my responsibility as part of the total fabric of our society to work co-operatively with my fellow citizens. I will keep the lines of communication open with those I disagree with, and not let friendship keep me from being objective with my friends.

The past has its lessons. The future has its promise. The past has been good, but the future can be the best if we remember that today is the first day of the rest of our lives.

At times, we might wish we knew in exact detail, or at least in general terms, what the coming year holds for each of us, for our families, for our businesses. Perhaps, it is best that we don't know, for there is nothing quite so exciting as hope and anticipation. One thing is certain— we will all have our share of laughter and our share of tears. Whether laughter or tears exert the most control on our lives will reveal our personal attitude toward life.

"The Wisdom of Solomon" is much more than a time-worn expression. The wisdom contained in Proverbs, Song of Solomon and Ecclesiastes is ageless and eternal. The following verses, particularly apropos as we enter a new year, have guided the lowly and the great for centuries:

> To everything there is a season, and a time to every purpose under heaven:
> A time to be born, and a time to die; a time to plant and a time to pluck up that which is planted;
> A time to kill, and a time to heal; a time to break down and a time to build up;
> A time to weep and a time to laugh; a time to mourn and a time to dance;
> A time to cast away stones and a time to gather stones together; a time to embrace and a time to refrain from embracing;
> A time to get and a time to lose; a time to keep and a time to cast away;
> A time to rend and a time to sew; a time to keep silence and a time to speak;
> A time to love and a time to hate; a time of war and a time of peace.
> What profit hath he that worketh in that wherein he laboureth?
> I have seen the travail which God hath given to the sons of men to be exercised in it.
> He hath made everything beautiful in His time: also He hath set the work in their heart, so that no man can find out the work that God maketh from the beginning to the end.
> I know that there is no good in them, but for a man to rejoice and to do good in his life.

The wisdom of Solomon suggests that we would be wise to live one day at a time; to take one step at a time; to live each hour for its total worth; to make the most of this new year.

T he world is a great book," it has been wisely said, "and the years are the pages. Page 'year-end' is closed. The entries have all been made and the accounts closed."

What a wonderful way for us to start the new year—to close all accounts and begin anew with our spirits and enthusiasm running high; to make plans and resolutions so that this year will be better than the last. As we look back on the pages of the past year, we see blots and erasures, corrections and mistakes. Somewhat sheephishly we have to admit that we handled ourselves and our lives like amateurs.

But as we enter a new year, the pages are clean and white. Let us mentally resolve to keep them that way, unblemished by the stain of failure or the smudge of omission. We seldom err with intent, more often with carelessness and neglect. Perhaps the following "Resolutions Concerning Myself" that I authored a number of years ago will provide you with some positive direction as you turn the pages of the coming year:

I will be joyful, that life may give me wings. I will be courageous, that there will be no binding fears. I will be balanced, that neither work, nor play, nor rest, nor worship shall lose its proper share. I will be self-reliant, that thoughts of failure shall not hold me back. I will be self-controlled, that emotions shall not be dominant. I will be intelligent, that straight thinking and knowledge shall direct all actions. I will be healthy, that my body shall not fail to respond. I will be clean in spirit, mind and action, that there shall be not shame. I will be good-tempered, that annoyance shall not irritate. I will be patient, that discouragement shall not seem final. I will be persistent, that my will may carry through to completion. I will be prepared, that an emergency shall not find me in confusion.

If we, as honest stewards of our time and effort, could live up to even half of these resolutions, this new year will be successful in spite of ourselves.

An anonymous writer gave us these words:

We are but minutes, little things,
And each is furnished sixty wings,
We are but minutes, use us well,
For how we're used, you'll one day tell.

The beginning of a new year is the perfect time to resolve to use time efficiently. Time, our only non-recoverable resource, lies before us as a new beginning. Of all my resolutions, I make none as often as the desire to use my time more wisely. Gerald B. Klein has these suggestions:

Today is here. I will start with a smile and resolve to be agreeable. I will not criticize. I will refuse to waste my valuable time.

Today . . . in one thing I know I am equal with all others . . . time. All of us draw the same salary in seconds, minutes and hours.

Today I will not waste my time because the minutes I wasted yesterday are as lost as a vanished thought.

Today I refuse to spend time worrying about what might happen . . . it usually doesn't. I am going to spend time making things happen.

Today I am determined to study to improve myself, for tomorrow I may be wanted, and I must not be found lacking.

Today I am determined to do the things I should do. I firmly determine to stop doing the things I should not do.

Today I begin by doing and not wasting my time. In one week I will be miles beyond the person I am today.

Today I will not imagine what I would do if things were different. They are not different. I will make success with what material I have.

Today I will stop saying, "If I had time" . . . I know I never will find time for anything. If I want time, I must make it.

Today I will act toward other people as though this might be my last day on earth. I will not wait for tomorrow. Tomorrow never comes.

If you are depressed or bored or disgusted, today is the exact and perfect moment to change all that. Right now, resolve to make this the best year of your life.

The race is not always to the sprinter, but to the one with endurance who becomes the finisher. Dr. Napoleon Hill, author of the classic book, "Think and Grow Rich," emphasized the importance of persistence. He wrote:

One of the most common causes of failure is the habit of quitting when one is overtaken by temporary defeat. Every person is guilty of this mistake at one time or another.

An uncle of R.U. Darby was caught by the "gold fever" in the goldrush days and went west to dig and grow rich. He had never heard that more gold has been mined from the thoughts of men than has ever been taken from the earth. He staked a claim and went to work with pick and shovel.

After weeks of labor, he was rewarded by the discovery of shining ore. He needed machinery to bring the ore to the surface. Quietly he covered up the mine, retraced his footsteps to his home in Maryland, and told a few neighbors of the "strike." They got together needed money for the machinery and had it shipped. The uncle and Darby went back to work the mine.

The first car of ore was mined and shipped to the smelter. The return proved they had one of the richest mines in Colorado! A few more cars of that ore would clear the debts and then would come the big profits.

Down went the drills! Up went the hopes of Darby and his uncle. Then something happened. The vein of gold disappeared! They had come to the end of the rainbow, and the pot of gold was no longer there. They drilled on, desperately trying to pick up the vein again . . . but to no avail. Finally they decided to quit.

They sold the machinery to a junk man for a few hundred dollars and took the train back home. The junk man called in a mining engineer to look at the mine and do a little calculation. The engineer advised that the project had failed because the previous owners were not familiar with "fault lines." His calculation showed that the vein would be found just three feet from where the Darbys had stopped drilling! That is exactly where it was found!

Success is a key word in America's language. We build statues of the successful. We hang portraits of the successful. We have annual banquets honoring the city's most successful of the year: "Outstanding Young Man." "Outstanding Salesman." "Outstanding Farmer." But you have the right to be a failure.

We believe we are people of free choice so that includes freedom to fail. It's not easy to be a failure for many forces of society keep pushing you upward. However, today we are doing a better job protecting the lazy and even making it possible in some instances to make about as much money not working as working.

To be a successful failure, you can't just drop out, grow a beard, and disappear. Doing this, no one will know you're a failure. The success of failing is when people recognize your achievement. You must be able to show your "dunce cap."

Following are some rules for failure:

Don't let the boss push you around! React negatively when you see that successful guy next to you taking orders from the boss. After all, you know your job as well as the boss, and if you try too hard, you'll get tight inside and be tense when you get home. You want to be where you can sleep at any time—even on the job. A real failure is able to daydream so effectively he can even create a human accident or ruin a machine because he's building dream castles.

To be a failure, it's easier if you have many jobs. After all, it's only when you go from job to job that you can prove you're failing. The habit of changing jobs probably started when you were small. You never finished what you started—whether it was a model plane, homework, painting, and so on. Being a failure means it doesn't matter to you that changing jobs means loss of retirement, loss of hospital benefits, or loss of respect for credit reference.

To be a failure who is really genuine, talk a good game. Talk, talk, talk about the new job you are getting, how you'll be rich tomorrow, how the big break is coming—but do nothing about it today.

Most of us will not accept failure. If we do fail, we'll start again. The true failure is different. He or she is a "Yeah, but . . ." person. "Yeah, I could do what he does but . . . ."; "Yeah, I could do that but it's five minutes before lunch . . . ."

The successful are thankful for the opportunity of saying, "Yes, sir, just give me the chance!"

We do like to worry, especially about tomorrow. J.C. Rice, a fine church-man of South Carolina, wrote the following article that hit me at the right time and I'd like to share it with you.

Life is a continuous adventure into the unknown. Although we do not know the future, we do know that to lose heart is to lose everything. Each new day is an unvisited country. There are at least three things about the future that are certain. It will not be like the past. It will not be like we think it is going to be. It will change faster than it has ever changed before. Progress demands change. We cannot and will not remain the same.

We should not be afraid of a new day, nor a new year. It has been said that a certain sign of growing old is when a person begins to talk more about the past than about the future. Let us, then, not linger on our thoughts of the past long enough to hinder thoughts of the future. We have drunk deeply from the fresh flowing fountains of the past. We have climbed some rugged hillsides toward the mountaintop. We have sat at the fireside of God's love and enjoyed its continuing warmth.

Now, we need to place our feet in the sparkling sea of opportunity, and resolve to run the race that is before us with poise, peace, patience and purpose. With faith in God we will anticipate, activate, and consummate the race. We can have faith, goodwill and hope. We can be generous, kind and thoughtful. We can drink deeply from the well of love and attempt to make each day better than was the day before for others and for ourselves. Each one has his own responsibilities. They belong to no other person.

Today's appointment is not tomorrow's. Tomorrow's appointment is not today's. Life is complicated. We cannot jump a mile, but we can take one step at a time. Moment by moment we can follow the Guide. Jesus said, "Follow Me!" If we halt, we become locked within ourselves; we will become stagnated. To face the future with faith and fervency will enable us to live the language of love. Someday to us, all things will be revealed. It's enough now to live and love with orders sealed.

Actually, we have security when we strive to live each day at a time and leave the worrying and planning to God.

My mother and father felt it was worth the high risk of pulling up stakes to move to Louisville, Kentucky, so Dad could study Greek and Hebrew under the tutelage of Dr. Hershey Davis. This renowned professor was dedicated to scholarship but he believed the words of Herbert Spencer, "Not education, but character, is man's greatest need and man's greatest safeguard." He defined his convictions in these words:

The circumstances amid which you live determine your *reputation*; the truth you believe determines your *character*.

Reputation is what you are supposed to be; *character* is what you are.

Reputation is the photograph; *character* is the face.

Reputation comes over one from without; *character* grows from within.

Reputation is what you have when you come to a new community; *character* is what you have when you go away.

Your *reputation* is learned in an hour; your *character* does not come to light for a year.

Reputation is made in a moment; *character* is built in a lifetime.

Reputation grows like a mushroom; *character* grows like an oak.

Reputation goes like the mushroom; *character* lasts like eternity.

A single newspaper report gives you your *reputation*; a life of toil gives you your *character*.

Reputation makes you rich or makes you poor; *character* makes you happy or makes you miserable.

Reputation is what men say about you on your tombstone; *character* is what angels say about you before the throne of God.

A.P. Gouthy said that "character is like every other structure; its weaknesses show up when it is tested. No man knows of what stuff he is made until prosperity and ease try him."

D r. Paul Tournier, a celebrated European psychiatrist, quotes a friend's whimsical observation, "God likes life; He invented it." Why then can life be so troubling and bewildering, so difficult and painful? Why isn't life filled with only sweetness and beauty, peace and happiness? Surely if we had invented life ourselves, we would have tried to make it that way. But God is in charge of the universe and thinks in much bigger terms than we can even remotely determine.

Life is a marvelous, bittersweet journey made all the more meaningful by its challenges. We can better appreciate the sunlight after we have been in the shadows. Our character grows and develops as it rises to meet life's difficulties and problems. God has built ruggedness within us to endure and keep going.

The true secret of happiness is to have something in your heart that lifts you above that which is contrary to happiness, above the frustrations, defeats and pain of human existence. We can learn to be happy in the midst of sorrow and affliction by trusting that all things work out for the best if we love the Lord.

Happiness comes, not from what we get, but from what we give. Being self-centered makes our lives small and makes us unhappy and even sick. Happiness is part of being normal; normal people experience sorrows and problems, but are able to handle and balance them.

A happy person has something real and vital to give to others. If you want to be truly happy, deliberately plan to see how much happiness you can bring to other people. Some of it will wash back on you. Knowing that we have been a part of another person's happiness is one of the greatest sources of personal happiness. Make that effort today!

Y ou might recall during World War II the campaign reminding service-men and civilians alike to guard against inadvertently aiding the enemy by divulging classified information. There were billboards picturing a sinking ship with the epitaph, "Somebody Talked," and posters of wounded troops with the reminder, "A Slip of the Lip."

The tongue, which can do so much good, can also be an instrument of destruction. This paradox is referred to in the Bible, which states, "If any man offend not in word, the same is a perfect man" and "The tongue is a fire, a world of iniquity." The same tongue that can encourage, also can discourage; the tongue that builds, also can destroy; the tongue that inspires, also condemns.

I have witnessed companies almost tumble because of a bad tongue. The near-disintegration of an entire organization may be traced to a whisper campaign aimed at the general manager; or jealous resentment vented against fellow employees; or confidential company business discussed on the street. Some mask their true intentions with the excuse, "Well, it's the truth!" The truth or falsehood of the statement does not matter if it is harmful or a detriment to their fellow man. Truth cannot be a license to injure.

Honestly ask *yourself* why you gossip. Isn't it to elevate yourself and appear somehow better than the subject of your gossip? In fact, gossip is a compliment to the person maligned, for we all tend to unite in opposition to someone we perceive as better than ourselves. We selfish beings resent genius or perfection or success in others.

The tongue also can be misused by the "needler," a coward who degrades his fellow man with thinly-veiled subtlety without calling his name. If the victim inquires, "Are you speaking of me?", the needler replies, "If the shoe fits, wear it." Wrapped in a feeling of smug security, the coward gains a perverse sense of pride and pleasure knowing that the individual attacked received the intended message. The needlers forget, however, that they are judged by the same standards they use to judge others.

Let us guard against injuring a loved one or friend or co-worker by a "slip of the lip."

Today's notion that money can solve all of life's problems is widespread and popular. Money has been described as the sixth sense without which the other five don't count. Cynics claim that money isn't the most important thing in life, but it's way ahead of second place. Money won't buy happiness, the joke goes, but it can be used as a down payment on a car to go looking for it.

These one-liners, while humorous, are erroneous. Money, of course, can buy the basic needs of the body and, depending on its abundance, provide a comfortable, secure lifestyle. But that is all!

Money will not buy self-discipline; in fact, money tends to work against the discipline needed for achieving excellence. Only the rarest individual can rise above a wealthy upbringing and live the self-disciplined type of existence that results in excellence. Money cannot buy encouragement, reassurance or satisfaction. These rewards come from God, usually through those who are his servants here on earth. Money will not buy good health. Vast amounts of money may be spent on doctors, but physicians themselves are the first to refrain from promising good health regardless of the fee. Money cannot buy peace of mind. Clinics, hospitals and the self-help section of bookstores are filled with people trying to buy peace. It can't be done! Peace stems from forgiveness, cleansing, a change of attitude and embracing a new set of values. It is God's grace, not money, which brings peace to troubled minds.

Money cannot buy real friendship—friendship must be earned. Money cannot buy good health—the secret of health comes from living right. Money cannot buy a clear conscience—the price tag is dealing honestly with others. Money cannot buy happiness. Money cannot buy golden sunsets or the singing of birds or the music of wind in the trees—these gifts are as free as the air we breathe. And money cannot buy character—character is what we are when we are alone with ourselves in the dark.

Are these the worst of times in our nation's history? I doubt it. But they aren't the best of times either. Maybe it depends on you. Faith sees the day—doubt sees the blackest night. Faith sees the way—doubt builds a dead end. Faith soars—doubt dives. Faith responds—doubt is deaf.

Let's compare our times. We are irritated when we're experiencing a blizzard and some old-timers say, "But sonny, you should have gone through the storm of 1908." We don't like having someone "top" each of our experiences, but history has a way of doing just that.

If we think America is struggling today, we should relive the dark moments of George Washington. He was leading the Colonists in a war that only one-third approved. One-third were loyal to England and the other third didn't care. General Washington's little army was torn by disease, dissension, and dissatisfaction. He pleaded with the Continental Congress for aid. He needed not only supplies but one thousand men to restore the diminishing ranks. Only one hundred raw recruits responded. History gives us a precise figure of two hundred sixty-one pairs of pants he requested. Because of not having pants in some tents, only one of ten men could respond to roll call.

Yet, it was this army that defended the cradle so we could birth our Republic over two hundred years ago. It would have been impossible except for the character and faith of the valiant few.

Today we have the supplies. We are a rich nation. But we need people of quality. We need people who cannot be bought, whose word is their bond, who put character above wealth. We need people who make no compromise with wrong, who take chances, who aren't lost in a crowd, whose ambitions aren't confined to selfish desires. We need people who do not have one brand of honesty for business and another for private life, who do not believe that shrewdness, cunning, and sharpness are the best qualities for success.

We are not in the best of times but probably not in the worst of times either. We are at a moment of history that gives our intentions and integrity a test which can be most satisfying—if we pass.

What pictures come to your mind with these words: courage, wholeness, aliveness, honesty, compassion, uniqueness, richness, reliability, understanding, reality? These words, if used to describe you, would be describing a good person . . . an admired person . . . an unusual person.

Do you remember the wealthy man who had three nephews but no sons? He wanted to leave his business and holdings to the nephew most able to carry it on. One day he summoned the three nephews to come to his office.

"One of you will be my successor . . . but only one of you," he said. "I am giving each of you a coin of great value. This room must be filled with something purchased by this coin. You must fill the room as full as possible but you cannot use any additional money. Return this evening with your report."

The nephews thanked their uncle for this trust in them, and then departed their separate ways to make their purchases.

At evening the three nephews returned to their uncle. The first nephew had bought two bales of hay and these filled half the room. The second nephew had bought two bags of thistledown which, when released, flew everywhere but, when it settled down, filled only about three-fourths of the room.

The third youth stood sadly, not anxious to report to his uncle. "And what did you purchase?" he was asked.

He replied with hesitation, "I gave half of my coin to feed a hungry child and most of the balance I felt urged to contribute to the church where I prayed. With the few cents I had left, I purchased these matches and a tall candle." With this report he lit the candle and the light filled every corner of the room.

"You alone have caused the room to be filled," said the old uncle approvingly. The young man fell to his knees as the old man blessed him and made him his successor. He demonstrated all the adjectives I used at the beginning of this story.

Longfellow wrote: "There is an honor in business that is the fine Gold of it, that reckons with every man justly; that loves Light; that regards kindness and fairness more highly than Goods and Prices or Profits."

Dear God: I'm sorry you made Sunday where you did. You see it is like this—we could attend church more regularly if your day came at some other time. You have chosen a day that comes at the end of a hard week, and we feel we should enjoy ourselves; therefore, we go out to a party, and often it is almost impossible to get up on Sunday morning. You have chosen the very day we want to sleep late. It makes it mighty hard to get the children off to Sunday school, especially when they have the dishes to wash—and we always have some things we have to wash out.

Then, too, you must think of John. He is cooped up in his office all week and Sunday morning is the only time he has to tinker with the car and to mow the lawn. When he gets into his old clothes and his hands are all greasy, you couldn't expect him to drop everything and go to church.

I am telling you these things, dear God, because I want you to get our viewpoint. It is not our fault that we are not able to get to church on Sunday morning or evening. We would like to go and need to go, but it must be clear to you that the real reason we cannot go is that you have chosen the wrong day. If you will select another day, we shall be glad to go to church and Sunday school and be more faithful.

Many of us might see ourselves in "An Open Letter to God" above, if we find ourselves searching for excuses to miss church or synagogue services week after week. We avow our desire not to influence our children in making choices and decisions in matters of religion. Yet there is no substitute for a good example. It has been wisely said that it's better to be a poor gardener than a poor parent, because we can throw out spoiled vegetables, but we have to keep spoiled children.

A person cannot make a withdrawal without first making a deposit. This elementary principle of banking carries over to other areas of living, as well. Specifically, we cannot constructively criticize another without first praising.

Praise, reinforcement, cheering and encouragement are ways to build up people and to build loyalty in people. We all cherish commendation. Praise makes us eager to give the second effort; a pat on the back translates to loyalty. Praise must be sincere, however, not empty flattery. Qualified praise can indicate that improvement is noticed, but a better job still needs to be done. Most of us need to learn one step at a time; well-placed praise can make that journey satisfying.

Criticism is difficult to take under any circumstance; it becomes impossible to take if we don't have confidence in and respect for the critic. When criticism must be made, the first step is to be controlled and collected enough to make it constructive. Unless the problem is glaringly self-evident, it is a good idea to ask questions and make certain that the facts are what they appear to be. You should be open to reasonable explanations, while rejecting weak excuses. Prior to confronting the individual, have in mind the result you want. Your goal is not to demoralize or destroy someone, but to honestly help a person see their error and learn from the mistake. You want to be perceived by people as a leader who wants to help them maximize their talents, not as a snoop constantly looking over their shoulders. Don't look for opportunities to be critical, but don't shy away from the caring that is an integral part of criticism.

Patience and understanding are the base upon which we build praise and criticism. We live on praise, but we also need criticism.

Many times each day, in the process of our day-to-day living, we exercise faith. Each time we get into a car or board a plane, we firmly believe we will arrive safely at our destination. We place trust in our doctors to treat our ills and heal us. On the job each day, we anticipate that we will successfully accomplish all we set out to do. These feelings of trust, anticipation and belief are faith in action.

Faith must precede fact if we are to function as human beings. But where to put our faith? Alastair Mac Odrum offers sound, practical advice in his essay, "The Daily Dozen":

1. Believe in yourself, for you are marvelously endowed.
2. Believe in your job, for all honest work is sacred.
3. Believe in this day, for every minute contains an opportunity to do good.
4. Believe in your family and create harmony by trust and cooperation.
5. Believe in your neighbor, for the more friends you can make, the happier you will be.
6. Believe in uprightness, for you cannot go wrong doing right.
7. Believe in your decisions; consult God first, then go ahead!
8. Believe in your health; stop taking your pulse, etc.
9. Believe in your church; you encourage others to attend by attending yourself.
10. Believe in the now; yesterday is past recall and tomorrow may never come.
11. Believe in God's promises; He means it when He says, "I am with you always."
12. Believe in God's mercy; if God forgives you, you can forgive yourself—and try again tomorrow.

Faith is worthy of the name only when it erupts into action. We can strengthen the muscles of our faith by first acquainting ourselves with God; by applying faith to problems of poverty, human ills, on-the-job troubles, tangled human relationships and the trials that beset us all. We exercise our faith when we act only with sincerity and honesty in the present, not waiting for tomorrow.

Gumption" is a somewhat old-fashioned word for a timeless virtue. In a bygone era, describing someone as having gumption was about the highest compliment that could be paid to another. Possessing gumption meant that someone was a competitor; that someone responded to a challenge; that someone ordinary acted in an extraordinary way.

While our usage of the word may have become passé, the need for gumption in modern times is as real as ever.

I am unimpressed when I hear people describe in detail the problems plaguing our country and dramatize the inequities and injustices. All that proves to me is that they read newspapers or listen to news commentators. I am truly impressed when I hear people outline how they, as individuals, are trying to do something good and worthwhile for America.

As Americans, we face many internal problems—poverty, hunger, pollution, crowded cities, drugs, crime, racial tensions, corruption, obsolete laws and confused morals. The answer is not in the reinvention of government cure-alls, but in the rediscovery of gumption by each of us individually. We can start on the blocks where we live, in our neighborhoods, in our schools, in our communities. We can begin to effect a cure as best we know how; we can begin to make a difference. Like it or not, our modern times demand that we reawaken the gumption that rests within each of us.

It has been said that the most common sin among all the people of the earth is that of ingratitude. Man becomes involved in his own selfish problems and his outlook becomes so narrow that he forgets that the very air he breathes is a free, unearned gift." These wise words are, perhaps, better illustrated by a heartwarming story.

Michael Dowling's position as a successful banker in a midwestern city led to an opportunity for him to be of help to his countrymen during World War I. He traveled to France to speak to and encourage wounded American soldiers.

He began one of his talks from the mezzanine of a large hotel. Below him on the lobby floor, on cots and in chairs, were the maimed soldiers, the crippled amputees, the blind. Mr. Dowling startled his suffering audience by belittling their injuries. His sarcastic tone quickly became insulting to his listeners. He continued on, criticizing the men for their pessimism and lack of spirit. To the growing accompaniment of boos and catcalls, he slowly began to descend the staircase. By then, the soldiers were almost driven to the point of throwing their crutches or anything within reach at him.

Unfazed, Michael Dowling continued to speak and sat down on the stairs. He began to twist his left leg with his hands and, with a quick jerk, he threw his artificial limb to the bottom of the stairway. The boos gave way to murmurs. Next, he removed his right leg and tossed it to the floor. The sheepish soldiers were dumbfounded. Now speechless, they watched as he unscrewed his left arm from its artificial socket and threw it on the heap below. Then, with a final dramatic flip of the wrist, his right hand fell to the floor. There he sat, a stump of a man. All breathing seemed to cease.

Then, in that perfect teaching moment, Michael Dowling told the story of his personal triumph over a seemingly overwhelming handicap. Eloquently, he urged the soldiers to be grateful for life and the opportunity to overcome adversity.

Few among us will ever have to make the sacrifice of Michael Dowling. Let us remember, in spite of our hardships, our suffering, our handicaps, to thank the Creator for our every blessing.

As a classroom assignment on anatomy, a 10-year-old boy described his body in detail, using a youthful imagination to compensate for shortcomings in grammar and spelling:

Your head is kind of round and hard, and your brains are in it, and your hair is on it. Your face is in front of your head where you eat and make faces. Your neck is what keeps your head out of your collar. It's hard to keep clean.

Your shoulders are sort of shelves where you hook suspenders on them. Your stummick is something that if you don't eat often enough, it hurts; and spinnage don't help it none!

Your spine is the long bone in your back that keeps you from folding up. Your back is always behind you no matter how quick you turn around.

Your arms you've got to have to pitch a ball with and also so you can reach the butter. Your fingers stick out of your hand so you can throw a curve and hold a pencil when you add up 'rithmatic.

Your legs is what, if you have not got two of you can't get to first base—neither can your sisters.

And that is all there is of you except what's inside—and I never saw that.

In the complex maturity of adulthood, we lose the refreshing simplicity of childhood. That is as it should be. And yet, we would do well to pause and seek simplicity in our thinking. Complex problems are compounded and complicated by complex answers; instead, seek solutions to complex problems with simple logic.

Of some people we say, "I liked him until I knew him better." Of others we say, "The more I know him, the better I like him." Dare I say the latter phrase is more often the case—if we take time or desire to really know someone?

In my mom's *Ole Poem Book* I found the following poem:

When You Know a Fellow

When you get to know a fellow, know his joy and know his cares
When you've come to understand him and the burdens that he bears,
When you've learned the fight he's making and the troubles in his way,
Then you find that he is different than you though him yesterday.
You find his faults are trivial and there's not so much to blame.
In the brother that you jeered at when you only knew his name.

You are quick to see the blemish in the distant neighbor's style.
You can point to all his errors and may sneer at him the while,
And your prejudices fatten and your hates more violent grow.
As you talk about the failures of the man you do not know,
But when drawn a little closer, and your hands and shoulders touch,
You find the traits you hated really don't amount to much.

When you get to know a fellow, know his every mood and whim,
You begin to find the texture of the splendid side of him;
You begin to understand him, and you cease to scoff and sneer,
For with understanding always prejudices disappear.
You begin to find his virtues and his faults you cease to tell,
For you seldom hate a fellow when you know him very well.

When next you start in sneering and your phrases turn to blame,
Know more of him you censure than his business and his name,
For it is likely that acquaintance would your prejudice dispel,
And you'd really come to like him if you knew him very well.
When you get to know a fellow and you understand his ways,
Then his faults won't really matter, for you'll find a lot for praise.

All of us will think of our church or synagogue as I list some "Things That Never Happen In Church."

Things that never happen in church:

- ushers calling for assistance in carrying the offering because of its bulk or weight.
- choirs pleading with the minister to permit them to sing at mid-week service.
- the church "sore-head" doubling his pledge to the budget.
- the finance committee rejoicing over a big increase in next year's budget without soliciting it.
- a dozen people asking the minister on Sunday for some definite church work to do during the week.
- five families arriving late and requesting the same usher at the same time to place them in the front pew.
- everyone reaching alertly for the hymn book when a number is announced and singing heartily on every stanza.
- every head reverently bowed during the prayer period.
- a volunteer choir that doesn't have one member who whispers during the service.
- the Sunday school director announcing the church has run out of room for the sixteen- to twenty-one-year-olds desiring to attend.
- "old timers" graciously enlisting newcomers for their jobs, believing they can do better.
- the minister saying, "I've never been so busy attending committee meetings, visiting the sick, calling on disgruntled members, reconciling members mad at each other, raising money for the needed new building. I really don't feel like preaching today and didn't have time to prepare, so you'll excuse this warmed-over three-year-old sermon."

Things that never happen in church—a bit of "kidding on the square" or maybe just some wishful dreaming.

A friend with keen insight told me some years back that people let me down because I believed more in them than they believed in themselves. Perhaps my friend was right; perhaps it is a fault to believe so strongly in people. My true concern is that you accept yourself and believe in yourself.

If the truth be known, I suppose I encourage others so strongly because I have struggled with self-confidence most of my life. I understand from personal experience how a lack of self-esteem can impair your life. The following suggestions have proven helpful to me, and may be to you:

1. Think more highly of yourself than you have in the past. Believe that God created in you a worthwhile, valuable person. When you view others with suspicion, you are really dissatisfied with yourself. Your attitude toward others is a mirror of how you view yourself. As you begin to respect yourself more, you will respect others.

2. Choose realistic goals for your life, goals you can achieve. Goals accomplished, no matter how small, make you feel worthwhile and, in turn, confident. Goals based on self-respect are attainable; goals that stem from self-exaltation are merely dreams.

3. Count what you do successfully and discount your failures. You can't overlook failures; rather, use them as effective teachers and learn from them. Don't dwell on your mistakes and allow them to haunt you.

4. Associate with people who are successful and self-confident. Let the positive attitudes of others rub off on you. Negative people will view you as a threat and will try to bring you down to justify their own low esteem.

5. Ensure that your job makes you happy. If your job pleases you, you will strive to be better at it, in turn gaining confidence. If your work makes you happy, you will find it easy to be productive, orderly, hardworking and honest.

6. Help others when the opportunity arises. Seeing the results of your assistance, you will gain confidence in your ability to contribute to mankind.

Believing in yourself doesn't make you a self-centered egotist. Believing in yourself gives you a sense of worth. And when you are worth more to yourself, you will be worth more to others.

Would you have had any reason to read the book *This Freedom Whence* by J. Wesley Bready? If you do see a copy, you might want to pick it up. The author is presumptuous enough to make the suggestion that our highway system, our educational system, our sanitation system and our hospital development were the result of the revival movement led by John Wesley and George Whitefield. However, I don't think that is being presumptuous. I'd rather think it is factual; and as we think ahead to this weekend and worshiping at the place of our choice, our religion has meant more to the United States than just worship centers. It has really been the basis of our freedom. Yes, there is a modern group of thinkers who try to suggest that religion may have actually prevented freedom, but such misconceptions need to be shattered because the idea of freedom came out of our religious experience. Our founding fathers believed that faith and freedom go together and one could not survive long without the other; that the founding of America's democracy and the survival of it is intertwined and intermarried with what we really believe about God and eternal matters. For years I did a lecture entitled "Patriotism Through Religion." I am a staunch believer in separation of church and state, but do not feel that means separating the state from God.

Another way to put it might be that I do not believe that God is just concerned about saving "the soul," if we consider the soul a part of a person and forget that it is the total person. When we see people as created beings of God, and see them as our brothers and our sisters, then we begin to understand why we were taught to love God with heart, soul and mind. The second commandment is very close to this . . . loving our neighbor as we love ourselves. We provide ourselves with food, clothing and shelter, so that must be our desire for our neighbor. That's why the great religious awakenings of this country have spawned the social improvements that make our nation the envy of the world.

Much has been written about the effects of change on us poor human beings. Change can be difficult for us to absorb and change can be viewed as a discomforting threat. But change is an inevitable fact of modern life.

Unfortunately, behavioral scientists have concentrated their studies too much on the change rather than on the more fundamental problem. As a society, we are not plagued so much by the change itself as by the loss of the linkage between the changes. Dr. Manfred Halpern, professor of politics at Princeton University, supported this contention when he argued that ours is the "age of incoherence" and suggested that we made a big change to the left and another big change to the right, but somewhere along the way we lost the connecting links.

Just what are the missing connecting links? Clare Booth Luce wrote that a nation cannot last long without a spiritual faith. We have been the generation of scientific achievement where the age of reason loses its reasonableness if it loses its moral and spiritual values. We are surrounded by evidence that we have allowed the lining of our moral brakes to wear out and are unable to control our mental horsepower.

To those without faith, every scientific achievement becomes a threat, every technological change becomes a hazard. Such people fear that the computer will strip them of their identity, turning them into mere numbers.

A strong personal faith is required to handle our electronic age. Without faith, we become servants of the creation, rather than using new equipment as a tool to make our work more effective. Faith in God allows us to take change in stride so we view it positively, not negatively. Faith enables us to see God as the source from which all new discoveries emanate, knowing He holds the universe in His hands. A strong personal faith lets us view all that is new as a challenge instead of a threat.

Good human relations skills come from the heart, not from systems and techniques. An academically brilliant human relations specialist can be totally ineffective in dealing with others. Methods of interpersonal relationships work only if they represent our honest feelings toward others.

Look inside yourself as you answer the following questions and you may discover insights into dealing with others:

- Are you open, direct and consistent?
- Do you have a balanced view of life, your job, of your own self-importance?
- Are you neat and well-dressed, neither slouchy or careless nor flashy or overdressed? Either extreme can create a hurdle to overcome.
- Do you stand and sit erect, confidently and at ease? Do you speak up and express your ideas clearly without talking too much or too loud? Do you get right to the point without rambling, using precise words and correct grammar?
- Does your manner bespeak friendliness, courtesy and consideration for others?
- Do you smile, reflect good health and physical energy? Can you analyze problems, sense tensions, get to the heart of the matter, and focus quickly on what is important?
- Have you cultivated a wide range of interests? Do you possess a strong curiosity? Are you a seeker? Are you well read?
- Do you possess an open mind? Are you actively seeking new ideas and new approaches? Are you threatened by new ways of doing things, or do you desire to perfect all you do? Are you flexible, readily adjusting and adaptable to change?
- Can you control your emotions, harness your temper and use it constructively? Are you able to maintain poise under pressure?
- Do you have a clear picture of your own strengths and weaknesses? Do you accept yourself, knowing your limitations? Do you have your basic goals and objectives in view?
- Most importantly, do you have a genuine interest in other people? This question is the beginning and the end of all you do with others.

I always marvel when I am reminded of a surprising statistic: 20 percent of the salespeople in America do 80 percent of the business.

What makes a successful salesperson? We cannot spot the most successful salesperson in a crowd; our preconceived notions based on personal appearance, style of dress, stature or personality have little to do with success. The following story gives a clue to the basic secret of success in sales.

A man arrived at his home one rainy evening to find a stray kitten taking refuge on his porch. The kitten was soaked and, when the man opened the front door, darted inside. The man chased the stray, caught it and put it back outside before the wet kitten could climb on any furniture.

Shortly thereafter, a pair of children came home from playing in the neighborhood and the kitten sneaked in behind them. Another chase through the house ended with the kitten being evicted once again.

The evening newspaper arrived with a thud on the porch and the children ran to retrieve it. Again, the kitten scampered in. While the youngsters chased the kitten and put it out for the third time, their father was down in the basement. The basement was warm and dry; he spotted a box in a corner and thought to himself, "We could probably use a cat around here, if for no other reason than to chase mice." He gathered some rags to make a bed in the box, creating a snug home for the wet kitten.

The plan was spoiled by one problem—the kitten didn't come back. The father and children went out in the rain searching for the kitten, but it was not to be found.

The moral of the story: if the kitten had made just one more call, it would have had a home for life. While oversimplified, this allegory underscores the essential component of sales success—persistence. Determined perseverance will win out over good looks and charm and stylish clothes every time.

With you, I live in a nation of problems; but I'm glad I'm alive and hope I can always be part of the solution and not part of the problem.

Birthdays aren't all bad—it certainly beats the alternative! However, on one's birthday you find yourself looking back, not to embellish but take inventory. Better still, you find yourself looking forward to the challenge of today and tomorrow.

Growing up like most of you, I had everything but money. Like millions of American youth, I had the privilege of working my way through college as my parents could give me only two dollars a week.

But what a legacy Mom and Dad left me. Make no mistake. I enjoy money and would have been glad had my folks been wealthy. I didn't enjoy patched breeches, darned socks, and frayed collars; but I still had the best—good motivation from godly parents.

Their gift to me can be found in three statements.

1. "Give God your life. He can do far more with it than you can." This was a statement by D.L. Moody, founder of the school Dad and Mom attended and where they met. My father felt God had so blessed him by guiding him to immigrate to America—a land beyond his fondest dreams—even with our problems.
2. "God is more interested in you than in what you'll ever do." My parents taught me I could never make up in "doing" what I lacked in "being." God is not fooled by flattery. A good deed does not give immunity to do wrong. My folks could agree with Albert Einstein: "Do not strive for success—strive to be a person of greater value."
3. "Do whatever you do well—no matter how menial the task—for you never know when God is standing in the shadows taking your measurements for a bigger opportunity." I resent striving for perfection, but my folks taught me to strive for quality.

You can readily see, I believe, that although I was raised poor in terms of money and material things, through my parents God gave me a rich legacy.

Often the most meaningful service is the easiest to render—if it comes from the heart, if it is given with love. Such was the case with Wilbur Pinney.

Wilbur spent his career in the food industry and died several years short of retirement. Like all executives, he had many demands on his time outside of business—community projects, Scouting, charitable groups—but his first consideration was his church.

As a long-time member of the Chicago Temple, the famous downtown United Methodist Church, he performed an unheralded service. On Sunday afternoons, he participated in a social program for senior citizens who lived in the neighborhood. Many were widows and widowers; most were lonely, forgotten and neglected.

Wilbur didn't develop or administer the program; he merely met the senior citizens when they arrived, mingled among them, and bid them farewell.

On the Sunday after Wilbur died, the pastor of the Chicago Temple unlocked his study and found a note slipped under the door by an earlier visitor. "Pastor, Wilbur Pinney died;" the note read, "now who will smile at us on Sunday afternoon?"

Such a simple ministry—no honors, no plaques, no citations. Wilbur just cared about those others forgot. He didn't cater to their self-pity and he didn't condemn others for not caring as he did. Wilbur Pinney just smiled warmly, simply, eloquently, lovingly, faithfully.

The decline of manners is a sad commentary on our American society in general; the decline of manners in the world of business is particularly distressing. Manners tell more than how we were raised or how nice a person we are—manners proclaim how much we respect one another. Manners are communicators, not decorations.

Ed Flanagan's practical comments on basic business manners highlight the need for respect and consideration, even in the workplace:

Those of us who have been in the business world a little longer than others remember the good old days. The days when people returned a phone call within a reasonable amount of time. At least before you forgot who made it. And promptly replied to your letter.

Many business executives with whom we are in contact agree that, in this era of instant communication, it's a growing problem.

Too busy? It's a sad commentary. And what are the effects on your company? Or on you as an executive? What type of reputation are you getting in the process? We think the answer is obvious.

Well, first of all, what's your policy? Have you gone on record saying, "All phone calls to our department are to be returned within 'X' number of hours, days, etc.?" Have you ever looked at the dates of the pink slips sitting on your employees' desks? Do you maintain a log of correspondence? Are letters date-stamped? What about your policy on answering letters? Is it in black and white? Do your people know about it? Some executives maintain a 'read' file on correspondence in and out of their departments. It's their way of keeping track, their pulse-taking.

Unreturned phone calls and unanswered correspondence can be damning. They're the life-blood of most businesses and it's your responsibility, as an executive, to set the policies and monitor the compliance. As the saying goes, "Are you part of the problem, or part of the solution?"

Most of us care more than we admit and, certainly, more than we demonstrate. We search for meaning in our lives, but are afraid of the commitment necessary. We are a generation that moves about easily, lives comfortably and eats well, but suffers from the emptiness of not knowing if we or life truly matter at all. We have become better at building barriers than stringing lines of communication.

Caring means making ourselves vulnerable. None of us would plan to be vulnerable; we have grown up learning that vulnerability is a sign of weakness. Despite currently popular management concepts preaching the "power of manipulation" and "enlightened self-interest," vulnerability is a strength. Vulnerable people are strong enough to place the needs of others ahead of their own wishes. Only the vulnerable have enough love to make a difference for the better.

We learn to like and enjoy ourselves only when we care, only when we see ourselves performing unexpected acts of kindness and generous acts of thoughtfulness. The traditional tenet of Scouting, to do a good deed each day, taught youngsters the only way to be proud of themselves. Our ruthlessness comes not from being without goals, but from having goals that only concern ourselves. We daydream of being wealthy, thinking this will allow us to be generous to others. Enormous wealth has made few people rich; usually, it just whets the appetite for more riches.

Caring means taking time to build friendships and repair the misunderstandings that damage relationships. Caring means being honest; honest in both tender, intimate moments and in moments of anger and frustration. The good and the bad must be shared if it is to lead to caring. Caring means focusing priorities on people rather than things. Caring means giving others freely of our time and purse, and accepting it as a privilege instead of an infringement.

Caring means having the courage to be vulnerable.

Every time we buy something—from a pack of chewing gum to clothing to appliances to cars—we cause America's wheels to turn. With every purchase, we demonstrate that we can earn money according to our abilities, buy what we want competitively, and enjoy the highest standard of living in the world. We call this the free enterprise system, but perhaps a better term is the private enterprise system.

Critics claim that private enterprise strangles us, but have they compared America to the Marxist countries they admire? Do we beg to buy wheat from Russia, or do they come to us? Do we enjoy telephones and televisions, mobility and leisure activities, or do we prefer a controlled society that equates to a low form of confinement?

Critics say that private enterprise exploits people, turning them into cogs in a machine. They have never witnessed a Soviet collective farm or factory. Certainly, we may punch a clock, but at least we can choose our careers and where we wish to work. And even if we punch a clock, we still have the time and opportunity to freely attend a football game or take a fishing boat to the lake.

Critics denounce the advocates of private enterprise as selfish and materialistic because of what we spend on ourselves. We are fortunate to have so much, even if we do overspend at times. But there is no other nation on earth whose citizens give like ours, give to churches and synagogues, to educational and charitable organizations. Add to all the dollars almost 40 million citizen volunteers who freely give their time and energy as hospital workers, Little League coaches, den mothers, and helpers to the disabled and elderly.

Critics charge that under private enterprise only a few have all the wealth. In truth, no country has wealth so widely distributed as the United States. And those who do have wealth have earned it through their own skills and abilities.

Critics attack the private enterprise system and choke our business with red tape and regulations. Yet they cannot offer a better example—not Russia, nor Yugoslavia, nor France, nor China. Let's not destroy what we have unless we have something proven better.

If you ever feel you have too much to accomplish each day; if you ever feel swamped and unable to keep ahead of your workload; if you sleep soundly but wake up more fatigued because of these pressures, the solution could be improved time management. The following ideas may help you better plan and organize your time:

1. *Identify your goals.* Just knowing what needs to be done is not enough—you must arrange priorities. You need to differentiate tasks that *must* be done from those that *should* be done if possible. If you are an employer, for instance, your primary obligation is to your employees. Yet you also have time commitments as a member of various civic, charitable and social organizations. You must guard against being over-involved in worthwhile activities that impair your leadership responsibility to your company and its employees.
2. *Write down your goals.* Jot down major goals for your job, such as sales targets, as well as the little things you do before and after work. Depending on your personal choice, you might want to make your list each night before retiring or each morning upon arising. Then, as you complete each task, check it off and feel the sense of accomplishment.
3. *Accept the unexpected.* Any goal is subject to the unexpected. Don't be discouraged by occasional detours or changes. Accept the unexpected as a matter of life, or even the spice of life that adds excitement to our existence. If you miss a goal, write yourself a note explaining why, and go right ahead from there.
4. *Don't look behind you.* If you are having a good day, don't fret about the bad day you had yesterday. If a task blew up in your face yesterday, don't let it haunt you today.
5. *Be honest with yourself.* Learn the difference between deliberation and procrastination. There are times when haste can make waste, but there are also times when delay can turn a small, insignificant task into one of gigantic proportions.

Learning to manage your time effectively is the first step in eliminating that "the faster I go, the behinder I get" feeling. But you still may need to lighten your load. Don't allow pride and ego to keep you from admitting that you have more work than you can handle effectively.

Opportunities to help another person crop up in the unlikeliest circumstances, as shown in a story about one of the nation's lesser-known presidents, Calvin Coolidge.

Mr. Coolidge was vice-president and had just become the 30th president following the death of Warren G. Harding. Mrs. Harding was still living in the White House and the Coolidges temporarily remained at the vice-presidential residence in the Willard Hotel. During the middle of the night, the new president awoke to find an intruder going through his clothing, removing his wallet and watch chain.

In darkness, President Coolidge calmly spoke up, saying, "About that watch, I wish you wouldn't take that." The startled thief regained his voice and asked, "Why?" The president answered, "I don't mean the watch and chain, only the charm. I am very fond of that charm; it means a great deal to me. Take it near the window and read what is engraved on the back."

The robber read the inscription, "Presented to Calvin Coolidge, Speaker of the House, by the Massachusetts General Court." With amazement, the young man asked, "Are you President Coolidge?" "Yes, I am, and I don't want you to take that charm," replied the president. "Why, son, are you doing this?"

"Mr. President, my friend and I came down from college to have a vacation in Washington. We spent all our money and haven't got enough to pay our hotel bill and get back to campus. If you don't mind, I'll just take the wallet."

President Coolidge was an old-fashioned, hard-headed Yankee and knew he had $80 in his wallet. "How much will it take to pay your hotel bill and get you and your friend back to campus? Sit down, and let's talk this over."

The president calculated the room rate and rail fare to the college at $32. "I'll give you the $32 as a loan, and I expect you to pay me back," he told the novice thief. "Thank you, Mr. President," said the astonished young man.

President Coolidge advised him to exit through the window he came in to avoid the Secret Service agent patrolling the hotel corridor. As the young man climbed over the windowsill, the president advised, "Son, you're a nice boy. You are better than you are acting. You are starting down the wrong road. Just remember who you are."

History makes no mention of whether or not President Coolidge ever received the $32 loan from the young man he helped and trusted. But I suspect that he did.

One of the bonuses of receiving an honorary degree from Salem College is receiving the alumni magazine. Some time ago this magazine printed a message written by a Doctor of Veterinary Medicine, Onwusongonye Boniface Okehi. I do not know him, but his plea caught my eye:

- Give me a real chance today, knock me not with bigotry that staggers my resolves and masks my real worth.
- Give me a real chance for my spirits to blossom, my true potential to come alive and my pride to emerge.
- Give me a real chance today, that my attributes may find expression, hid not in sweet words or in beautiful churches, for my chances are in the tabernacles of thy soul.
- Give me a real chance to squeeze out the achievements ingrained in my genes. Block not my chances for my worth is itching to burst out.
- Call it equal education opportunity, my abilities are ready to be purified. Call it equal employment opportunity. My ingenuity has long been caged.
- Worry not what thy neighbors might think or say, only put thyself in my stead and thou will overcome the hesitation.
- Give me a real chance today for I hate to divert my energies to things other than constructive and be a liability to myself and neighbor.
- Dribble me not with hypocrisy for my needs are urgent and my appeals legitimate, and give me that chance today.

I oppose giving or forcing opportunity on people who reject accepting responsibility. I equally oppose denying opportunity to those who thirst for it.

As you're enjoying the last of your weekend, are you dreading tomorrow—"Blue Monday?"

Through the years Monday has been identified as the start of drudgery. Monday is the day the assembly line starts up—everyone goes back to work as the stenographer, teacher, file clerk, button pusher, paper shuffler, money counter, retail clerk, people manipulator, nurse, stamp licker.

If we have trouble facing Monday, perhaps it's because we haven't learned how to relax and use our weekends properly. We tend to do things in excess and play too hard on the weekend.

On weekends the extra time makes us face problems we evade during the work week. Marital or family problems can't be sidetracked when we face each other, so often Mom and Dad long for Monday when the job becomes an escape.

The most difficult weekend time is during January, February, and March. Depression, like the flu, is a wintertime illness.

How do you spend your weekends? Do you sit around in a mood, talking little and staring much into space? Do you drink too much and much more than you ever would on a work day? Do you sleep beyond a normal "sleeping in?" Do you overschedule social and recreational activities?

A couple of generations ago the weekend centered around church attendance. This gave the family something to share together without even considering the spiritual aspects.

If we plan, but not overplan our weekends, they can be a time of uplifting experiences. Few of us die from overwork, but many are destroyed by boredom.

We are much more health conscious today, and rightfully so. If you're bored or depressed or even overworked doing household chores that must be done on weekends, take a break from the routine and walk through your neighborhood this Sunday afternoon. It's good exercise. It will clear the cobwebs and maybe you'll even meet a new neighbor you've been curious about. Whatever you decide, make it fun, and just maybe Monday morning will be a day you look forward to with excitement.

We often hear someone wish that we could get "back to basics," professing a longing to return to a simpler, more tranquil way of life. Such a journey through time is not only impossible, but it is the wrong reason to want a return to basics.

The true underlying reason to return to basics is so that, despite our technological advances, we do not let ourselves become so preoccupied that we overlook and neglect the character that brought us to where we are. Neither time nor technology changes the primary needs of today's world. Certain values and virtues are everlasting, such as those basic attributes I would look for in an employee:

1. *Dependability.* Perhaps loyalty is a better description, but too often it is coupled with the word "blind." Blind loyalty suggests forfeiting your honor and becoming a mere robot to your employer. Looking for dependability, I would want your independence, your integrity. I want to know we are both working for the same goals. Dependability refers more to commitment than to activity; it means you are assuming responsibility for your company's success. At the end of the day you walk away from your work, never leaving your pride of employment.

2. *Ability.* Few of us look for geniuses to hire. On the contrary, the person with normal, average abilities, but maximum desire, makes a winning employee. Plus, ability is not so predestined that each day cannot bring improvement. In fact, individuals with limited abilities may be moved to prove themselves worthy of an employer's trust.

3. *Teachability.* This natural third step must be matched by the availability of a willing and able teacher. A company cannot expect its employees to learn if the company doesn't carefully explain, define and teach. Teachability ensures growth, both for the individual and for the company.

When jobs are scarce, work is always available. Perhaps not the job you want today, but you can make that job grow to meet your vision and use it as preparation for the next opportunity. All it takes is getting back to the basics of dependability, ability and teachability.

Certain great individuals possess an unusual lasting quality in what they say. The Rev. Peter Marshall, chaplain of the United States Senate, was such a person. The following prayer, delivered before the Senate well over 30 years ago, still expresses our feelings today:

"Our Father, we pray for this land. We need Thy help in this time of testing and uncertainty, when men who could fight together on the field of battle seem strangely unable to work together around conference tables for peace.

"May we begin to see that all true Americanism begins in being Christian; that it can have no other foundation, as it has no other roots.

"To Thy glory was this republic established. For the advancement of the Christian faith did the founding fathers give their life's heritage, passed down to us.

"We would pray that all over this land there may be a return to the faith of those men and women who trusted in God as they faced the perils and dangers of the frontier, not alone in crossing the continent, in building their cabins, in rearing their families, in seeking out a livelihood, but in raising a standard of faith to which men have been willing to repair down through the years.

"Make us, the citizens of this land, want to do the right things. Make us long to have right attitudes. Help us to be Christian in our attitudes. Let all that we do and say spring out of understanding hearts.

"Make us willing to seek moral objectives together, that in united action this nation may be as resolute for righteousness and peace as she has been for war.

"Bless those who bear responsibility. May they be led by Thee to do that which is right rather than that which is expedient or politically wise. Save us from politicians who seek only their own selfish interests. Illumine the minds of management as well as labor, that there may be an end to selfishness and greed, to the stupidity of men who are unable to find in reasonable agreement solutions to the problems that plague us.

"Bless this land that we love so much, our Father, and help her to deposit her trust, not in armies and navies, in wealth and material resources, or in achievements of the human mind, but in that righteousness which alone exalteth any nation, and by which alone peace can finally come to us. This we ask in that name that is above every name, Thy Son, Jesus Christ, our Redeemer. Amen."

John Doe makes America great!

No, he won't appear on any "most admired" list. He represents the average Americans, the hard-working men and women who are the backbone of our country. The average folks who love their families, are good neighbors, respect the law, work hard at their jobs, pay their bills and pay their taxes. Not the headline-grabbers, just ordinary people, often overlooked and usually taken for granted.

We have built a society of misfits who demand that perversion be accepted—chronic criminals are given light sentences and early paroles, drug addicts are given wrist-slaps while the pushers go undetected, drifters are financed by welfare, the dependent live off the workers.

And what of our average Americans? They could feel penalized for working hard and just say, "What's the use?" Instead, they are faithful to their jobs, even if bored at times. They work hard, not to please an employer, but to satisfy their integrity. They start out to do something and they accomplish it. They have compassion for their neighbor's failings, but won't allow their values to be compromised to make him look good. They help the weak by setting an example of strength.

God bless you, the average American. You might have enjoyed an extra hour of sleep, but didn't; you might want to quit, but won't. You are what makes America great.

In the Eskimo culture, there is a popular saying: "We are here to help each other, to try to make each other happy." What a simple yet sublime philosophy to live by.

When you commit your life to others, you invite them to step inside the wall of your life. You are now giving. Givers find joy—getters usually don't. To be a giver, you merely have to give a bit of yourself—a kind deed, a warm word, a helpful suggestion, a lift over a rough spot, a strong shoulder, an understanding nod. With a simple act, you transmit a feeling from your mind and heart into another's mind and heart.

Speak to people. A warm greeting brings cheer.

Smile at people. It takes nearly 60 fewer muscles than a frown and it brings light.

Call a casual acquaintance by name. The sweetest sound is one's own name.

Be cordial and friendly. Make it evident that your acts of kindness are a genuine pleasure.

Be quick to praise and equally slow to criticize. Praise lights fires; criticism smothers them. Anything scarce, such as praise, is of great value.

Be conciliatory. There are three sides to any argument—yours, theirs and the middle ground where you resolve your differences.

Be attuned. Look for ways to be helpful; seek opportunity instead of waiting to be asked.

Be humble. If fortune has come your way, resist the tendency to be arrogant. Though you work hard, most good things come from circumstances of good fortune.

Be faithful to your friends, to your beliefs and convictions, and to yourself.

At times, we may feel the whole world is wrong. Even so, it will change another day. Good things await the giver—the giver of joy, of compassion, of warmth, of kindness. Be a giver today!

Life has its ups and downs—sometimes even by the barrelful. For a needed smile on this last day of the workweek, let's review the following unsigned letter, ostensibly from a bricklayer to his construction firm, quoted in the *Manchester Guardian* as an "example of stoicism":

Dear Sir:

When I got to the building, I found that the hurricane had knocked some bricks off the top. So I rigged up a beam with a pulley at the top of the building and hoisted up a couple of barrels full of bricks. When I had fixed the building, there was a lot of bricks left. Then I went to the bottom and cast off the line.

Unfortunately, the barrel of bricks was heavier than I was, and before I knew what was happening the barrel started down, jerking me off the ground. I decided to hang on and halfway up I met the barrel coming down and received a severe blow on the shoulder.

I then continued to the top, banging my head against the beam and getting my fingers jammed in the pulley. When the barrel hit the ground it bursted its bottom, allowing all the bricks to spill out.

I was now heavier than the barrel and so I started down again at high speed. Halfway down, I met the barrel coming up and received severe injuries to my shins. When I hit the ground I landed on the bricks, getting several painful cuts from the sharp edges.

At this point I must have lost presence of mind because I let go of the line. The barrel then came down, giving me another heavy blow on the head and putting me in the hospital.

I respectfully request sick leave.

What makes an artist? I feel I know Bernard Stern of London, England, because I know his son, Mark; his mother; and best, I know his sister, Mrs. Colin Lindsey of Tampa, Florida. Bernard Stern is the true artist who has turned his successful lighting ornament companies to others so he can bury himself in his art. Why do we admire the true artist?

We are having a renaissance of the arts in the Western World, and I'm delighted. One of these bright lights is Bernard Stern. When I said this successful businessman buried himself in his art, I misspoke. He has actually found himself and resurrected himself in his art.

I've always been fascinated with the artist. Their mysticism frightens me a bit, yet challenges me. They appear to hear the inaudible while I hear the shouts.

Get a feel of Bernard Stern as he says, "Drawing is for me the universal language—the essence of visual communication as well as the 'shorthand' of life movement. That's why I draw more easily than I write. A simple line, traced in a single movement is time and motion suspended, expressed through the perception of the mind. How fast goes the pen, the pencil? How deeply does the camera feel? I love the spontaneous surge of an unimpeded line, free of constrictions, where the supreme technique is simplicity distilled."

Bernard Stern reveals his own honesty in his art. He has seen anti-human forces and zoological attitudes invade the realm of art. Ugliness has destroyed beauty. Cruelty has taken the place of compassion. Sex has replaced love. Matter has conquered spirit. Mr. Stern feels that art in its traditional sense is the love of creation. It is the miracle of God. Art fills the need of human reaction to the beauty and mystery of life, to give life form. Art is a way to communicate our experiences to each other.

Simplicity might perhaps best describe Bernard Stern's art. It reveals hope maintained when war years were cruel to his family and, for awhile, they were fleeing pilgrims. Stern's art shows he knows sorrow. He knows the frustration of a youthful painter of lampshades to keep body and soul together as his family fortunes were lost in war. Most of all, his painting shows the simple faith that his goals would be reached. Disappointment taught patience and humility to handle his present success.

We need the communication of young artists like Bernard Stern, a man who could not be kept from his ideals.

Some of the happiest moments of my childhood were spent as a family gathered around the old piano. Well do I remember when it came as a gift from my grandfather. It cost him all of twenty-five dollars. We had it in the family for over fifty years and it is still being used in a Sunday school classroom of an Atlanta church.

My parents believed that music was one of the delightful aspects of worship and second only to memorizing Scripture was the value of knowing the words of the hymns of the church. These hymns were written by people of conviction, not so much to make money as writers, but to express the overflow of their hearts. Still, they are only as valuable as our acceptance of the message. Thus I couldn't help but chuckle when several years ago I found these observations:

We sing "Sweet Hour of Prayer," and then content ourselves with ten to fifteen minutes a day—or no time.

We sing "Onward Christian Soldiers," and then wait to be drafted into His service.

We sing "O for a Thousand Tongues," and we do not use the one we have.

We sing "There Shall Be Showers of Blessings," but do not come out when it's raining.

We sing "Blest Be the Tie that Binds," and let the least little offense sever it.

We sing "Serve the Lord with Gladness," and gripe about all we have to do.

We sing "We're Marching to Zion," but fail to march to Sunday school and church.

We sing "I Love to Tell the Story," and never mention it all year.

We sing "Cast Thy Burden on the Lord," and worry ourselves into nervous breakdowns.

We sing "The Whole World Wide for Jesus," and never invite our next door neighbors to church.

We sing "O Day of Rest and Gladness," and wear ourselves out traveling, cutting grass, or playing golf.

We sing "Throw Out the Life Line," and content ourselves with throwing out a fishing line.

For someone who started out life as a boy soloist and has ended up not even singing in a good monotone, I take comfort that although the notes of the song are important, it's the words that convey the message—and what good memories come to all of us as we recall the hymns of the church.

One of the marvels of the workplace is how well employees usually get along with one another. When you consider that we spend more time with our co-workers than with our families, you might suppose that such contact would lead to problems. Even the closest of families can get on one another's nerves when they spend long periods of time together, yet we can work next to the same person for years and maintain a pleasant relationship.

To have that kind of ongoing, cordial, interpersonal relationship with a co-worker takes a special attitude toward people, incorporating some or all of these outlooks:

1. You accept the fact that people are different—different from you. Acknowledging and accepting that fact, you anticipate a difference of opinion and grant others their rights without becoming defensive or offensive.
2. You view each person's job as important—as important as yours. You see no insignificant or menial jobs where you work. You realize that company success depends on the floor sweeper as well as the president. You see each job as part of the overall system.
3. You expect that each employee wants to work hard—just as hard and conscientiously as you. Mutual trust results from the good work habits of each.
4. You realize that work is not the place for small talk, but without being nosy, you exhibit a real concern for each other's problems.
5. You are willing to join in overall goals and even throw out challenges to each other. All good employees know that productivity leads to security.
6. You consider the other person's feelings first when a co-worker appears to be slacking off on the job, rather than criticizing or containing your resentment. It could be that the person has suffered a personal disappointment or is unfamiliar with doing the job. Whatever the cause, your encouragement helps the employee be self-motivated.

Using a little concern and compassion, we can make every day on the job pleasant and productive.

King Solomon said of man, "As he thinketh in his heart, so is he." Ralph Waldo Emerson updated the philosophy, "A man is what he thinks about all day long." And John Miller further modernized the concept, "The way we think determines happiness. It doesn't depend upon who you are or what you have; it depends solely upon what you think."

What do you think? How do you see yourself? How do others see you? What do your actions tell others about you? For an insight into why we succeed or fail, see which of the following characteristics identifies you:

- I walk, talk and look enthusiastic. Or, I walk, talk and look as though today will be a bad one.
- I look and dress the part of a neat, well-ordered person. Or, my personal appearance is sloppy because I figure no one will notice me anyway and the type of work I do has little to do with being neat and clean.
- I am a student, no matter my age, trying to learn each day how to do my job better. Or, I am satisfied I do my job the best it can be done, so I just try to be pleasant and defeat boredom.
- I am kind to my competitors, believing I can win the sale on merit, personal service and product quality. Or, I am a gossip, constantly dropping innuendos about my competition, whether accurate or not; I think I can rise by pushing everyone else down.
- I am able to face disappointment and dissatisfaction as a challenge, a mountain to climb. Or, I run from any trouble and, if it overtakes me, I feel sorry for myself; I am convinced the other person's success comes from good luck while mine comes from hard work.
- I am always interested in the well-being of my family, the strength of my company, the problems of my customer. Or, I am interested only in myself, believing my strength is the best thing my family, company or customers have going for them.
- I am taking time to make pleasant calls, to send birthday greetings, to send small gifts so my friends and associates know I see them as real people. Or, I am always wondering why someone has overlooked me or slighted me or left me off an invitation list.

Think about what you think, for it provides a mirror to the world of your heart and soul.

President Calvin Coolidge has been rediscovered, much to the surprise and amusement of many. "Silent Cal" is the personal hero of no less eminent an American than Ronald Reagan. This new-found popularity has made the 30th president better known today perhaps than during his administration.

President Coolidge's common-sense observations and philosophies, especially his economic restraints, illustrate why he is regaining respect and popularity:

- If you see ten troubles coming down the road, you can be sure that nine of them will run into the ditch before they reach you.
- Americans have not fully realized their ideals. There are imperfections. But the ideal is right. It is everlastingly right. What our country needs is the moral power to hold it.
- There is no dignity quite so impressive, and no independence quite so important, as living within our means.
- The only way I know to drive out evil from the country is by the constructive method of filling it with good. The country is better off tranquilly considering its blessings and merits, and earnestly striving to secure more of them, than it would be in nursing hostile bitterness about its deficiencies and faults.
- It has always seemed to me that common sense is the real solvent for the nation's problems at all times—common sense and hard work.
- Industry, thrift and self-control are not sought because they create wealth, but because they create character.
- Prosperity is only an instrument to be used, not a deity to be worshipped.
- People criticize me for harping on the obvious. Perhaps someday I'll write an article on "The Importance of the Obvious." If all the folks in the United States would do the few simple things they know they ought to do, most of our problems would take care of themselves.
- There is no right to strike against the public safety for anybody, anywhere, anytime.
- The meaning of America is not to be found in a life without toil. Freedom is not only bought with a great price: it is maintained by unremitting effort.

These words, though spoken many decades ago, still ring true today.

In his book titled *Servant Leadership*, author Robert K. Greenleaf underscored his premise that "the great leader is seen as a servant first" and that simple fact is the key to a great leader's greatness.

All of us would agree that there is a dearth of great leadership in our country. We have a disproportionate number of executives, but don't feel led. We have a higher ratio of officers to enlisted personnel in our armed forces than ever before in our history, yet we feel militarily weak.

Perhaps what is missing from our leadership is the great leader seen first as a servant. The heart-warming story of William E. Dearden illustrates the point.

Bill Dearden was raised and educated at the Hershey School for needy orphan boys; he attended college on a Hershey scholarship that supplemented his athletic grant. His brilliant corporate career was well under way when the Hershey School asked him, at economic sacrifice, to return and serve as the financial officer. He heeded the call to serve, acknowledging a debt to his alma mater for his early upbringing. He plunged into his work, not merely to establish a sound fiscal policy, but with a sincere dedication to use the Hershey Trust to do the best for the most youth.

Bill Dearden would have willingly spent his life serving the school, but he literally outgrew the job. He moved over to Hershey Foods, rose to chief executive officer, and used his leadership to guide this major corporation to remarkable success. He also ensured that the dreams of the company's founder were fulfilled—for Milton Snavely Hershey had enabled Bill Dearden's dream to become reality.

Mr. Hershey, late in his life, was asked if he ever regretted willing his fortune to the Hershey School for needy children. "No," he replied, "for someday one of these lads, fatherless or from a broken home, will attend our schools, graduate and come back to lead our great company."

Bill Dearden fulfilled Mr. Hershey's vision and exemplified the ideal of servant leadership.

Children have such a wonderfully naive notion of age. They think 30 is ancient and 50 is beyond imagination. I know from firsthand experience that turning 40 and then 50 isn't all that bad. In fact, I feel better past 50 than I did at 35—which means I am either in better physical shape or my memory is fading.

Do you feel your age? Do you feel you are getting older minute by minute? If you think time is flying by, just consider this. A billion seconds ago, World War II ended. A billion minutes ago, Jesus was on earth. A billion hours ago man was not yet created. But a billion dollars ago was just yesterday afternoon in Washington, D.C.

If that analysis doesn't make you feel old, this will. You know you're getting older...

> When almost everything hurts, and what doesn't hurt, doesn't work anymore.
> When it feels like the morning after the night before, but you didn't go anywhere.
> When all the names in your little black book end with the initials M.D.
> When you're winded just playing checkers.
> When you look forward to a dull evening.
> When you turn out the lights for economic, not romantic, reasons.
> When your knees buckle, but your belt won't.
> When you're 17 around the neck, 40 around the waist, and you shoot your weight around the golf course.
> When you sink your teeth into a steak and they stay there.
> When you reach to pull your socks up and find you forgot to put any on.
> When a little gray-haired lady tries to help you across the street.

Age is more a matter of feeling than years, but years do enter the picture. A.P. Gouthey wrote, "Only years make men. Rarely do the great men of history distinguish themselves before they are 50, and between 50 and 80 they do their best work...both as regards quality and quantity."

So don't worry about age and the passing years, the best is yet to come!

We in the United States are considered to have the poorest reading habits in the civilized world. That's hard to believe when you see the mass buying of paperback books. Even counting these, we are not reading, comparatively speaking.

In our world a new book is published every minute. One half of the world is saturated while the other half is starving for reading.

Copies of printed books exceed eight billion a year but four of five are printed in the U.S., Canada, New Zealand, Australia, Russia, and a half dozen European countries.

What bothers me is that while we're indifferent to books, the developing countries have an insatiable demand for literature and are rapidly providing schools to encourage literacy. Taking into account adults who become literate and children attending school, the world's reading population has more than doubled in the last twenty years. In Asia, Latin America, and parts of Africa, there is an acute shortage of books. Low production, inadequate distribution, and the high cost of importing a sufficient number of books combine to deprive people of reading.

What about our country? Television may give our children awareness of current events, but leaves them woefully ignorant of knowledge. We have a statistics generation as opposed to a philosophy people. We are concerned how our news can be managed, controlled, and prejudiced. The fault isn't only intemperance by the media. It takes place because people who don't read, lack adequate basis for judging.

How do you create an atmosphere of reading in your home? Have books available. Make them the center of attention and decorating in the family room. Let the children see you reading, especially books you're proud of. Better still, discuss the book you're reading with the children. When your children are reading, ask them about the book, even if it's one you've read. It is interesting to get their impression. Also, I feel there must be times when parents insist that children read, and monitor the subject matter.

Knowing only what is happening today can frustrate and confuse. When you read great books you build a philosophy that gives you stability and strength. We have to be cautious that we don't become a nation that bought books and built libraries for status, but only admired the covers.

It takes young people to relate to young people. Right? Wrong. Let me tell you about the influence of one man upon young people—some fifteen years ago when he was sixty years of age. This essay should be titled "The Second Time Around."

In Rhinelander, Wisconsin, they were desperate for a Scoutmaster for an established but failing troop. After being turned down by all the recommended choices, the troop discovered Harvey Martin, a delightful sixty-year-old janitor. Surprised by the committee's request, Mr. Martin begged off reminding them he was sixty. He had been active with his two sons, whom he had sent through college and they were now active in Scouting. The committee prevailed on Harvey Martin—and he accepted.

At the first meeting there came a lad shabbily dressed from an alcohol-broken home. Unable to buy a uniform, he asked Mr. Martin if there was any way he could earn one. Harvey said, "I'm allowed to employ help to take care of the school so I'll hire you if you'll work hard." The lad did and soon joined his fellow Scouts with proper uniform.

Sometime later the same lad asked, "Mr. Martin, how do you know God?" Harvey said he didn't have the education nor ability to answer but it was a good time to ask because Easter was near and why didn't the lad come to church and hear the sermon? Harvey had forgotten about the invitation until he and his wife drove up to church Easter morning and found the lad waiting for him. He had the same clothes on he had worn all week to school and while doing his janitorial duties, but they were washed and pressed. Harvey figured the boy did it himself.

Months later the Scout office received an application from this boy. In his reason for wanting to be an Eagle Scout he wrote: "I feel I should improve my life every way I can and working on my merit badges to be an Eagle will help me. My ambition is now to prepare to become a minister. I learned about Jesus from my Scoutmaster, Harvey Martin, and I will be satisfied as a minister if I can find just one boy and do for him what Mr. Martin has done for me."

The story of Harvey Martin is one of many reasons I believe in Scouting and make it my hobby. In 1974, Harvey Martin received his Scout Council's highest award. Long after raising his own sons, he took a Scout troop no one wanted and served it as his contribution the second time around.

People seldom take pride in their blunders or announce their failures. Realizing that "to err is human," we can profit by our mistakes. Mistakes can be our enemies or they can become our allies, depending on our outlook and inner strength.

Someone once philosophized that Benjamin Franklin was the only man in history to get good news out of bad weather when he sent his kite into an electrical storm and gave mankind a tiny look at the power and potential of electricity. This parable underscores the need to gain hope out of discouragement, optimism out of adversity.

Every day, any number of disagreeable things happen to us. We miss appointments and lose things, we suffer pains and develop symptoms, we are treated unfairly and used by others. Some of us take these affronts to heart and brood over them all night, only redoubling their load the next day. Others erase these unpleasantries as they occur and do not "let the sun go down upon their wrath." These special few have developed a positive outlook on life and use it to conquer fear and disappointment.

Overcoming the forces of discouragement in your daily life makes you stronger in character and moral power. Your difficulties are transformed into dividends. Overcoming temptation this hour makes you mightier for the next hour. In the end, you become a spiritual master. If you let failure after failure keep you down, you become a spiritual slave. We have all visited shut-ins and received a blessing from the gentle, uncomplaining attitude of one who has placed their trust in God, and been equally frustrated by another who bitterly complains about their bad luck.

The story goes that Stonewall Jackson, an elder in the Presbyterian Church, was asked to deliver the prayer one Sunday morning. This legendary general made a mighty first effort, but failed miserably. He refused to let his first failure overcome him, however, and he later became as well known for his praying as his military exploits. Likewise, Peter the weakling became Peter the Rock; Saul the murderer became Paul the Apostle.

Let us, as well, learn to develop the inner spirit and positive outlook that can turn stumbling blocks into stepping stones.

One thing in this world is certain—trouble comes to all of us. Adversity never leaves a person unchanged. It either makes the individual bigger or it makes them smaller. Professor Arnold Toynbee, the eminent historian, stated that civilizations rise to greatness only when faced with some desperate challenge, some dire threat to their existence. That same concept is applicable to us as individuals. Adversity can be the abrasive that hones an edge on courage. It can be the trumpet that calls forth the latent nobility in man.

No two troubles are exactly alike, so there is no infallible formula for dealing with adversity. These five common-sense suggestions can prove helpful in facing our troubles and using adversity to our advantage:

First, face up to your problem! It will not go away by ignoring it. Admitting that an emergency exists is the first step in mobilizing the great defensive forces within each of us. So stare trouble in the eye. Take its measure. Once dissected, it will not seem so formidable.

Next, take an equally hard look at yourself. People in trouble often find the trouble is really in them. A troubled emotional condition can impair judgment, cloud reason and drain energy. We must recognize and deal with the trouble within ourselves, before we can effectively deal with external adversity.

Third, take some kind of action. Action is a great confidence builder. Inaction can be the result of fear, but also its cause. The course of action you take may be successful, perhaps not. But any action is better than no action at all.

Next, seek help with your troubles. Trouble is neither a disgrace to keep hidden nor a burden to stoically bear alone. None of us are truly self-sufficient; we all need help from others every day of our lives. In virtually every problem area there are experts to offer help—your doctor, lawyer or clergyman. And non-experts can help by listening sympathetically and providing support and encouragement.

Lastly, and surprisingly, beware of falling in love with your trouble. Trouble can give us a kind of melancholy importance, soothing to a shaky ego. Some people actually "enjoy" poor health, dwell on it and make it the unhealthy axis around which their lives revolve. Trouble can become a convenient alibi for our failings and shortcomings.

The essence of genius, according to William James, is knowing what to overlook. Let us apply this principle to our troubles. Overlook the small ones and meet the big ones head on, deal with them swiftly and be done with them.

Calvin Coolidge stated, "Work is not a curse; it is the prerogative of intelligence, the only means to manhood, and the measure of civilization." Using less lofty prose, the great philosopher Elbert Hubbard remarked, "Folks who never do any more than they get paid for, never get paid for any more than they do."

Wiser words were never spoken in the working world. Today's top executives are all-around men and women who have proven themselves capable of handling any assignment and willing to tackle any challenge.

Many of us envy the top executives who seem to live in ivory towers, do little but sign papers with a flourish, and enjoy the wealth and perquisites that come with their positions. One unknown author provided the following insight into the misunderstood role of the executive:

> An executive has practically nothing to do except decide what is to be done; to tell someone to do it; to listen to reasons why it should not be done or should be done by someone else, or done in a different way; to follow up to see if the thing has been done; to discover that it has not; to ask why; to listen to excuses from the person who should have done it; to follow up to see if the work has been properly done at last, only to discover that it was done incorrectly; to point out how it should have been done; to conclude that as long as the work has been done to let it stay as it is; to wonder if it isn't time to get rid of a person who cannot do a thing right, but also to reflect that he probably has a wife and 10 children and that, anyway, someone else would be just as bad if not worse; to consider how much simpler and better the work would have been if one had done it himself in the first place; to reflect sadly that one could have done it right in 20 minutes and that, as things turned out, one has had to spend two days to find out why it has taken three weeks for someone else to do the work the wrong way.

Being in a top executive position is never as easy as it might appear. Executives are up there because they tried a little harder, worked a little longer and gave a lot more of themselves.

More often than I would like, I find myself feeling ashamed for having misjudged another person. There is no excuse for judging another, yet we all do it. Before hastily passing judgment on someone, let us remember that we often criticize in others what we fear is true about ourselves or what we dislike about ourselves.

The victorious Duke of Wellington, after his retirement, used to invite the officers who served with him in the Battle of Waterloo to a yearly banquet, where they discussed the exciting experiences of other days.

At one of these annual events, the Duke produced a lovely jewel box— small, but encrusted with diamonds. The box was passed around the table for the guests to admire.

After some time, the Duke asked for the return of the jewel box. His guests were startled, as no one remembered who had held it last. A careful search of the table and floor revealed nothing. At this stage in the proceedings, someone suggested that all the guests present submit to being searched. Two raised objections to this proposal—one who would not agree to being searched; the other, the Duke himself, who flatly refused to have his former officers suffer this indignity.

The banquet ended with the box still missing. The guests departed, including the one who had refused to be searched (and consequently, was regarded with suspicion). Some days later, the Duke found his jewel box in an inside pocket of his coat! It had been returned to him the night of the banquet; and, while engaged in conversation, he had picked up the box without thinking and slipped it in his inside pocket.

At once the Duke set out to find the guest who had declined to be searched. He found the officer living in a poor section of the city nursing his sick wife. After informing him that the missing box had been found, the Duke inquired, "Why did you object to being searched, thus drawing suspicion to you?"

The officer replied, "In my pocket that night was a large part of my meal, slipped from the plate into a paper bag, that I might take food to my wife."

How often, when we criticize unfavorably, we do not know all the circumstances.

Communication is the act of accurately and effectively conveying information from one person to another. *Good* communication is the art of getting the right message to the right person at the right time.

In this definition of good communication, much emphasis should be placed on timing. Timing alone often spells the difference between good and poor communication. All too often, we say what needn't be expressed and leave unsaid words that would warm an indifferent heart or lift a troubled spirit. This concern rests at the heart of B.W. Spilman's essay, "Say It":

> You have a friend—a man, a woman, a boy, or a girl. For some reason, you love him very much. Have you ever told him so? Perhaps he would like to have you *say* it! Your friend has helped you along the way in the days gone by. Gratitude is in your heart. Do not let it lie buried there—*say* it! Some joy has come his way. You rejoice with him. But he will never know it unless you *say* it. An honor comes to him. He wins in the game of life and you are glad—*say* it. Your friend succeeds in some task which he has undertaken. You feel a grateful pride that he has done it—*say* it.
>
> A sorrow comes his way. He may have lost his property. Some of his loved ones may have gone wrong. Disease may have laid its hand on him, taking away the glow of health. You would share the sorrow with him—*say* it. Old age, or perhaps a breakdown in the human machinery, may shut in your friend so that he can no longer fare forth among his fellows. Perhaps the end draws near. In your heart you wish him bon voyage as he nears the sunset gate. A word of kindly sympathy would brighten the way—*say* it. The messenger of death may have knocked at his door and borne away into the unseen world some loved one. A word of sympathy would help to lighten the load and brighten the way—*say* it.
>
> A personal word, a telephone call, a post card, a letter, a telegram, and only a few minutes of time. Silent sympathy. Your own life may be better because of it; but your friend may go to the end of the journey and never know. You may add to the joy; you may lighten the load; you may brighten the way if only you take time to *say* it.

The words we speak in kindness and love live in the memory forever.

A retired business executive said it, "I discovered at an early age that most of the differences between average people and top people could be explained in these three words—'and then some.'" By the phrase "and then some," he meant people were more thoughtful of others, they were more considerate—"and then some." They met their obligations and responsibilities fairly, squarely, on time—"and then some."

Of the many quotes made by the late World Heavyweight Boxing Champion, James J. Corbett, during his colorful career, one was preeminent. When asked by a reporter what was most important for a man to become a champion, Corbett replied, "Fight one more round."

This was Jim Corbett's way of saying, "and then some."

You remember that the Lord Jesus asked his followers the test question, "What do ye more than others?"

We have our heroes and we find that most of these who have excelled could be identified by the three words, "and then some."

Thomas Edison, seeking a proper filament to light his incandescent lamp, failed month after month; but one day his efforts were successful. The world was presented with the electric light. He knew the meaning of "and then some."

S.N. Behrman, one of America's outstanding playwrights, turned out manuscripts for eleven years before he finally sold his first play—"and then some."

Fannie Hurst wrote more than 100 stories before one was ever accepted—"and then some."

Somerset Maugham was a failure for ten years, earning five hundred dollars in all that time. A producer hard put for a play dug out the forgotten manuscript, "Lady Fredrick," and Maugham became the toast of London—"and then some."

We have become computerized workers who are clock watchers. There is no romance in working overtime nor is there any reason we shouldn't leave on time. But if you measure your performance by the clock, it usually indicates just getting by with the least effort. Personal satisfaction comes when we leave knowing we've put forth the extra effort.

For some unexplainable reason, many projects are successful when someone has felt he could and then he gives it that one more effort—the finest tradition of "and then some."

Do you remember as a child when the circus came to town? I've always loved a circus—the animals, the color and glamour, the clowns, the popcorn! I love a circus except for the tightrope. The tightrope makes you tense and maybe it too strongly reminds you of a basic principle in life.

Even though the tightrope act may make us too tense, it is one of the most popular acts of the circus. We recognize the skill involved—and the danger. More than that, it may remind us that life is a tightrope. We must keep ourselves in balance, careful not to lean one way or another. We have been described as civil wars with internal pressures always seeking to make us lose balance. The Apostle Paul wrote about doing what he didn't want to do and being unable to do what he knew was right.

We admire the ability of anyone who can keep life under control and hold dangerous forces in balance. The tightrope walker can never stand still. As we learned riding a bike, we must keep moving to retain balance. Proper balance requires action, but the action must be with caution. Some of us tend to go to extremes. Any problem causes us to over react. We enjoy hysteria or making mountains out of mole hills. As I kid a dear friend, if he can't find a crisis, he will create one. Such conduct impairs judgments and makes fantasies. Others of us, when we have a problem, become super cautious. We want to stand still, hoping the problem will evaporate before we awake in the morning. But the tightrope walker who stops, falls—so in life.

As the tightrope walker and the bike rider must have balance, so must the team player. The baseball star must be able to hit, run, and throw. The basketball player must be able to playmake, pass, rebound, and score. Also, a big score in one inning or one quarter does not win the game. The same is true of good companies and their employees. Not enough that you know your job well or one phase of it. The total company must be of concern to you.

Most importantly, to be of value to yourself, your family, and your company, you and I must stay individually balanced. Accepting the fact that life is a tightrope, we cannot survive standing still, wishing, or reacting violently; but we must carefully keep walking forward.

The balanced life contains submission to God, love of family, and dedication to work. Such a person always seems to walk across the problems without too often falling in the net.

Communication is so basic to all relationships. Basic, but often overlooked. We all must learn to express our honest feelings; to lovingly, kindly, but honestly, talk to one another.

Do you and your spouse communicate? I feel my wife and I really do, but there is always room for improvement. Not long ago, I confided that I would like a two-door car for a change, although I knew she truly preferred a four-door. "Tom, the only reason we always have a four-door is to satisfy you," she replied, "in fact, all I ever had were two-door cars until I married you." A trivial matter, but we had gone for years assuming it was the other person's preference to have a four-door. All we had to do was communicate.

We assume too often what each other likes or wants without asking. Couples need to openly and sympathetically discuss what is in their hearts. To communicate effectively, neither person can be defensive. If we take ourselves too seriously, it leads to arrogance that can flare up over any criticism. If we are quick to accuse, we become equally quick to defend ourselves. And open communication suffers.

Any couple needs to cultivate a mutual sense of humor. Laugh together, laugh at each other, laugh at yourself—but all without cruelty. A while back, my wife and I were running late for a banquet and, in the tradition of all good husbands everywhere, I took a shortcut over a mountain. It turned out to be the worst road I had ever seen. My wife could have joined me in getting down on myself, but instead she had me laughing with her, and a miserable mistake became a joke to remember and share.

Effective communication depends on equally effective listening. We all have the tendency to form a reply while our mate is still talking, so we never really hear. And listening includes looking. The words may say one thing, while the look in the eye may give a totally different signal.

The foundation of any communication is enhanced if the communicators share a deep affection and a desire to know more about each other. Love is the greatest thing we can communicate.

During more than a quarter century of daily radio broadcasts, one particular script received the most audience response, and I was requested to repeat it annually. For many years, I told listeners the author was unknown, but I later met him—an authentic Colorado cowboy by the name of Jess Kenner. The message contained in "The World is Mine" can help us all put things back in proper perspective when we are feeling sorry for ourselves:

Today upon a bus, I saw a lovely maid with golden hair; I envied her—she seemed so gay—and wished I were as fair. When suddenly she rose to leave, I saw her hobble down the aisle; she had one foot and wore a crutch, but as she passed, a smile. Oh, God, forgive me when I whine; I have two feet—the world is mine.

And then I stopped to buy some sweets. The lad who sold them had such charm. I talked to him—he said to me, "It's nice to talk to folks like you. You see," he said, "I'm blind." Oh, God, forgive me when I whine; I have two eyes—the world is mine.

Then walking down the street, I saw a child with eyes of blue. He stood and watched the others play; it seemed he knew not what to do. I stopped a moment, then I said, "Why don't you join the others, dear?" He looked ahead without a word, and then I knew, he could not hear.

Oh, God, forgive me when I whine;
I have two ears—the world is mine.
With feet to take me where I'd go,
With eyes to see the sunset glow,
With ears to hear what I would know,
Oh, God, forgive me when I whine;
I'm blessed indeed. The world is mine.

A company's profits are its very lifeblood, providing its employees with healthy jobs. A company losing money is mortally sick and, without a quick reversal, places its employees' futures in jeopardy. You are linked in a very personal way to your company, beyond just a place to work. Your survival spurs you to work for a profit and to feel proud when the company achieves profitability.

Profits—a nickel on every dollar of sales for the average industrial enterprise—enable a company to fund many vital activities:

- Profits are used to replace old machinery with new and competitive automated equipment.
- Profits allow for the building of new plants and expansion of existing plants that create additional job opportunities and promotions.
- Profits are used in research and development activities to create new product lines and keep current products competitive.
- Profits pay dividends to shareholders—the people who believe in you enough to invest their savings in your company.
- Profits pay federal, state and local taxes.

Or as a major auto manufacturer simply stated, "The company that fails to earn a profit hires no new people, develops no new products, pays no dividends or taxes, trains no new employees and makes no contribution to the community."

Making a profit is more than simple productivity, producing goods, selling goods; profits are linked to quality products at competitive prices. Quality is achieved when:

- You take personal pride in every aspect of your work, even the most routine, and never settle for less than the best.
- You do the job right the first time, realizing that duplication wastes valuable time and money.
- You admit your mistakes, learn by them and determine not to repeat them.
- You declare your own personal war on waste and see how each day you help cut costs.

Good companies—profitable companies—don't come about by accident or luck. Good companies—profitable companies—result where employees feel self-worth and take a fierce pride in their work.

Some people just know how to live. As Uncle Colin Lindsey likes to say, "I'm not concerned about putting years on my life, but putting life into my years." Some enviable people appear to squeeze the most out of every moment—they walk into a room and bring with them a certain warmth and exhilaration. Some people are passionate about what they do and seem to get more done, laugh more, whistle more, play more, think more.

A common characteristic among people who thoroughly enjoy life is that they keep life simple. They may face complicated problems on the job, but when they leave work, they do just that. They go home to an uncluttered simple life; often sharing not only a warm romance with their mates, but equally important, sharing a genuine friendship.

These upbeat people who get the "biggest bang for the buck" out of life, have accepted life as it is. They are far from docile—just the opposite— they are aggressive. They accept the fact that life is never static, so they are undaunted by the unexpected. They accept change as a way of life, rather than accept frustration as a daily companion.

Upbeat people are highly flexible. They roll with life's punches while looking for the opening to score a knockout. They know that people, just like giant skyscrapers, have to sway to keep from crumbling.

There is nothing boring about living. We are in charge of our lives when we view each change as a greater personal opportunity. Any change contains a risk factor, but not as much risk as standing still and letting the world pass us by. The very uncertainty of living can help keep us awake and alert and upbeat—and that's life.

A rut is an open-ended grave," someone once said, while another observed, "The only difference between a rut and a grave is a matter of inches."

In truth, it is only a matter of inches or degrees that separates the routine from the rut. We all have parts of our lives that are routine and repetitive; we fall into a rut only if we let ourselves. We allow ourselves to become easily bored because we seek one peak of excitement after another. We want to be entertained and amused, then afterwards find ourselves dull and neutral.

We have to admire people who stimulate themselves from within; people who take their mundane circumstances and turn them into positive opportunities. United Technologies Corporation, in its series of thought-provoking ads, offered this sage advice:

> Oscar Wilde said, "Consistency is the last refuge of the unimaginative." So stop getting up at 6:05. Get up at 5:06. Walk a mile at dawn. Find a new way to drive to work. Switch chores with your spouse next Saturday. Buy a wok. Study wildflowers. Stay up alone all night. Read to the blind. Start counting brown-eyed blondes. Subscribe to an out-of-town paper. Canoe at midnight. Don't write to your Congressman . . . take a whole Scout troop to see him. Learn to speak Italian. Teach some kid the thing you do best. Listen to two hours of uninterrupted Mozart. Take up aerobic dancing. Leap out of that rut. Savor life. Remember, we only pass this way once.

Weekends are designed to refresh us in body and spirit. But weekends only rejuvenate if they are days spent in recharging the human batteries and using our creative juices. This weekend, climb out of your rut; do the unusual; savor life; refresh yourself!

Certainly we can eat small amounts of delicious food, but we must burn up those calories afterward. Swim, walk five miles, anything to use those leg muscles," said the late Dr. Paul Dudley White. We are a country of fad diets and spectacular exercises but Dr. White said simple walking could be a life saver.

"The Battle of the Bulge" may be the biggest problem facing many of us. No matter the cost of food, we are determined to dig our own graves with our teeth.

Dr. Paul Dudley White became a household name when he guided the late President Eisenhower back from a heart attack. The Boston physician was always a strong advocate of exercise as a means of keeping physically fit and preventing heart disease. Dr. White didn't let us off with just walking, which he called the road to life, however. In addition to daily exercise he urged that we eat sparingly and drink only moderately.

Health is very important in our fast-paced life. Physical fitness determines how well we carry ourselves, how ready we are for action, and how long we can endure. Exercise isn't only for overweight but for toning muscles, strengthening fiber, and building stamina.

The American Medical Association reports that "the man or woman who takes regular exercise will maintain a better state of physical fitness, will keep active longer and is more apt to be resistant to the degenerative diseases of middle and later life, especially disease of the heart and blood vessels."

AMA even suggests that recent studies seem to indicate that the lack of physical exercise is more often the cause of a person being overweight than overeating.

When recommending walking, I mean more than a leisurely stroll. Walking should be long enough and strenuous enough to produce a sense of healthful fatigue. One report says a mile a day of walking takes care of at least five hundred calories a week.

Bill Maness, author of *Exercise Your Heart,* writes: "The primary benefit of walking is that the largest muscle groups in the body are in the legs and thighs. When these are exercised the heart gets a workout."

Is there such a thing as Ole Tyme Religion? The following gleanings might give us insight:

Favorite Hymns: Which hymns do Americans most enjoy singing? The Gallup Organization reported these were the top five:

1. Amazing Grace
2. How Great Thou Art
3. Rock of Ages
4. Battle Hymn of the Republic
5. The Old Rugged Cross

Fast Facts:

- Percentage of Americans who believe in heaven—71%
  who believe in hell—53%
  who believe in reincarnation—15%
- Percentage of income given to charitable causes by households with incomes below $10,000: 2.8%
  by households with incomes from $50,000 to $75,000: 1.5%
- Percentage of baby boomers (ages 22–42) who say they have had a religious or mystical experience—a moment of sudden religious insight or awakening: 33%

Statistics are interesting, but to most of us our faith is a private affair—a personal relationship with our God.

The champion isn't necessarily the person who has the most, but the champion is the person who gives the most." These are the observations of Dr. Laurence E. Morehouse of UCLA's Human Performance Laboratories. My champions are not the sports stars, but the individuals who go to work each day and to that work give their very best effort.

My champion is the old man who, year after year, had a line waiting for him to shine shoes at the Peabody Hotel in Memphis. When asked how he could shine shoe after shoe with such vigor and determination, he smiled with a warm, wide grin and said simply, "I'm not just shining your shoes, I'm working to make you proud of how you look."

My champion is the working wife and mother who manages a delightful home, raises good children and still handles an outside job to perfection. My champion is the salesperson who patiently works to satisfy the potential buyer, even when the time it takes is unreasonable. My champion is the woman who becomes vice-president of the bank; a woman who started as a teller and always had the longest lines waiting because she was so pleasant.

My champions are those who give good effort to any job they have.

My champions are those who give each day their best effort.

My champions are those who, when they fail at a job or feel they did less than their best, take a deep breath and try again.

My champions respect the company they work for, but also know that no matter who pays them, they still really work for themselves.

My champions are people who have so much pride in their work that they would willingly sign their names to any work they do.

My champions are the ordinary Americans who never make the headlines, yet undergird the foundation of our great country.

Do you find yourself moaning the old line, "The faster I run, the farther behind I become?" Do you occasionally feel like a gorilla is standing on your chest, jogging in place? Do you keep waking up and wondering where you've been? Do your goals that seem challenging, yet attainable, keep slipping farther away? Then you are one of the harried horde living a merry-go-round existence in the pressure cooker of modern life.

Much of our pressure results because we put emphasis on *doing* instead of *being*. We should get caught up in our work, but not at the expense of losing ourselves. We should stop worrying about what we will be and where we will be a year from now; we need only to live one day at a time.

Many of us have an insatiable desire for ego-massaging, but we want the reward without the risk. We want to play it safe and still be popular. If placed in a situation where we could be criticized, we search for someone to blame.

Then, some of us have the same social drives and needs, but are willing to take a few more risks if for no other reason than to attract attention to ourselves. Still, our biggest problem is that we are satisfied to *look* effective rather than *be* effective.

We could all be the most effective if we could be so caught up in our cause, our work, our profession that we neither question nor fear the risks involved. In truth, self-actualization is never plotted by us, but awarded by those we lead. When we perform for the success of others, we don't worry about covering our tracks. In the end, we accomplish more than we mess up, and even turn our failures into the mix for the next success.

All we need are well-established goals, standards, ethics, guidelines. Goals are objectives; standards define quality; ethics describe the heart's intent; and guidelines are the process. So, when next you feel ready to cave in, take a deep breath; rethink what you're doing; realize that you should act and work, not with regard to the impression you make, but so the heart is revealed.

Private or free enterprise is a great economic system, but it is neither perfect nor flawless. Our system of economics contributes to individual worth, individual vitality and individual freedom, but still it has its liabilities. Perhaps we expect too much out of the system and not enough from the people involved in it.

Adam Smith, the proponent of private enterprise, feared its dangers from the beginning. Private enterprise must include a support system that provides virtue, morals and ethics. The business of private enterprise is neither good nor bad by itself, but is regulated by the inner being of the people who work within the system. Too easily, we tend to blame our transgressions on the system instead of examining the hearts of the workers and managers.

Morals and ethics are of the soul, not the system.

We cannot expect the system to be perfect when it is managed by imperfect people. Yet we must not put ourselves down so much that we tarnish our worth. Neo-conservative Irving Kristol attributes our national negative attitude to the fact that we are always beating up on ourselves. If we continue to put ourselves down, we at once become the victim and the culprit, the savage and the savaged. A society is both good and bad, hot and cold, positive and negative. To take only one side creates imbalance.

While not overlooking or excusing the wrongs of private enterprise, neither should we isolate them. When we balance the virtues and the vices, we discover that America's private enterprise system remains the best of those offered. The United States is like a journey to travel, not a destination realized. We travelers who criticize the system must also turn our efforts toward making it better.

An error commonly made by anyone in a position of leadership is to spend too much time commiserating with the losers instead of praising the winners. Leaders tend to be subconsciously negative, reaching down instead of pushing up.

Whatever their role, leaders want their people to succeed. The seemingly logical practice is to give full attention to the losers, thinking the winners are doing fine on their own. In truth, there is logic for helping the weak. Think of the mother of a dozen children who, when asked which one she loved most, replied, "The one who needs me most." Yet in helping the weak, we must not neglect the strong, assuming—perhaps falsely—they are somehow less sensitive.

In the days when I served as a local parish pastor, I was careful never to talk about the members who were absent from the church. If I talked about the missing, those present might conclude that the only way to gain attention was to miss the next Sunday.

The same principle holds true in the world of business. Executives talk so much about their non-productive workers, their absentees and their ineffective salespeople that the capable employees begin to feel they can gain recognition only when they become a problem. Even if not taken to that extreme, effective employees may lose their incentive and initiative because inspiration from the top is lacking.

An article in the *Wall Street Journal* strengthened this argument. A sales manager, fed up with listening to excuses and buck-passing by his low producers, decided to devote the same time and energy to helping his best performers. As a result, 80 percent of his time was given to the top third of his sales force—helping them, praising them, listening to them, urging them on. The other two-thirds felt neglected and jealous; some quit and were replaced, while most stopped feeling sorry for themselves and took on an "I'll show them!" attitude. Before long, two-thirds were winners and even those in the lower third were more productive than before.

The key to motivation is to appeal to the natural competitive nature of people; to challenge the less effective workers, without putting them down, by using the better workers as examples. Insist they too can win—and they will!

A perfectionist" a humorist once claimed, "is someone who takes pains and gives them to the rest of us." All of us have a bit of the perfectionist in us, that urge to straighten a crooked picture even in a public place.

But perfection can be a club; perfection can be the ultimate crutch. Perfection can be a rejection of self. To gain insight into our desire for perfection, we would do well to ask ourselves the following:

1. Do I procrastinate, delay or put things off until I feel just right or inspired to act?
2. Do I surrender to inaction because I am afraid I will be rejected or unpopular?
3. Do I finish a job and then keep tinkering with it until I become totally frustrated?
4. Do I put myself down for missing a goal that was far beyond anything I had accomplished previously?
5. Do I strive to be like someone who has abilities well above mine?

Within reason, any task worth doing is worth doing right. "Within reason" is the key. We must measure the purpose of the job against the plan for doing the job. The way we carry out the garbage, for instance, varies greatly from the way we would carry a priceless antique. Reason requires that effort match the challenge; reason requires extreme care with the antique and not wasting energy and effort on mere garbage.

Perfection is the desire to give our best effort. The effort of today should be improved by the effort of yesterday. What we do today not only has a finished quality all its own, but prepares us for improvement in doing the same task tomorrow. Progress, not perfection, is the key. The test is whether the quality of a task lessens or increases with repetition; whether we view the repetition as boredom or as an opportunity to perfect our abilities.

The quest for perfection must never make us cower, afraid to learn from our mistakes. Remember, Thomas Edison tried 10,000 unsuccessful filaments before he found the secret and perfected the light bulb.

I believe one of the things right with America is her youth. Young people are concerned, questioning and seeking what is right in our kaleidoscopic world. Young people deserve the best answers we can give.

People who solve problems, young or old, usually have a sound basis for their judgments and decisions. Maybe you put it in creed form—maybe not. Walderman Argow did design a "Youth's Credo" which may express your feelings:

I believe in the greatness of myself, and that I am in this world for a purpose, that purpose being to put back into life more than I have taken out.

I believe in the integrity of other people, assured that they try as hard to follow the gleam, even as I.

I believe in the gallantry of older people whose seasoned experience and steadfast devotion have preserved for me the precious heritage of the past.

I believe in the magnificence of the past, knowing that without its storied wealth I would possess nothing.

I believe in the challenge of the future, fully realizing there will be no future except it become alive through me.

I believe in the sacredness of duty, through which I must do those things that are expected of me, and above all, fulfill the purpose for which I am here.

I believe in the nobility of work as the creative expression of the best within me, and as my share in easing the common load of all.

I believe in the enrichment of play and laughter as the means of cleansing my body of staleness and my mind of dullness.

I believe in the contagion of health, and that I can spread it through cheerfulness, wholesome habits, sensible expenditure of energies, and wise use of foods.

I believe in the holiness of friendship, knowing that my life is a tapestry woven from the threads of many beautiful lives.

Because I believe these things, I therefore believe in God, who justified all my beliefs; He is the still small voice within, ever urging me toward the unattained. Since He cares for these things, I believe that even death cannot steal these priceless possessions from me.

And whatever more I believe is entwined in those precious feelings that lie too deep for words.

A free society depends on builders of thoughts to match or undergird our building of mortar. A free society is built by adults and youth of goodwill, "brick by brick in the heat of the day."

D o you have to psyche yourself? I do. Each day I have a routine of discipline to get myself going, and so here are some thoughts for next week:

Monday's thought is from Charles Spurgeon: "Labor to have but one object and one aim. And for this purpose give God the keeping of thine heart, that thy soul, being preserved and protected by Him, may be directed into one channel, and one only, that thy life may run deep and pure, its only banks being God's will, its only channel the love of Christ and a desire to please Him."

Tuesday's comes from the *Herald and Presbytery* magazine: "Life must be lived on the installment plan. God gives and requires just so much at a time, no more, no less. Life is made up of so many successive installments of opportunity, of duty, and of grace. It is impossible, therefore, to live life in the future tense. All that men have and all that they are asked to attend to is the present. And the present in its demands is vigorous enough. Take care of the *now* and the *future* will take care of itself."

John Ruskin for Wednesday: "He only is advancing in life whose heart is getting softer, whose blood is getting warmer, whose brain quicker, and whose spirit is entering into living peace."

Thursday, John Locke: "In morality there are books enough written both by ancient and modern philosophers, but the morality of the Gospel does so exceed them all that, to give a man a full knowledge of true morality, I shall send him to no other book than the New Testament."

The great Bible teacher, F.B. Meyer, for Friday: "God's will comes to thee and me in daily circumstances, in little things equally as great. Meet them bravely. Be at your best always, though the occasion be one of the very least. Dignify the smallest summons by the greatness of your response."

The week is concluded with Charron: "He who receives a good turn should never forget it; he who does one should never remember it."

You probably have your own collection of good thoughts. Try reading one for each day—we are as we think.

One secret of success is not so much people believing in what you do as it is people believing that *you* believe in what you do. The best argument for convincing others is for them to see the fire of conviction in your eyes.

One of the great sales counselors and motivators was Ernest Dichter, thought by many to be the father of motivational research. What made him so effective was that he had learned the basic lesson by hard personal experience.

Ernest Dichter's academic preparation consisted of a doctorate in psychology earned in his late 20s. Unable to find work in education, he took a job selling woven labels for a small firm in Paris, thinking the job would at least keep body and soul together.

Weeks went by and the fledgling salesman hadn't made a single sale. He grew discouraged, but didn't blame himself. Instead, he went to the boss and complained that the price of the labels was too high. He couldn't peddle the merchandise with such an expensive price tag.

The boss must have been wise. Instead of arguing, he made a bargain with his young employee, saying, "Ernest, I'll tell you what I'll do. I'm not saying you're right, but I'll cut the price in half for one week. Now rush out, sell all you can, and ruin me."

Dichter hurried back to call on his potential customers. But after giving it his best shot, even at half price he couldn't move any of the the labels. He reported his frustration and failure to his boss, who smiled and said, "Ernest, I'm not laughing at you, but you won't sell until you believe in what you are selling." The boss had known that Dichter honestly thought his failure was due to the price, so he gave him the latitude to go out and prove himself right. When Dichter proved himself wrong, the boss had his attention and helped develop a sense of worth and value about his product. And sales resulted at the full price.

People are attracted to us, not because we are a "bargain," but because we believe in who we are and what we are doing. People believe in others who believe in themselves.

At one time or another, I suppose all of us daydream about living our lives over again and making major changes. While realizing it is a waste of time to seriously consider reliving our lives, it does help to reflect on our past as a means of living better in the present and assisting our children in the future.

One of the truly great men it has been my privilege to know was the late Walter McPeek. God had given him the gift of writing and he felt committed to using his talented pen to help youth, particularly the Boy Scouts.

In one of his musings, Walter wrote, "If I had my life to live over, I'd pay more attention to my friends, and to acquaintances that might have become friends. I fear that if most of us didn't work any more thoughtfully to cultivating the grass on our lawn than we do in cultivating friendships, we just wouldn't have much of a lawn.

"If I could live my life over, I'd pay more attention to people. I'd try to keep close to them and express the warmth and affection that I really felt for them. I'd try more often to send a note of good wishes when good things happened to them, or say a word of congratulations when I saw them.

"I wouldn't be satisfied to send a perfunctory greeting at Christmastime. I'd write a personal note; I'd set up a birthday file for a few of my closest friends and let it help me to remember to speak or to write a word of encouragement to them at birthday time...

"I'd be more careful to answer every personal letter promptly, to keep the channels of communications open and to keep friendships expanding. I'd take the initiative in making contacts with those acquaintances whom I regarded highly.

"When I met a person whom I admired, I would not keep my regard for him a secret. I'd show him that I truly respected him and enjoyed being with him...

"If I had my life to live over... there's little I can do about the part of it that is gone... but for the remaining years that I have to live, I'm going to try harder."

Typical of Walter McPeek, he never worked for material possessions or honors, but for greater relationships with his fellow man. Rather than mourn our past failures or oversights with people, we can begin today building the bridges of meaningful relationships.

Research indicates that few Americans devote more than two minutes a day to reading economic material. As a result, most citizens are woefully ignorant as to how our economic system works. When people verbally attack companies and their "obscene" profits, they may be hurting themselves.

Profit is what remains after the costs of producing, manufacturing, selling. Profit, in most cases, is the very reason a business was started.

Much profit is put back into the business for capital improvement in order to modernize the plant or store, and to help create even more profit in the future. When money is plowed back to improve the business, it often creates more jobs, higher salaries, additional benefits and retirement funds.

The reverse is true when a company loses money. Morale drops, jobs are threatened and the company's very existence is in jeopardy. It becomes apparent why working hard and productively comes back to benefit the worker.

By working hard, the company makes a profit and you are paid. And that pay provides your car, vacation, new television and even makes it possible for you to invest in a company and receive a greater share of the profits.

Some profit also goes to shareholders, the individuals who invest in a company by purchasing stock. They deserve a return on their investment in the form of dividends for the risk they have taken. If a company borrows from a bank, the investors have to pay the money back; if the company loses, the investors lose with the company.

In a system such as free enterprise in the United States, everyone shares the profits—owners, employees, shareholders. We all profit from profits.

If you see two people chatting in a corner, looking in your general direction, are you convinced they are whispering about you? If you have to wait for a clerk to take your order, do you feel slighted and convinced that other customers would have been waited on immediately?

None of us are free from an occasional negative thought. But if thoughts such as these often race through your mind, you are carrying the weight of a heavy psychological load. The suspicions we have about others only mirror the way we think about ourselves.

The following simple principles may help you keep your equilibrium and your perspective:

- If you are criticized, you must have done something worthwhile—keep it up.
- If you are jealous of your neighbor's new car, it doesn't make yours any older. And keep in mind who owes the most.
- If somebody calls you a fool, check the facts for accuracy before denying it.
- If your competitor cheats to take business away from you, remember someone will cheat and take it away from him. With so many good, potential customers to sell to, you don't need a customer who can be bribed.
- If the news media misquotes you, don't worry. Your friends won't believe it and the misquote might be better than what you actually said.
- If you don't get everything you want, cheer up. Think of all the things you wanted that you now wish you didn't have.
- If you have tried something and failed, think how much better off you are than the bored individual who tried nothing and succeeded.

Would you truly trade in your life on another one? Is there someone you would truly like to change places with? Instead, just enjoy who you are and what you can become by the grace of God.

One of this country's most prolific writers, Thomas Wolfe, claimed there is no way to recapture the past, no way to go home again. And yet the past seems to hold a magnetic attraction for us and we go through periodic crazes of nostalgia.

If pinned down, we readily admit we wouldn't really want to return to the past. We enjoy the very conveniences we condemn. Still there is an understandable logic to our nostalgia. Whenever we become uncertain or fearful of the future, we crave a return to the comfortable confines of where we've been before. We want the dusty old road where we know the potholes, instead of the new interstate highway with the unknown over every hilltop. What we forget is that the old road no longer exists—the highway has been built over it.

Memory plays tricks and our imagination has a way of romantically painting the past. The homes of our childhood expand in our minds until, when we return one day, we find it so much smaller we think someone has played a cruel joke.

Nostalgia, perhaps, got its start with Adam. We can imagine him, at the close of the day, strolling back to the gates of Paradise and looking longingly through to the past. Earning his bread by the sweat of his brow, Adam could remember the days gone by when the trees were heavy with fruit, the rivers flowed clear as crystal, and meadows were bejeweled with wildflowers. Adam must have kicked himself for the mess he had made under the guise of progress and wisdom he had expected to receive from the forbidden fruit.

But man cannot return to what he thought was paradise. Our destiny is in the future, not anchored in the past. Each of us has a choice. We can experience grief in a vain attempt to recapture the imagined glory of yesterday, or we can faithfully believe God has an even better future awaiting us if we move forward with our lives today.

Growing up I was always fascinated by older people. My grandpa and his contemporaries were my heroes. Living gives wisdom and I was attracted by the natural conversation of older people. Also, history has been my "bag" and these people have lived it.

Fifteen years ago, a great-grandmother, Ina Cozby Tygett, of Anna, Illinois, sent me these lines:

> Be kind, not jealous, for your eyes reveal it;
> Be feminine, not boisterous, we must conceal it.
> Be friendly, not bossy, if you're to succeed;
> Speak clearly and softly, for the charm that you need.
> Never shout, "I don't care," for you should care a lot.
> Everything that you do must be given much thought!
> Speak kindly of parents, it's a sign of good breeding,
> Cling on to their love which I know you'll be needing.
> It's time in your life you should seek out the Lord;
> He will soften your tempest and send His reward.
> School will be fun and your girl friends, too;
> Boys shouldn't be chased by young girls like you!
> When with your friends you can't seem to agree,
> Just ask yourself, "Could the fault be with me?"
> Tell all to your mom, with tears, not rebellion;
> She'll help solve your problem, you'll both feel like a million.
> Lots of money to spend, fine clothes to wear,
> Just a casual friend will get you nowhere.
> Deep love and understanding with God, Mother, and Dad
> Are the greatest possessions pre-teens ever had.

In our day when there is no much uncertainty, I'm especially pleased I have so many older friends. You've lived through crisis upon crisis—crime of the Roaring Twenties, depression, world wars. You've seen the Ship of State through some treacherous waters.

In this poem, you've seen that attitude and needs of youth are the same from generation to generation.

Most of us are determined to make our own mistakes. We seemingly want to have our own miseries. The wise youth learns from the experiences of others.

From the First United Methodist Church of Winder, Georgia, comes the following:

Americans are very religious.
   Some play golf religiously.
   Some follow baseball religiously.
   Some wash their cars religiously,
   Or care for their lawns religiously,
   Or keep up with the stock market religiously,
   Or watch television religiously.
Americans are most religious.
   Some are religious about house cleaning.
   Some are religious about family activities.
   Some are religious about their jobs,
   Or about how they brush their teeth,
   Or about getting enough rest and relaxation,
   Or about being in church and doing God's work.
I guess it depends
   On what your religion is—
   On what your god is—
   On what your priority is.
A person's religion or god is whatever he or she has time for when time is
   short and running out.
About what are you religious?

The more I live, the more I sense that life is measured by my choices.

We are all a bit uneasy giving or taking criticism. Strange as it seems, there are those who have even more difficulty accepting genuine compliments. You might be one who gets nervous when someone speaks about you in flattering terms.

One reason might be the unrealistically high goals and standards you have set for yourself. There is nothing wrong with wanting to be your best, the best you are capable of being. However, your standards may be beyond your capacity and, if so, you reject compliments because your performance or your appearance is still below your own expectations. No amount of praise or flattery can convince you otherwise.

Another reason for an inability to accept compliments might be feelings of rejection or non-acceptance. In your childhood days, you didn't receive the acceptance you craved; now you cannot accept a compliment as genuine. To do so would symbolize acceptance, and you don't feel it can be yours.

Or perhaps you cannot accept a compliment because of self-hatred. Self-hatred can stem from being made to shoulder too much guilt as a child or being ridiculed by peers or parents as a youngster. Now, you continue to see yourself as awkward, imperfect and unattractive and, therefore, you are certain compliments are only in jest.

Humility has nothing to do with rejecting compliments. The humble person will be honest enough to recognize the compliment as deserved, without being misled or distracted.

You are a person, one of a kind. You are you. You are capable of loving; you are capable of giving compliments. In turn, you are worthy of being loved; you are deserving of compliments.

Suspicion of the rich has long been a vice of the jealous. Prominent people make easy and convenient targets for our own inadequacies. Denouncing the wealthy, whether or not justified, somehow excuses our own lack of success. But, consider the personal philosophy of the late John D. Rockefeller, Jr.:

I believe in the supreme worth of the individual and in his right to life, liberty and the pursuit of happiness.

I believe that every right implies a responsibility; every opportunity, an obligation; every possession, a duty.

I believe that the law was made for man and not man for the law; that government is the servant of the people and not their master.

I believe in the dignity of labor, whether with head or hand; that the world owes no man a living but that it owes every man an opportunity to make a living.

I believe that thrift is essential to well-ordered living and that economy is a prime requisite of a sound financial structure, whether in government, business or personal affairs.

I believe that truth and justice are fundamental to an enduring social order.

I believe in the sacredness of a promise, that a man's word should be as good as his bond; that character—not wealth or power or position—is of supreme worth.

I believe that the rendering of useful service is the common duty of mankind and that only in the purifying fire of sacrifice is the dross of selfishness consumed and the greatness of the human soul set free.

I believe in an all-wise and all-loving God named by whatever name, and that the individual's highest fulfillment, greatest happiness, and widest usefulness are to be found in living in harmony with His will.

I believe that love is the greatest thing in the world; that it alone can overcome hate; that right can and will triumph over might.

It is tragic when a person feels he or she has outlived their life. Those who have lived long have so much to share from their experience. The following poem was reportedly found among the belongings of an elderly woman who died in a nursing home in Ireland:

What do you see, nurse, what do you see? What are you thinking when you look at me?

A crabbit old woman, not very wise, uncertain of habit, with far away eyes.

Is that what you're thinking, is that what you see? Then open your eyes, you're not looking at me.

I am a small child of ten with a father and mother, brothers and sisters who love one another.

A young girl at sixteen with wings at her feet, dreaming that soon now a lover she'll meet.

A bride soon at twenty, my heart gives a leap, remembering the vows that I promised to keep.

At twenty-five now I have young of my own, who need me to build a secure happy home.

A woman of thirty, my young now grow fast, bound to each other with ties that should last.

At forty my young now soon will be gone, but my man stays beside me to see I don't mourn.

At fifty once more babies play around me knee, again we know children my loved one and me.

Dark days are upon me, my husband is dead, I look at the future, I shudder with dread,

For my young are all busy rearing young of their own, and I think of the years and the love I have known.

I'm an old lady now and nature is cruel, 'tis her jest to make old age look like a fool.

But inside this old carcass a young girl still dwells, and now and again my battered heart swells.

I remember the joys, I remember the pain, and I am loving and living life over again.

I think of the years all too few, gone so fast, and accept the stark fact that nothing can last.

So open your eyes, nurse, open and see. Not a crabbit old woman, look closer . . . see ME.

Maturity or emotional growth has little to do with one's age or growing old. On his 70th birthday, the late T.S. Eliot remarked, "I'm just beginning to grow up, to get maturity. In the last few years, everything I've done up to 60 or so has seemed very childish."

Maturity comes to each of us in varied patterns. Some bloom early, having adulthood thrust upon them by circumstance, while others bloom late, living somewhat sheltered lives.

Ben Holden has given us the following practical description:

Maturity is the ability to control your anger and settle differences without violence or destruction.

Maturity is patience, the willingness to pass up immediate pleasure in favor of the long-term gain.

Maturity is perserverance, the ability to sweat out a project or a situation in spite of opposition and discouraging setbacks.

Maturity is unselfishness—responding to the needs of others, often at the expense of one's own wishes or desires.

Maturity is the capacity to face unpleasantness and frustration, discomfort and defeat, without complaint or collapse.

Maturity is humility. It is being big enough to say, "I was wrong." And when right, the mature person need not say, "I told you so."

Maturity is the ability to make decisions and stand by them. The immature spend their lives exploring endless possiblilities then doing nothing.

Maturity means dependability, keeping one's word, coming through in the crisis. The immature are masters of alibi—confused and disorganized. Their lives are a maze of broken promises, former friends, unfinished business and good intentions which never materialize.

Maturity is the art of living in peace with that which we cannot change.

Some of us may relate maturity with growing old. Actually, the mature person often lives longer because he or she accepts life as it is, excited by the daily journey into new areas of adventure and personal growth.

In recent years, we have tended to focus our parental concern on the problems of teenagers. But, by the time your child goes off to first grade, it might be too late. Dr. Burton White of Harvard University pinpoints the period from 8 months to 18 months as the most decisive in a child's life.

During this time, a child begins to grasp our language, to move about independently, to reach out in curiosity. Curiosity is the door to discovery, learning and growing. An infant needs to touch, feel and chew so we must provide an assortment of harmless playthings. As a child begins to talk we must do our best to understand and respond.

When both parents are in the workforce, a child can be somewhat cut off from our greatest help—parents' time. Out of guilt, working parents may use affluence to buy too much and too many toys. Out of guilt, working parents may tend to overlook a child's temper tantrums and pouting. But no child needs spoiling. The best teacher is our personal example, as outlined in the "Parent's Creed":

If a child lives with criticism, he learns to condemn.
If a child lives with hostility, he learns to fight.
If a child lives with ridicule, he learns to be shy.
If a child lives with shame, he learns to feel guilty.
If a child lives with tolerance, he learns to be patient.
If a child lives with encouragement, he learns confidence.
If a child lives with praise, he learns to appreciate.
If a child lives with fairness, he learns justice.
If a child lives with security, he learns to have faith.
If a child lives with approval, he learns to like himself.
If a child lives with acceptance and friendship, he learns to find love in the world.

A child seeks to discover the world. Such discovery is filled with excitement, laughter, disappointment, tears, frustration, warmth and hurts. All are necessary for well-rounded growth.

Did you have a tough week? Disappointed? It's easy these days to feel depressed when things don't go exactly as we would have them. Success is a goal which under normal circumstances is not obtained easily. Failure, in many instances, is just around the corner. The old saying, "Quit while you're ahead," is by no means the exact formula for success. It has it's merits for certain situations, but just how many really get to the top of the ladder in their fields without taking a chance here or there or struggling along when things seem darkest?

Along these lines, the famed "Author Unknown" has a few words to say:

Don't quit when things go wrong, as they sometimes will
When the road you're trudging seems all uphill,
When the funds are low and the debts are high,
And you want to smile, but you have to sigh,
When care is pressing you down a bit.
Rest if you must, but don't quit.

Life is queer with its twists and turns
As every one of us sometimes learns
And many a fellow turns about
When he might have won had he stuck it out.
Don't give up though the pace seems slow;
You may succeed with another blow.

Often the goal is nearer than
It seems to a faint and faltering man;
Often the struggler has given up
When he might have captured the victor's cup.
He learned too late when the night came down
How close he was to the golden crown.

Success is failure turned inside out,
The silver tint of the clouds of doubt.
And you never can tell how close you are;
It may be near when it seems afar;
So stick to the fight when you're hardest hit;
It's when things seem worst that you mustn't quit.

As children we were taught never to quit, never to say "I can't," always to say, "I think I can." As adults we need to be reminded once in a while that true success stems from undying effort.

We are to be our brothers' and sisters' keeper, but we're sometimes reluctant to accept that responsibility. Cain got the question right—but had already flunked the test. Perhaps our reluctance is not because we don't want to help, but we don't know whether we're capable of supplying what is needed. Suppose you suddenly find yourself in the position of managing people. You're responsible for building a team and hiring the right people. Let me suggest that you don't hire clones because you don't want everyone to be like you. You want people who complement you and your talents while bringing their own fresh ideas.

We have to be careful about partiality; and this is true whether we're dealing with our children or people who work around us.

Also, very little is gained by yelling at people. Positive instruction should be given calmly and clearly because most foul-ups result due to a lack of communication up front.

Then remember that just as you expect to be trusted by those around you, you have to show trust. That reminds me of a story out of the Old West where the word "trust" literally meant survival.

A wrapping paper message was found in a baking can attached to a pump. The message read:

> This pump was alright as of June 1932. I put a new sucker washer in it and it ought to last five years, but the washer dries out and the pump has to be *primed*. Under the white rock I've buried a bottle of water, out of the sun and the cork end up. There's enough water in it to prime this pump, but *not* if you drink some first.
>
> Pour in ¼ of it and let'er soak to wet the leather, then pour in the rest and pump like crazy. You'll get water—the well never has run dry, but when you get watered up, fill the bottle again and put it back like you found it for the next feller.

The old cowpoke was truly "his brothers' keeper" and his trust in the next man at the pump could determine whether other thirsty travelers survived or not. He passed the test.

Someone once asked a successful man the secret of his success and the key to his accomplished career. "I'll tell you," he replied. "It was a small trick I played on myself. No matter where I worked, I pretended that I owned the business. I pretended that I owned the whole place—lock, stock and barrel!"

Volumes have been written about how to succeed in business, but his simple, positive approach effectively summarizes all the theories. If everyone who receives a paycheck from a company—any company—took as much interest in the business as the owner, many of the internal problems that plague businesses everywhere would be eliminated. Everyone would work together; everyone would share common goals.

In the very strictest sense, many employees of a great many companies are owners of the business. These employees own shares of stock and, as shareholders, are partners in the business. These employee stockholders have invested their money for the opportunity to share in potential profits. In a much broader sense, *all* employees of a company are owners, whether or not they own any stock. For these employees have made an even greater investment. They have invested their time and energies, their efforts and creative talents to help make the business successful. They have invested themselves.

All too often, we think of "The Company" as an abstract impersonal entity. We tend to forget that the company is a corporation—a body of *people* sharing the common goals of service and profit. As employees, we are members of that body, each playing a vital role in making the company successful. Each role, each job, each position in the company is essential. The ultimate success or failure of the business depends directly on how well each employee accepts the responsibilities associated with his position.

In other words, how well *you* do *your* job determines the success of *your* business! If you just "work there," putting in your time and going through the motions, try pretending that you own the place. When you realize that you work for yourself as well as the company, when you understand that you profit as well as the company, then your job takes on new meaning and importance. To gain a new perspective on your work, put yourself in your employer's shoes—and take a long, hard look at yourself!

Tuesday, Week Thirteen

Years wrinkle the skin, but to give up enthusiasm wrinkles the soul," said Samuel Ullman. Have you retained the enthusiasm of youth, or is your soul beginning to show the years? Do you truly love your work and face each day with anticipation and enjoyment? If your wrinkled view of your job is "just the same old grind," you are missing something—something you can change.

Put your heart into your work. When viewed in terms of what it means to others, the work you are doing will take on a larger dimension and give you greater satisfaction. When you stop thinking about your job or daily routine in terms of drudgery and view your work as part of a great enterprise that helps people, you can awaken the enthusiasm within yourself.

Don't think of the day ahead as just another day. Anticipate having a good time at work. Wake up your enthusiasm each morning, remembering you are going to serve people. Call to mind those you serve—think how to bring a smile to their faces; think what special problem each bears; think what topic will help them talk with you. Not every individual you come in contact with will match your enthusiasm, but getting yourself in the proper frame of mind will enable you to conquer any adverse situation, handle it with humor and turn it to your own advantage.

In every phase of life, the individuals who continually raise their own sights emerge as the experts and the leaders. The successful salespeople are their own most exacting sales managers. The wisest scholars are the ones who set tasks for themselves beyond any assigned by their superiors. According to the old adage, "Whatsoever your hand or mind finds to do, do it with all your heart." We do well what we enjoy doing most. Put your heart into your labor and enjoy the fruits of it abundantly.

A lack of communication or a breakdown in communication is often used as a scapegoat for many of our errors. Yet, the truth remains that we *do* have trouble understanding one another. In our business relationships, as well as in our personal relationships, the basic requirement is that we understand each other.

This basic need to communicate effectively and be understood is aptly illustrated by the following satirical spoof—"The Chain of Command and How It Works: Operation Halley's Comet"—which came out of the military service, always a hotbed of humor:

A colonel issued the following direction to an executive officer: Tomorrow evening at approximately 20:00 hours, Halley's Comet will be visible in the area, an event which occurs only once every 75 years. Have the men fall out in the battalion area in fatigues and I will explain this rare phenomenon to them. In case of rain, we will not be able to see anything so assemble the men in the theater, and I will show a film of this.

Executive officer to the company commander—By order of the colonel, tomorrow at 20:00 hours, Halley's Comet will appear above the battalion area. If it rains, fall the men out in fatigues, then march them to the theater where the rare phenomenon will take place—something which occurs every 75 years.

Company commander to lieutenant—By order of the colonel, in fatigues at 20:00 hours tomorrow evening the phenomenal Halley's Comet will appear in the theater. In case of rain in the batallion area, the colonel will give another order, one which occurs every 75 years.

Lieutenant to the sergeant—Tomorrow at 20:00 hours, the colonel will appear in the theater with Halley's Comet, something which happens every 75 years. If it rains, the colonel will order the comet to the battalion area.

Sergeant to the squad—When it rains tomorrow at 20:00 hours, the phenomenal 75-year-old General Halley accompanied by the colonel will drive his Comet through the battalion area theater in his fatigues.

Laughter is a precious gift, and like a gift, laughter is best when freely given and shared with others. A laugh can brighten our day, make us feel better or help us overcome a difficult situation. An unusual look at the funny side of laughter is provided by Joe Bayly, whose own sense of humor emerges from the following analysis of humor:

"Laughter is a gift of God, a good gift. Yet most of us in the 'household of faith' don't laugh enough, especially at ourselves!

"God has a sense of humor. There are the ordinary evidences of it, such as His design of the camel, dolphin, penguin and monkey. But there are the laughing spots of history as well, ancient and modern. For example, monks in a monastery who have taken the vow of silence spend long hours in their cubicles reflecting, meditating, seeking the presence of God. But in the kitchen is the cook, a man who has to forego the vow of silence; after all, someone has to cook three meals a day, scrub the pots and pans, and deal with tradesmen. God must have laughed when out of that kitchen, and not from the cubicles of a hundred monasteries, came the great devotional classic of the late Middle Ages, 'Practicing the Presence of God.' I think God must have laughed when an Italian Communist produced that most Biblical of modern films, 'The Gospel According to St. Matthew.'

"Laughter is a personal thing. What seems funny to the British isn't funny to many Americans. And the standard of humor even varies from family to family.

"Any good gift can be perverted. There's danger in humor; our laughs can hurt a person created in the divine image. Laughter can destroy. Laughter can also short-circuit times of potential value. Have you ever been in a Christian gathering, perhaps after service on Sunday night, when risqué jokes eliminated any possibility of spiritual fellowship? Some Christians cover up their feelings, even their real personalities, with the mask of humor. Perhaps we fear that others will not accept us as we really are, so we must cover ourselves with the garb of a clown.

"Life begins and, in most instances, ends with tears. In between is the possibility for laughter, especially for those 'who examine everything for the fingerprints of God.' That's a marvelous way to enjoy genuine good humor. That's why we are made to laugh, but we must learn how and for what reasons."

Some years ago, when a prominent man in our city died, there were those who were surprised that I sorrowed at his death. For this individual had given me a great deal of trouble a decade earlier. I reminded them that, in order to hurt me, this man had to first be my friend. And it was far more pleasant to recall those days of friendship rather than the distress he caused later.

Charles Tennent expanded on this idea in his "Little Lessons in Rotary":

> Man's real enemy is not his fellowman, however loathsome he may appear through biased lenses that portray him as such, but rather the circumstances and conditions that make it possible to view him in that light. Man's real enemy is not his fellowman, but attitudes born of ignorance, greed, selfishness, fear, and prejudice.
>
> A friendly smile, a warm handclasp, a kind word, a good deed, even a good wish or silent prayer in a man's heart for his fellowman, ripples on and on to the ends of the earth.
>
> Understanding is a mental process which enables one to: read between the lines on a man's face; see him as he is; know why he thinks, talks, and acts as he does; grant him the right to do so; accept him as a brother.

Our shrinking world is too small for walls of animosity. The longer I live the more I realize that we cannot afford the luxury of holding a grudge; we cannot allow a momentary deed of ill will cause us to resort to vengeance. If, instead, we bend with temporary injustices, we transform an enemy into a potential friend. Cultivating friends—even from among the weeds—is far more satisfying than magnifying enemies.

According to a West German medical magazine reporting the results of life insurance studies, the husband who kisses his wife every morning before he leaves for work will probably live five years longer, earn 20 percent to 35 percent more money, lose up to 50 percent less time because of illness, and be involved in fewer auto accidents. How about those statistics!

The old line goes, "Behind every successful man is a dedicated wife and a surprised mother-in-law."

Every marriage has different requirements. We probably all think our spouse is the greatest. With my constant travel between High Point and Chicago, as well as speaking and industry-related meetings, I think my wife, Buren, not only adjusts, but actually builds up my confidence so I can maintain the erratic schedule. Self-confidence is the mainstay for a man or woman doing a job. Mine would be in serious trouble if upon returning home from a week of constant travel, I took a verbal mauling and was made to feel guilty about being gone so much.

Not only can your partner increase your self-confidence, but Buren also spares me the flood of petty problems. These she handles in my absence.

A helpful spouse also stays on the safe side—never spending the maximum nor afraid of losing face when there's a need to cut back.

The real test of a helpful marriage is when you feel your mate is not competing with you, but would rather you look good in a given situation, instead of himself or herself. This reveals a generous, inner confidence.

On our trips I especially feel flattered by Buren's commitment to my work and the people we come in contact with. She's always willing to help me do a better job.

Most of us can face just about anything as long as we feel, in the words of the song, "Long as I know I have love I can make it . . ."

If the German study on the benefit of a morning kiss is correct I'm in trouble with my travels—but I'm not complaining. It sure makes coming home worthwhile!

Upon speaking one Sunday for my friend, Pat Patterson, at the St. James Presbyterian Church in Greensboro, North Carolina, Colonel William Goode, then Dean at A & T University, lead the morning prayer. I share it with you below.

Dear Heavenly Father, give us more charity, more self-denial, more likeness to Thee.

Teach us to sacrifice our comforts to others, and our likings for the sake of doing good.

Make us kindly in thought, gentle in word, generous in deed.

Teach us that it is better to give than receive, better to forget ourselves than to put ourselves forward—better to minister than to be ministered unto.

Eternal God, Father of mankind, who has created thy children to be a common family; increase among all nations, we pray Thee, the sense of brotherhood and the spirit of goodwill.

Remove from them bitterness and intolerance.

Take from our leaders all unholy ambitions, unworthy motives, and perilous jealousies.

We commend to thy loving providence our brethren in every land, who are bound with us in the bonds of common faith. Supply them with the courage and the loyalty through which their fathers found the glorious liberty of the children of God.

When doors are closed against the outreach of our hands in ministries of friendship, keep open the highway of the spirit on which we journey with them toward the City of God.

We ask Thee, Dear Heavenly Father, to instill in the heart of every parent the will to discipline and to guide their young into the paths of respect, dignity, and good moral standards.

Monday, Week Fourteen

Self-respect cannot be hunted. It cannot be purchased. It is never for sale. It comes to us when we are alone, in quiet moments, in quiet places, when we suddenly realize that knowing the good, we have done it; knowing the truth, we have spoken it."

An inner feeling of self-respect is what separates the winner from the loser. Here is a thought from the "American Salesman":

> When a winner makes a mistake, he says, "I was wrong."
> When a loser makes a mistake, he says, "It wasn't my fault."
> A winner goes though a problem.
> A loser goes around it and never past it.
> A winner says, "I'm good, but not as good as I ought to be."
> A loser says, "I'm not as bad as a lot of other people."
> A winner says, "I'll be glad to do it."
> A loser says, "That's not part of my job."
> A winner listens.
> A loser just waits until it's his turn to talk.
> A winner feels responsible for more than his job.
> A loser says, "I only work here."

When I think of the loser, I am reminded of what Rudyard Kipling wrote with tongue in cheek, "I never made a mistake in my life; at least never one I couldn't explain away afterwards." And George Bernard Shaw, commenting on winning or leadership, said, "Power does not corrupt men; fools, however, if they get into a position of power, corrupt power."

A leader or a winner is defined as one "who knows the way, goes the way and shows the way." A leader or a winner truly deserving of the role is noticed for his or her calmness and steadiness. Long ago, Samuel Johnson observed that the more uncertain people are, the louder they shout, saying, "You raise your voice when you should reinforce your argument."

As someone who's been on the platform since age twelve, and is not considered very shy and retiring when in private, I've done my share of talking and would be the first to admit that it is much easier than listening. Knowing that I have a tendency to "face every issue with an open mouth," I read carefully the words that Key Powell sent me from an unknown author:

When I ask you to listen to me, and you start giving advice, you have not done what I asked.

When I ask you to listen to me and you begin to tell me why I shouldn't feel that way, you are trampling on my feelings.

When I ask you to listen to me and you feel you have to do something to solve my problem, you have failed me, strange as that may seem.

All I asked was that you listen, not talk or do—just listen to me.

Advice is cheap: twenty-five cents will get you both Dear Abby and Billy Graham in the same newspaper.

And I can do for myself: I'm not helpless. Maybe discouraged and faltering, but not helpless.

When you do something for me that I can and need to do for myself, you contribute to my fear and weakness.

But when you accept as a simple fact that I do feel what I feel, no matter how irrational, then I can quit trying to convince you and you can get about the business of understanding what's behind this irrational feeling. And when that's clear, the answers are obvious and I don't need advice. Irrational feelings make sense when we understand what's behind them.

Perhaps that's why prayer works sometimes, for some people, because God is mute, and He doesn't give advice or try to fix things. He just listens and lets you work it out for yourself.

So please listen and just hear me. And if you want to talk, wait a minute for your turn; and I'll listen to you.

Well over 200 years since the birth of our nation, there still exist minute men. These are the people who either say, "Wait a minute," or launch into every task at the last minute. A fictitious boss supposedly became so weary of hearing lame excuses, he made a list and told his employees not to bother saying the excuse, just refer to the appropriate number. See if your favorite excuse is on his list:

1. That's the way we've always done it.
2. I didn't know you were in hurry for it.
3. That's not in my department.
4. I'm waiting for an O.K.
5. No one told me to go ahead.
6. How did I know this was different?
7. That's his job, not mine.
8. I guess I should have read the details.
9. I forgot.
10. I didn't think this was important.
11. I've been so busy, I couldn't get to it.
12. I thought I told you.
13. I wasn't hired to do that.
14. I thought George was going to take care of it.
15. I got pulled off the job by my DE.
16. I meant to get it later, but . . .
17. I must have misunderstood you.
18. Nobody said anything to me about any change order.
19. They gave me the wrong instructions.
20. Somebody, I can't remember who, said he thought it would be O.K.
21. Wait until the boss comes back and ask him.

As the old saying goes, "Success comes in cans, failure in can'ts." Casey is the only individual who became famous by striking out. Excuses mean you don't even want to step up to bat.

Alcoholics Anonymous is a proven, worthwhile organization, whose principles apply to any set of personal problems. An A.A. member, anonymous of course, compiled the following resolutions:

Just for today I will try to live through this day only, and not set far-reaching goals to try to overcome all of my problems at once. I know I can do something for 12 hours that would appall me if I felt that I had to keep it up for a lifetime.

Just for today I will try to be happy. Abraham Lincoln said, "Most folks are about as happy as they make up their minds to be." He was right. I will not dwell on thoughts that depress me. I will chase them out of my mind and replace them with happy thoughts.

Just for today I will adjust myself to what is. I will face reality. I will try to change those things which I can change and accept those things I cannot change.

Just for today I will try to improve my mind. I will not be a mental loafer. I will force myself to read something that requires effort, thought and concentration.

Just for today I will do a good deed for somebody—without letting him know it. If he or she finds out I did it, it won't count.

Just for today I will do something to improve my health. If I am a smoker, I'll make an honest effort to cut down. If I'm overweight, I'll eat nothing I know is fattening. And I will force myself to exercise—even if it's only walking around the block, or using the stairs instead of the elevator.

Just for today I will be totally honest. If someone asks me something I don't know, I will not try to bluff; I'll simply say, "I don't know."

Just for today I'll do something I've been putting off for a long time. I'll finally write that letter, make that phone call, clean that closet, or straighten out those dresser drawers.

There is plenty of food for thought contained in those suggestions, regardless of our personal problems or lifestyles. Hannah Moe wrote, "The keen spirit seizes the prompt occasion; makes the thought start into instant action, and at once plans and performs, resolves and executes." Today is the occasion to begin putting your life in order—don't wait.

With the harried existence we moderns live, we can lose sight of how easy we really have it. Certainly, we live under pressures and stress unknown to our forebears, but the physical strain of our labors has diminished considerably. Here is a classic tribute, by an unknown author, to the hard work performed by our ancestors:

> Mama's mama, on a winter's day, milked the cows, and fed them hay,
> Slopped the hogs, saddled the mule, and got the children off to school.
> Did a washing, mopped the floors, washed the windows and did some chores.
> Cooked a dish of home-dried fruit, pressed her husband's Sunday suit,
> Swept the parlor, made the bed, baked a dozen loaves of bread,
> Split some firewood, and lugged it in, enough to fill the kitchen bin.
> Cleaned the lamps and put in oil, stewed some apples she thought might spoil,
> Churned the butter, baked a cake, then exclaimed, "For mercy's sake,
> The calves have got out of the pen!" Went out and chased them in again.
> Gathered eggs, locked the stable, returned to the house and set the table.
> Cooked a supper that was delicious, and afterward washed all the dishes.
> Fed the cat, sprinkled clothes, mended a basket full of hose.
> Then opened the organ and began to play, "When you come to the end of a perfect day."

And we all think we have too much to do!

Aren't the seasons beautiful? It would be interesting if we could find out how many times the words "Spring is here" have been used. So many people take weekend drives in the fall to our North Carolina mountains to see the turning of the leaves. They are beautiful, but as I look at them, I'm reminded that they are also announcing the death of a season. Spring not only brings the pastels of blossoms, but also the weeds and dandelions. Still it is my favorite season because it announces life, a new beginning, a series of resurrections, a chance to start anew.

As spring relates to our homes, it indicates we've shoveled our last snow of the winter. We can make those repairs that resulted from winter damage. Spring cleaning is still a ritual to some. It is a time for painting, fixing up, freshening, and for our highway system, filling potholes.

Still there is another aspect. Spring is a time of planning. Those of us who grew up around a farm know it's also a time for planting, the turning of the earth—the smell of fresh soil. In our planning we're even thinking about the end of school, what the children will do in the summer, where we'll go on a vacation. Yes, spring is a busy time. There is such a thing as spring fever where we stare out the office window, wishing we were hiking in the woods or lazing by a singing brook and gazing at the clear, blue sky.

In order to add freshness and vitality to spring, I would make these suggestions:

- Spring is a time to work; that gives us a sense of achievement.
- Spring is a time to plan; it gives us a sense of power.
- Spring is a time to play; for a sense of youthfulness.
- Spring is a time to laugh; it is music for our souls.
- Spring is a time to dream; that's the step toward reality.
- Spring is a time to pray; that gives us a sense of worth.

For many of us, Sunday worship would not be the same without praying together the familiar "Lord's Prayer." Yet, anything done regularly carries the danger of becoming commonplace and losing its meaning. Rediscover the meaning of this marvelous prayer through the following:

I cannot say OUR, if my religion has no room for others and their needs.

I cannot say FATHER, if I do not demonstrate this relationship in my daily living.

I cannot say WHO ART IN HEAVEN, if all my interests and pursuits are in earthly things.

I cannot say HALLOWED BE THY NAME, if I who am called by His name, am not holy.

I cannot say THY KINGDOM COME, if I am unwilling to give up my own sovereignty and accept the righteous reign of God.

I cannot say THY WILL BE DONE, if I am unwilling or resentful of having it in my life.

I cannot say ON EARTH AS IT IS IN HEAVEN, unless I am truly ready to give myself to His service here and now.

I cannot say GIVE US THIS DAY OUR DAILY BREAD without expending honest effort for it or by ignoring the genuine needs of my fellowman.

I cannot say FORGIVE US OUR TRESPASSES AS WE FORGIVE THOSE WHO TRESPASS AGAINST US, if I continue to harbor a grudge against anyone.

I cannot say LEAD US NOT INTO TEMPTATION, if I deliberately choose to remain in a situation where I am likely to be tempted.

I cannot say DELIVER US FROM EVIL, if I am not prepared to fight in the spiritual realm with the weapon of prayer.

I cannot say THINE IS THE KINGDOM, if I do not give the King the disciplined obedience of a loyal subject.

I cannot say THINE IS THE POWER, if I am seeking my own glory first.

I cannot say FOREVER, if I am too anxious about each day's affairs.

I cannot say AMEN, unless I honestly say, "Cost what it may, this is my prayer."

This wonderful prayer embodies our spiritual needs as we sincerely repeat it and provides a model for our spontaneous prayer.

Carelessness on the job cannot be blamed on the worker, regardless of how simple it seems or how much we would like a pat answer. Just as we give equal credit to both employer and employee for good production, we must challenge both employer and employee to correct poor work habits.

A generation ago, we literally threw people into jobs. Your ability was hired, and it was up to you to sink or swim. Today, we apply technology to even the simplest jobs, making training absolutely mandatory. Whether the employee is a bagger at the corner grocery or a computer operator, training is a must. Employers are quick to complain that good people are hard to find, but they need to widen their vision and see whether an individual *is* good or *became* good because of the training opportunities a company offers.

When an employee fails, it costs everyone. More often than not, the marginal employee could become exceptional with a little more interest and a little more instruction. Employees who aren't quite sure what the boss expects or don't feel comfortable that they know how to do it become tense and tentative and, as a result, accident-prone.

Too often employers offer a job with excitement and the employee responds with enthusiasm and anticipation. But then, the first day on the job, the employee feels lonely and abandoned. No letdown quite matches the one that follows a big buildup.

Effective companies utilize a buddy system for new employees. They make sure there is enough work to do to make the employee feel worthwhile, and use this support system to help employees see themselves as worthy. They don't expect new employees to act like veterans, but they ensure the rookies have a job in keeping with their initial enthusiasm.

Walter Dill Scott believed, "Success or failure in business is caused more by mental attitudes than by mental capacities..." An effective employer can enhance and ensure a positive attitude by simply remembering that the first day on the job often determines the last day on the job.

M y life is my own and its my own business." We have all heard such a statement; some of us have even uttered such a declaration. Such a thought, however, is erroneous. The great Greek philosopher Plato proclaimed to the people of his day, "I do not belong to myself alone. My family owns a part of me, my city, my land and my country; my friends are mine and I am theirs."

As wise Plato knew, all of life is a family affair—business, education, government, religion, even death. If you work at a job, you work for another; you receive a paycheck from the boss. The boss, then, is a part of your life and you labor to satisfy the boss. Even the top executive with wealth and power must depend on employees for the operation of a business and would be helpless without them.

All who have bosses—and indeed all of us do—may be interested in the "Ten Commandments by the Boss":

1. Don't lie. It wastes my time and yours. I'm sure to catch you in the end, and that's the wrong end.
2. Watch your work, not the clock. A long day's work makes a long day short, and a short day's work makes my face long.
3. Give me more than I expect and I'll pay you more than you expect. I can afford to increase your pay if you increase my profits.
4. You owe so much to yourself that you can't afford to owe anybody else. Keep out of debt or keep out of my shop.
5. Dishonesty is never an accident. Good men, like good women, can see temptation when they meet it.
6. Mind your own business and in time you'll have a business to mind.
7. Don't do anything here which hurts your self-respect. The employee who's willing to steal for me is capable of stealing from me.
8. It's none of my business what you do at night. But if dissipation affects what you do the next day and you do half as much as I demand, you'll last half as long as you expected and hoped.
9. Don't tell me what I'd like to hear, but what I ought to hear. I don't want a valet for my vanity, but I need one for my money.
10. Don't kick if I kick. If you're worth correcting, you're worth keeping. I don't waste time cutting specks out of rotten apples.

The cartoon depicted a couple sitting on a park bench, she in a tattered evening dress and he in a battered tuxedo, holding the remnants of a cigar on the end of a stick, as he remarks, "We sure gave the Joneses a run for the money for awhile, didn't we?"

No problem perplexes couples as much as money matters. Most young couples experience failed marriages because of financial difficulties. Couples blame personality differences, sex, parental failure, but all these are only by-products of money problems.

As a nation, we do not save; we are infected with a "buy now, pay later" mentality. The bankruptcy law is abused as an easy way out of money problems, and there are few traps as easy to fall into as the credit trap.

It is no wonder that couples, particularly young couples, find themselves in a financial bind. The following thoughts may save you from getting in over your head:

1. A bargain may be a real buy, but only if you need the item. If you buy on credit, you must add the interest onto the price and the bargain may no longer be a great buy. So don't buy compulsively—today's bargain will probably be repeated at a later date.

2. Pride dictates many purchases. If you move into a new home, your impulse is to fill it with furniture immediately. Remember, furniture of good quality is the best buy. And there is something admirable about walking into a living room and finding only a single chair, because you are buying quality and only each piece as you can afford it.

3. Realize that the salesperson's job is to sell. You admire the aggressive salesperson without falling for what you don't need. Also, remember the word "barter." The best bargain can usually be obtained from the super salesperson, whose ego won't let you say "no" and walk away. So bargain for the best price.

4. The foundation of good economic planning is to live on the income you make. Choose a lifestyle that fits your budget. Income has little to do with saving—you save when you think enough of yourself and your family to plan for the future.

5. When you receive a windfall such as an overtime check or year-end bonus, save it. Don't allow your lifestyle to be spoiled by temporary increases. Self-indulgence is vogue—don't indulge yourself to your own ruination.

The biggest problem facing America today is loneliness. Economic problems, energy and other nationwide concerns come and go, only amplifying the feeling of loneliness that people share. Lonely people feel that no one cares about them, that tomorrow will only be worse than today.

Loneliness is the most graphic evidence of someone feeling they are without love.

Sociologists profess that people feel lonely and unloved because our society moves so fast—computers have turned us all into mere numbers; we are the by-products of an impersonal plastic-card society.

These are only symptoms. The loneliness of America comes from having lost *true* love. Love in our society has been reduced to the sensual, the measuring of what you can do for me. We cannot even term it "shallow love" because it lacks any of the qualities of true love. What has happened to love?

1. Most love today is the selfish gratification of an undisciplined appetite. When a young man says, "Prove you love me by satisfying my needs," he knows nothing of love. Love is not asking; it is giving space to the other's feelings and convictions. Selfish love is really lust.
2. We are told that most love today is the result of atmosphere—the soft music, full moon, exotic perfume. Certainly, circumstances enhance a relationship. To some, marriage is a letdown after the excitement of courtship.
4. Love today cannot withstand the unpleasant. Our society's catch phrase has become, "I loved him until he did something I didn't like." Love is acceptance—not changing another for your own satisfaction. True love changes anything it touches for the better.

We in America are a lonely people because we are living outside the glow, the warmth and the uplift of feeling loved. Once our country smiled, felt good about herself and reached out to the world. Now, we are introverted, scared, tentative, confused and polarized. We have become masses of lonely islands instead of communities of concern. Our salvation will not come from sociologists or the government—love will draw us together and strengthen us.

E ach of us has our own personal Achilles' heel. I am a self-confessed
workaholic, fueled by a streak of ambitiousness, but my real weakness is a desire to be lazy. So the following article really touches my sore
spot, and perhaps yours:

It's wonderful to be lazy—if you know how. It spares your heart,
saves your energy, relaxes your mind, and you needn't feel at all
guilty about it if you confine laziness to these approved ways:
Be too lazy to frown, fidget and worry.
Don't wear yourself out carrying needless weights of grudges,
prejudices and envy.
Listen more than you talk, and see how much better you feel after
almost any meeting or gathering.
Don't run to catch a bus. The next one will get you there and it's
better for your heart.
Don't rush for a bargain that takes more out of you than it saves
for your pocketbook.
Don't knock yourself out trying to park your car in a space too
small for a scooter. Better to pay a parking fee than a bill at a
hospital.
Don't bother to quarrel over small things. Let the other fellow
think he's right when it really doesn't matter.
Conserve your mental muscles for things that count; and never
bother to wrestle with the inevitable, the imponderable or the insignificant.

It all depends on outlook. Laziness can be a virtue if we are lazy
enough to choose the right priorities and expend our energies on things
that really matter.

Agnes A. Kubitz shares some interesting thoughts about the use of a broom:

As I placed brooms on several floors of a dormitory, I thought of the good work they would do, the joy they would bring to the housekeeper. In the library I read about broom and broom corn, learning that any climate and soil suitable for maize is suitable for growing broom corn. I became a broom enthusiast.

But brooms are not ornaments. They are made to do a useful work. Until one needs a broom badly and cannot get one, one forgets how necessary, how helpful a broom can be.

A few years ago when I visited England, I asked for a broom to sweep the rugs in my room. I was given a long-handled brush. Objecting, saying a broom would serve me better, I learned that in England there are no brooms as we know them in America.

Katherine Buchanan was a housewife who knew when to use the broom. One day she heard a crash of thin glass shattering on her kitchen floor. She knew without looking that it was a tall, slender vase with a wild rose painted on it.

Many years before she had bought that vase. She was a young mother with an invalid husband and four hungry mouths to feed. It took careful planning to buy bare necessities. On one of her shopping trips to the city she had managed to find some marked-down clothing for the children. Preparing to return home, she found a fifty-cent piece in her purse, still unspent. Her eye caught sight of a table on which stood some slender, tall vases, decorated with a single wild rose. The children needed mittens and other things that the half-dollar would buy. She picked up the vase and saw it reflect the gay lights of the store. It was hers! And through the years when she had been weary and discouraged, she had reached for the vase, admired its grace and beauty, and then, strengthened, she had resumed her work.

She now gazed at the broken pieces of glass and felt as if a part of her lay there shattered on the floor. She says: "It had been a vital part of my life. A hyacinth to feed the soul." But it had served its purpose, and she reached for the broom.

In His wisdom God often lends us props to support our weakness, our weariness, our lack of faith. These props are but crutches that, in time, must be removed when we are able to stand without them. The shattered vase may appear to us to be a tragedy whereas it has really done its work and is no longer needed.

God make us brave enough to use the broom to sweep up the broken fragments of the vase we no longer need.

How fortunate one is when people believe in him. Unlike most speakers, I do not use booking agencies to arrange my personal appearances. Ours is the simple result of one group hearing me and believing in what is being said and recommending me to others. One such believer was Phil Berg while serving as vice president of the Colorado Association of Real Estate Boards. Phil had that splendid talent of making a voluntary association function as a huge state-wide team for the betterment of Colorado in all areas of life.

A bit of Phil's wit comes through in the Board Executives' Prayer which he sent to me:

Dear Lord, help me to become the perfect executive. Give me the mysterious something which will enable me at all times to satisfactorily explain policies, rules, regulations, and procedures to everyone concerned.

Help me to teach and to train the uninterested and slow-witted without ever losing my patience or temper.

Help me to understand perfectly all fields of specialization and endow me with inventive and innovative genius.

Instill into my inner being tranquility and peace of mind that no longer will I wake from my restless sleep in the middle of the night crying out, "How can I please my members, balance the budget, and get everyone to love the board?"

Teach me to smile if it kills me.

Make me a better leader of men by helping develop larger and greater qualities of understanding, tolerance, sympathy, wisdom, perception, equanimity, mind reading, and second sight.

And when, dear Lord, Thou hast helped me to achieve the highest pinnacle of administration and when I shall have become the paragon of all executive virtues, in this mortal world—then, dear Lord, move over.

Amen and Amen!

As we begin a new week, here are several thoughts worthy of our contemplation; the first from Dr. Roscoe D. McMillan:

May we be able during this week to:

Take time to work; it is the price of success.
Take time to think; it is the source of power.
Take time to play; it is the secret of youth.
Take time to read; it is the foundation of wisdom.
Take time to laugh; it is the music of the soul.
Take time to be friendly; it is the road to happiness.
Take time to dream; it is the highway to the stars.
Take time to look around; it is the shortcut to unselfishness.
Take time to pray; it is the way to Heaven.

And this from W.R. Hunt:

Dear Lord, please give me . . .

A few friends who understand me and yet remain my friends.
A work to do which has real value, without which the world would be the poorer.
A mind unafraid to travel, even though the trail be blazed.
An understanding heart.
A sense of humor.
Time for quiet, silent meditation.
A feeling of the presence of God.
And the patience to wait for the coming of these things, with the wisdom to know them when they come.

Fred Herzberg is given credit for defining and applying "hygiene to the corporation." He was not speaking of cleanliness but the good health of a company that gave its attention to the human needs of the individual employee. His thoughts of three decades ago birthed "job enrichment," "participative management," "work circles," "shared decision-making," etc.

The cynic would say that we have not improved the working atmosphere of our companies. They even seem to have statistics to support their skepticism. They refer to a survey conducted by Louis Harris for Steelcase, Inc. Over one thousand people were polled. Basically employees echoed what has been observed for years. Once pay is considered comparatively, adequate dollars and cents are not an overpowering motivating force. You have to call up someone out of the Great Depression to hear: "I don't care what they want as long as they pay me." Don't misread—68 percent of the respondents gave some importance to pay, but 76 percent said it was very important to have the opportunity to contribute significantly to their company.

The survey indicated gaps between expectations and reality:

- 80 percent felt a challenging job was very important, but only 63 percent felt they had one.
- 75 percent want the freedom to decide how they do their work, but only 55 percent thought they enjoyed that luxury.
- 61 percent wanted participative decision-making with only 28 percent believing they had it.

The poll indicated we were making progress in employee satisfaction ten years ago, or at least 70 percent of the employees thought so. Now we have declined to 56 percent feeling we are improving worker hygiene.

What can we do? Management, according to the poll, has different priorities. Is it time for Dr. Herzberg to lecture again? The merger-mania, the LBOs, and the takeovers have the managers scrambling to save their own hides. The executive suite is becoming internalized and paranoid. Would an appropriate question be:

What does it profit a leader if he should temporarily save his job and lose the loyalty of the employees who made him productive?

Do you know someone who *enjoys* getting angry? Such people are not the gruff and grizzly people who act angry to cover up their soft hearts. People who truly enjoy being angry walk around with a chip on their shoulder and, if someone doesn't knock it off, they bend over so the chip will fall off.

Here's a classic story that illustrates this type of personality:

One of the passengers on the old Boston, Hartford and New Haven Railroad was commuting from Boston to New York. He finished his meal and wanted to top it off with plum pudding. When told there was no plum pudding, he became irate and stated, "You always have plum pudding on this train. It's one of the few decent desserts you have. Do you realize my company is one of the biggest users of this sorry railroad?" By this time the chief steward came to the aid of the porter and assured the customer he'd try to get some plum pudding when the train stopped at New Haven. As promised, when the train pulled away from New Haven, the waiter announced they now had plum pudding, which he graciously placed before the man. The fellow looked at it . . . pushed it away . . . flung down his napkin and snorted, "Heck with it. I'd rather be mad at this—railroad!"

At one time or another, we've all met this man on the railroad. Only, we've met him at the airport, in a parking lot, at the grocery store, at work. Under a very thin layer lies a smoldering volcano. Some people simply enjoy being angry.

These people don't like themselves, so the anger directed at you is really meant for themselves. Or, they have a personal problem they are ducking and, ashamed of themselves for not facing it, they get angry at you. Or they feel inferior and instead of trying to make themselves more acceptable, they are deliberately obnoxious hoping you will dislike them and give them an excuse for not improving.

If you have been angry, allowing your temper to run loose, hurting those who love you—forgive yourself and begin enjoy living.

The teen years are the hard years. And without a doubt, that time when we leave childhood behind and struggle to become an adult is fraught with heartache and confusion and wonder. Dr. Frank Howard Richardson, a Baptist physician and counselor, lists a dozen guides to help teenagers over the rough spots:

1. You are very important. Don't underestimate your abilities.
2. Growing up is a tough job. Teenage years bring weighty problems.
3. Your parents are longing to help you succeed. You and your parents, working together, can be the greatest team the world has known.
4. Never let the good things of life take the place of the best. Standards you make today mold your life tomorrow.
5. Blessed are they who hear the word of God and keep it.
6. Petting is an enemy of both dating enjoyment and popularity.
7. Going steady is not as good as it looks. It probably would prevent your selection of the best possible marriage partner.
8. Teenagers can be our best drivers. But owning a car may cost you your education.
9. You don't have to smoke or drink. Weigh carefully the cost before you decide to do either.
10. Make friends with everyone you meet. Put yourself in the other person's place.
11. Look toward the future and be prepared for it. Ups and downs of the present seem trivial when compared with future goals.
12. The future is yours. What you make of it will be handed down from generation to generation.

Being a parent and guiding our young on the journey from infancy to adolescence to adulthood is an awesome responsibility. Instilling in our young the virtue of responsibility is, perhaps, an even greater challenge.

The following "Twelve Rules for Raising Responsible Children," written by Robert D. Norton, may offer some guidance:

1. Begin with infancy to teach the child he cannot have everything he wants.
2. When he picks up bad words, correct him.
3. Give him spiritual training early in life.
4. Make frequent use of the word "wrong" in correcting bad acts.
5. Make him pick up his own things and do as many other things for himself as he can.
6. Be careful what you let him read.
7. Keep the home atmosphere pleasant and warm.
8. Make him earn his spending money.
9. See that sensual desires and cravings for food, drink and comfort are satisfied only in moderation.
10. Back him only when he's right and let him know you won't back him when he's wrong.
11. Accept your responsibility for his actions until he's of an age to accept them himself.
12. Prepare for a life of satisfaction with your child. You are likely to have it.

Teaching responsibility can begin by teaching ourselves—a good example is still the best teacher.

If I were to ask which major city in the United States is most difficult to drive in, I believe there would be a single "hands down" winner. Note that I said "major city" meaning seven hundred fifty thousand and more. The winner of the most difficult city in which to drive would be Boston—the city of my youth.

In honesty I must admit Boston is a bit better today. At least you can drive through on the Interstate Highway but it is still difficult when you get into the city. The old story is that while the Colonists did business and worshipped they let their cows roam wild. Then in later years, they put roads where the cows had roamed. Along with the narrow and crooked streets there is also the confusing naming. You may have driven on Water Street, then go another block and suddenly you're on Milk Street.

When we moved to Massachusetts, Dad asked one of the church's deacons if he would teach him Boston. The deacon said, "Pastor, I've worked in Boston for a quarter of a century but I've never driven inside the city limits. I drive my car to Ashmont Station and catch the subway to work." This seemed odd until we drove into the city. My Mom realized she was fortunate when growing up as a girl in and around Boston. She didn't drive but depended upon the subway and trolley.

Along the way I'm sure the city planners knew they should do something about the meandering streets but felt maybe it would be easier later. Here is a lesson for our lives. Many of us have complex and difficult lives. Tomorrow we're going to simplify. We know we're injuring our health. Tomorrow we're going to practice better discipline about sleeping and eating. Tomorrow we'll straighten the crooked. We'll confess our sins and make right the injuries we've imposed upon our neighbors.

Boston could have simplified their streets easily years ago but each passing year made it more complex and costly. So with our lives. Delay is seldom on the side of correction. Today is the best time to form straight living.

On the sundial in Harvard Yard the students are reminded constantly with the inscription: "On this minute hangs eternity." Carlyle puts it this way: "One life, a little gleam of time between two eternities, no second chance for us forevermore." Today is the best day to make a better tomorrow.

Among the unsung heroes of this world are the Sunday school teachers; those wonderful, wonderous, sacrificing individuals who, as one anonymous author claimed, need:

The education of a college president.
The executive ability of a financier.
The humility of a deacon.
The adaptability of a chameleon.
The hope of an optimist.
The courage of a hero.
The wisdom of a serpent.
The gentleness of a dove.
The patience of Job.
The grace of God, and the persistence of the devil.

Billy Graham has this to say about Sunday school teachers:

I want to say to every Sunday school teacher that he is just as much called of God as a missionary to some remote land. He needs to prepare just as diligently—he needs to labor just as earnestly—as if he were carrying the gospel to the most remote spot on the globe.

I believe that out of the tragedy of this hour, pastors and parents and Christian workers are once more beginning to be in earnest about Sunday school. They are once more taking the offensive—going out to do visitation work; winning boys and girls to Christ. They are seeing that Sunday school should be something more than just a place where church members send their children for an hour every Sunday morning.

God doesn't intend that revival should be limited to evangelistic campaigns. He can send revival through Sunday school. He is waiting today for men and women who will work and pray for sacrifice, waiting for those who have a consuming desire to see others brought to Christ. God is waiting for Christians who will yield to the cleansing and energizing fire of His Holy Spirit.

If you are an unhappy employee, discontent because you feel unfair practices are allowed to continue at your place of work, speak up and talk to your supervisor about it. If you remain silent, you will either become totally dissatisfied and quit your job or your productivity and value to the company will slip. You cannot be filled with resentment without hurting both yourself and your employer.

We all probably know capable, hard-working individuals with skills and talents who have spent their careers moving from one job to another. In each new job, they amass a list of gripes and grievances; but instead of voicing their concerns, they pull up stakes and move on. With each move, they add to their reputations of being unreliable malcontents.

If you are unhappy with your job, here are several suggestions:

Be certain your criticism is honest. Many of us are burdened with quick tempers, feelings of superiority, stubborness to suggestions and change, a false hautiness hiding pride and sensitivity. If you honestly believe you are above such feelings, then you must decide how to proceed.

It could be that you want everyone to share the work load, but you don't want to be branded a squealer by your co-workers or a troublemaker by your employer. You may fear that, if your manager or supervisor doesn't agree with your observation, you could be cutting yourself off from future opportunities.

If constructive criticism on your part will jeopardize your position and future, then you are working for the wrong company. Companies are only improved when they listen to their employees.

There is an alternative. Instead of reporting a fellow employee, face the individual yourself with an attitude of sincere helpfulness. Perhaps you can correct the work habits that are aggravating you—then you have corrected a problem and probably made a friend.

There are few jobs in this world where merely being a good worker is sufficient—there are deeper matters of loyalty, enthusiasm, honesty, sincerity and cooperation. You cannot shy away and rage within yourself. You have a duty to help your fellow employee or, if that fails, you have an obligation out of fairness to the company to express yourself to management.

If asked the question "Are you honest?" the majority of us would answer with an emphatic "yes" and some might even be insulted by the very question. While proclaiming our basic honesty, we might admit to not being "totally" honest, supporting such an admission with explanations and rationalizations.

None of us can doubt that one of our nation's greatest needs is a return to truth and honesty. What we call "white collar" crime is actually dishonesty practiced by basically honest people.

Dishonesty may begin with something as seemingly innocent as taking cookies from the cookie jar during your parents' absence. Next, perhaps, dishonesty is changing your answer on an exam after accidentally seeing the answer written by the student next to you in class. Shrugged off and laughed off, dishonesty can rapidly become habitual.

Later in life, dishonesty can take the form of underpaying employees when their hard work and productivity should dictate a raise. On the other side, dishonesty can take the form of employees giving less than their best work to their employer.

The breakdown in general service in America is an indication of widespread dishonesty—we have difficulty finding a neat carpenter or a reliable plumber or a skilled electrician or a competent appliance repairman; we have difficulty getting the car fixed properly or getting a good meal in a restaurant. Honesty is the foundation for successful skills.

Turn another page, and dishonesty might take the form of our not returning what we have borrowed or not paying our debts. Widespread income tax evasion is another sign of our national dishonesty. We quickly excuse ourselves, citing how corrupt other government agencies are when they overlook internal scandals.

Justification for dishonesty is impossible. Our actions are not predicated or excused by the actions of others, but by the dictates of our conscience. If we feel smug when headlines cite violent crimes, we had best examine our own hearts. There are no shades or degrees of dishonesty. There is, however, a need for a pure heart in America.

For many Americans, the word "profit" has an adverse connotation, especially when linked to a word such as "corporate." And yet, profits—fair, ethical, deserved profits—are essential to a corporation. Profit is to a corporation what breathing is to a living thing. While profit is not the sole purpose of a company, choking off profits will result in extinction as surely as choking off oxygen to a living creature will result in death.

The dictionary defines profit as deriving from the Latin word "profectus" meaning to advance or progress. Our lifestyle exists because industry is making a profit, in turn bringing advancement. The purpose of a profitable business is to meet the needs of people by manufacturing products and providing services. In short, it is the organized effort to create something out of raw materials.

In analyzing what profit is, it is imperative to discuss what profit is not. Profit is not funds pocketed by a select few at the expense of others. Profit is not mad money to be spent on unproductive frills. Profit is not a stockpile of funds kept out of circulation as a cushion against hard times.

Profit is what remains after all the expenses of operating a business have been paid. Part of the profit is returned to investors in the form of dividends. This determines the true value of a company, since investors look for companies that will yield the most return on their investment.

Profit is also reinvested in the business for future growth. A responsible company has a duty to its employees now and in the future. American industry created approximately 20 million new jobs between 1978 and 1985, at an average cost of $25,000 per job. New jobs cannot be created overnight and they cannot be created without profits. No profits, no jobs. It's that simple.

True to the Latin word "profectus," profit is progress. Profit is needed to continue jobs and create new ones in the future, to safeguard the savings of individuals, and to improve the general welfare of the world.

Self-assessment can tell us a great deal about ourselves. It can be frightening to look deep within ourselves; realistic self-assessment can reveal flaws and remind us of past mistakes. Honestly evaluating ourselves, however, can also make us grateful for the potential we have.

As you seek a better understanding of yourself, what questions do you ask? Here are some that will get you started:

Am I creative? If my current job has become routine, is there an innovative way to do my daily work?

Do I look for new approaches to old problems or have I given up in futility, accepting "what will be, will be"?

Do I prefer a settled routine or am I willing to take a slight risk or even a big gamble?

Do I feel more comfortable presenting my ideas or am I more at ease implementing the ideas of others?

Do I enjoy giving orders and the feeling of power and authority?

Do I get along well with others? Do I compromise basic convictions to achieve popularity? Do I constantly wonder what others think of me? Do I placate or pacify those who manage me?

Do I resent supervision? Am I suspicious of those in authority over me or those below me in the organization?

Do I want to complete a work project before leaving for the day or am I comfortable to walk away at quitting time and begin again the next day?

Do I want my job clearly defined or do I appreciate the challenge of an open-ended assignment?

Do I act well under pressure? Do I think I ought to have pressure or should someone else?

Too many individuals are miserable in their jobs, long ago having accepted the security of a job they didn't like instead of facing the challenge of looking for another job or seeking ways to make the current job more enjoyable. By suppressing their true feelings and trying to work like robots, these unhappy people are opening the door to serious physical and emotional problems.

It is imperative that we keep our self-identity. We cannot live just for the expectations of others; we must live so that we are satisfied within. To see ourselves and accept our strengths and weaknesses is half the battle. Knowledge of ourselves becomes the cornerstone for building goals and aspirations.

Most of us share a natural inclination and longing for a long life. Dr. Alexander Leaf, former chief of staff at Massachusetts General Hospital and professor of medicine at Harvard University, made a lifelong pursuit of investigating the reasons people achieve long life. He identified three areas of the world, each highly removed from the others, where its citizens lived long lives—Hunza, a remote area lodged between Pakistan, Afghanistan and China; Georgia in the southern reaches of Russia; and Ecuador in South America.

Dr. Leaf discovered four reasons for long life, common to each of the areas' residents:

1. Old parents. Long life seems to run in families and even tribes of families. Dr. Leaf felt that long life was an inherited trait, much like facial similarities or intelligence.
2. Simple diet. People who live long are not overweight; they eat relatively simply and don't clog their arteries with animal fat. Our good, rich food can shorten our lives.
3. Activity. Dr. Leaf's subjects remained active and vigorous well into old age. We too often confuse endurance and strength; rippling muscles are fine, but the real test is being able to last.
4. Attitude. People who live long lives, Dr. Leaf found, did not worry about things they couldn't change. This may be the most important factor. As a nation, our greatest illness comes not from physical ailments, but from psychological and emotional problems.

We all want to live a long life. Only God knows whether we will, and it's too late to choose our parents. But we can do something about our diets, we can exercise more, and we can change our attitudes.

It's not easy working together daily with the same people, and I admire those who do so in harmony.

We also know that it takes a heap of living to make a house into a home. This means you have to work at bringing a family together in loving harmony. The same is true in a plant where the same people work side by side daily. The success of the company depends upon harmony among employees. The company can maintain helpful policies but in the final analysis, harmony is the result of the attitude of the individual employee.

I enjoy addressing company dinners; and the reason is that I gain confidence about America as I meet employees face to face.

Cicero, the philosopher, hundreds of years ago outlined six mistakes we make, and I feel that most employees who have worked at the same plant for years must have a similar attitude:

1. The delusion that personal gain is made by crushing others. Employees all want to advance but long term employees don't seek advancement at the expense of others.
2. The tendency to worry about things that cannot be changed or corrected. Some employees "nit-pick" to find things about their work they deplore. Good employees start the day with a positive attitude and feel, on balance, their company is better than any other.
3. Insisting the thing is impossible because we can't accomplish it. When other employees accomplish what we couldn't, we ought to admire it rather than be jealous.
4. Refusing to set aside trivial preferences. When you work daily with people there will be little irritations, but these must be dismissed quickly.
5. Neglecting development and refinement of the mind, and not acquiring the habit of reading and study. Employees I admire do not become obsolete because they keep learning about their job.
6. Attempting to compel others to believe as we do. When you work side by side you must let others believe as they will and respect them for their beliefs.

There is too much talk about people not wanting to work. I feel sorry for these but I admire you production people who make our nation such an industrial giant.

Without apology I admit to being an enthusiastic Bible reader. No other book in my rather large library gives me something fresh each time I read (and now re-read) it.

Among my favorite Scripture chapters is 1 Corinthians 13. It makes clear that love is not merely emotion. Love is literally life flowing out of you to help others. Paul in the thirteenth chapter of 1 Corinthians defines what love is and isn't; what it does and doesn't do.

Here is a modern translation of 1 Corinthians 13:

> Love is very patient . . . Love is gracious . . . It looks for a way of being constructive . . . Love never boils with jealousy . . . not anxious to impress . . . makes no parade. Love is never boastful . . . is not arrogant, not conceited. It does not put on airs, nor does it cherish inflated ideas of its importance. Love is never rude, or unmannerly or indecent; never selfish. Love does not insist on its own way or rights . . . is never self-seeking.
>
> Love bears no malice, never reckons up her wrongs, not quick to take offense; is not irritable or resentful. It is not touchy. It does not keep account of evil. Does not gloat over other men's sins; never glad when others go wrong, but rejoices at the victory of truth. She can overlook faults . . . always slow to expose, always eager to believe the best. It bears up under anything. There is nothing that love cannot face . . . knows no limit to its endurance . . . always hopeful. Love shall never pass away.
>
> The time will come when we outgrow prophecy. Strange languages— ecstatic speaking—will stop. As for knowledge, it will be superseded . . . swept away . . . faith, hope and love . . . these are the great three, but the most important of these is love.

After such reading all you can do is say with a prayer: "Give me love and help me love another." As Goethe believed, "We are shaped and fashioned by what we love."

We all need to be corrected from time to time; and we will usually accept correction, however unpleasant, if it is handled properly. If you are involved in managing and leading people, you undoubtedly have a need to correct them on occasion. Following are several common mistakes to avoid:

1. Never belittle a subordinate. Higher rank gives no one the right to humiliate another person. And higher rank does not necessarily indicate higher intelligence. I recall an executive who lost his lofty position after a subordinate he had belittled ended up as chief executive officer of the company and remembered well the incident.

2. Never criticize a subordinate in front of others. Criticizing in public broadcasts the negative message that you are interested in demonstrating your authority rather than helping your subordinate.

3. Never fail to spend time with subordinates when things are going right. This personal interaction may prevent things from going wrong.

4. Never give your subordinates reason to feel that your primary interest is in feathering your own nest and protecting your own image. Giving that impression creates resentment and casts them in the role of scapegoats.

5. Never play favorites. This is a difficult task since, in any group of people, some are more likable, more capable, more dedicated. However, you must make every effort to treat subordinates fairly and equitably.

6. Never dull your sensitivity to the small things. A shy person can blossom with a little well-placed attention; an angry individual can mellow with a little caring guidance.

7. Never lower your personal standards. Lowering your standards, even at a casual gathering or social function, can compromise your position and impair your ability to lead.

8. Never delay decision making. Make decisions promptly or explain the reasons for the delay. Otherwise, the delay will be taken as a sign of weakness.

Charisma, magnetism, radiance, charm—all are terms commonly used to explain the popularity of some well-known celebrity. More often than not, such lofty acclaim stems from the pages of a fan magazine or the puffery of a press agent. We have to wonder who the real person is behind the facade.

No one can be happy all the time; that depends on the happenings of one's life. Life's building blocks are not constant smiles; they can't be, as Job was to learn. Great songs come out of the dead of night; sensitive poetry is written in despair; tears become the release valve of the heart when too much pressure is placed on it. Life's joys are enhanced by life's blows. Such a joyous person possesses true charisma or charm, magnetism or radiance.

The only prescription I know for actual joy was written by the Apostle Paul to the church of Thessalonica. He counseled, "Rejoice evermore. Pray without ceasing. In every thing give thanks: for it is the will of God in Christ Jesus concerning you." Simply, I believe we cannot be thankful and depressed at the same time. Depression and frustration, even in small doses, belittle our full personality. Thanksgiving purifies our spirit and prevents our feeling sorry for ourselves. It means seeing the best side of even a bad problem; it means overshadowing bad thoughts with good.

Test my premise. For the next two weeks, begin each day by writing down three things for which you are thankful. You may write some of the the same things over and over; new items will undoubtedly be added. You may start with thanks for family, country, job, income, a child's good grades or a much-needed vacation. Don't just think them—write them down, look at them, remember them throughout the day. In so doing, make them the basis for a thanksgiving prayer. If you are thankful in everything, you will be praying without ceasing and, as Paul suggests, you will rejoice evermore.

During a hike in the country, a troop of Boy Scouts came across an abandoned section of railroad track. In turn, each tried walking on the rails, but eventually lost their balance and tumbled off. Suddenly, two of the boys, after considerable whispering, bet that they could both walk the entire length of the track without falling off. Challenged to make good their boast, the two boys jumped up on opposite rails, extended a hand across the gap to balance each other, and walked the entire length of track without difficulty.

We *can* learn from our children. With their innovative solution to a problem, the pair of Scouts have illustrated the principle for successful living—a principle that works in a family or business or community. Make no mistake, reaching out your hand to another is more than generosity or compassion—it is survival. As the Scouts discovered, when we hold another in balance, we have the prop to balance ourselves.

On the homefront, household chores can turn into fun when the family joins together. An even stronger bond develops when older children help their younger brothers and sisters with homework and other childhood problems. Husbands and wives who have helped their mate through a crisis share more than love.

In the workplace, when people freely and willingly help each other, a spirit of teamwork emerges that can make a department or entire company take off. When work becomes happy and enjoyable, business booms.

At home or office, thankless jobs and undesirable chores become almost pleasant when done together. Misery loves company, so the saying goes. But when misery *has* company, the misery element usually disappears.

Time is more than the shadow on a dial or the striking of a clock. Time is more than the passing of the days and the seasons. Time is the life of the soul.

If we squander time, we waste the stuff of which our lives are made. We squander time if we let miserable misunderstandings continue from year to year, intending to clear them up "someday." We squander time if we keep wretched quarrels alive because we refuse to swallow our pride and end them. We squander time if we pass people sullenly on the street, refusing to speak to them out of some silly spite. We squander time if we let our neighbor starve until we hear they are dying of starvation. We squander time if we let a friend's heart ache for a word of appreciation or sympathy which we mean to give "someday."

If only we could know and see and feel that time is short. One day, it shall be no more. There is too little time, too little of the stuff of which our lives are made. Let us not squander the life of our souls.

The Book of Ecclesiastes describes time and in so doing, gives us a definition of life.

Or, as Charles Caleb Colton wrote: "Time is the most undefinable yet paradoxical of things; the past is gone, the future has not come, and the present becomes the past even while we attempt to define it, and, like the flash of lightning, at once exists and expires."

So we are reminded by Leigh Richmond: " 'There is a time to be born, and a time to die,' says Solomon, and it is the memento of a truly wise man; but there is an interval between these two times of infinite importance."

"Friendship," like "love" and "happiness" and "success," is among those commonly used words that we just as often misuse and abuse. We have come to take such words so lightly that they almost lose meaning and definition. This essay on friendship by Harry B. Hayes can help us redefine friendship and evaluate our personal worth as a friend:

All that can be expected of any man is to make the best use of the things that are within his power.

Only the contented man is rich; so we must look for the things that bring contentment.

The first of these is to find a friend; and if you find two friends you are indeed a lucky man, and if you find three friends—real friends—then you are a rich and powerful man.

In prosperity it is easy to find a friend, but in adversity it is the most difficult of all things.

No matter how small a man's means may be, if he gives of what he has to his friend, it is the same as if it were a great amount.

A man's pleasures are insured by sharing them with a friend, and his griefs are reduced by securing the sympathy of a friend.

The counsel of a friend is the best counsel because it will be true advice; for when received from a mere acquaintance, it may be so filled with flattery that its value will be destroyed, and faithful and true counsel rarely comes excepting from the true friend.

It is said that in youth we have visions and in old age dreams, and the vision and the dream may give us an ideal of perfection; but experience and large contact with men compel us to accept the man who measures in his virtues only to the substantial average.

If we view a man as a whole and find him good as a friend, we must not be diverted from the happy average—the every-day, human average—by using a magnifying glass upon his faults or frailties.

We must, in order to have and hold a friend, accept him as he is, demanding but one thing in return for our affection—his fidelity.

Do you ever have to make a speech? Teach a Sunday school class? Make a presentation at work? Speechmaking is not an easy task but the effective speaker makes it look easy.

Speaking has been a large part of my life, and I'm surprised by the response of many people when they are called upon to speak publicly. Their usual reaction is HELP! The general put-down of one's self is: "When I stand up, my mind sits down." This I doubt. The real problem is that you speak infrequently but feel you should speak as well as someone who does this all the time.

May I make some general suggestions?

Understand who your audience will be. Don't be surprised by the size or age of your listeners. Know exactly how much time you are allotted and abide by it.

Agree to speak on subjects of interest to you. This isn't always possible if you're speaking for a business group and maybe the boss assigned the subject to you because he didn't want to do it.

Organize your material. My recommendation is to put into one sentence what you want to say and be sure your comments surround that sentence. Also, I strongly suggest you work on the conclusion before the introduction. Blame it on the attention span, but speeches are judged on their beginning and ending more than the content.

Study your speech over and over until you feel married to it. Even if you're using notes, still know your material.

Work to establish eye contact. If using notes, lift your eyes up periodically. Pick a few faces around the room to look at.

Use personal references for identity, but not too many, and tell clean jokes— but only if you have joke-telling ability.

If you speak infrequently, but still on the same general subject, remember an audience would rather hear a good speech twice than a half dozen poor speeches.

D r. Albert Schweitzer has been called "The Great Man's Great Man." He took the teachings of Christ literally; and he obeyed the call of Christ. "If any man will come after me, let him deny himself, and take up his cross, and follow Me. For whosoever will save his life shall lose it: and whosoever will lose his life for My sake shall find it" (Matt. 16:24–25).

That's exactly what Albert Schweitzer did:

> He FOLLOWED Christ
> He DENIED HIMSELF
> He TOOK UP HIS CROSS
> He LOST HIS LIFE BUT FOUND IT

Albert Schweitzer was born in Alsace, January 14, 1875, the son of a Lutheran minister. In his boyhood he heard little of liberty and more of discipline. The suffering and pain of people developed in him early a keen sense of the extreme sorrow of the world. This sensitivity grew more acute and as he put it, "The inner voice would not let me rest on a cushion of roses."

Albert Schweitzer earned four doctorates and had innumerable honorary doctorates conferred on him by such renowned universities as Zurich, Prague, Oxford, Chicago, and Edinburgh. He served as a minister, university professor, was one of the world's greatest pipe organists, and was a skillful physician.

When Dr. Schweitzer was thirty years old, he announced that he must go as a medical missionary to Africa. This announcement came as a bombshell to the academic, literary, and musical worlds. His friends thought he was crazy, wasting his training. They asked "Is not scholarship service?" "Is not teaching service?" "Is not preaching service?" "Is not music service?"

He answered, "Of course, but too easy. It is not really service unless the giving hurts."

So Schweitzer returned to the university and enrolled as a medical student, receiving his M.D. in 1913 when he was thirty-eight years of age. On Easter 1913, Albert Schweitzer sailed for Africa.

War broke out in 1914. His mother was trampled to death by cavalry in a village street; old friends were killed; his health declined, the hospital ruined; no income and high debts. He felt he had failed. But he didn't quit. He invested his life in Africa. He lost his life but found it.

To young men he said, "I don't know what your destiny will be. But one thing I know: the only ones among you who will be really happy are those who will have sought and found how to serve."

Winning and losing, succeeding and failing are closely linked, beyond the obvious connotation of opposites and extremes. For only a person willing to risk losing can ever win. We learn from our failures, using them to succeed the next time. Perhaps what we truly need are a few well placed failures in our lives.

There is an old Norwegian tale about a fisherman and his two sons. Every day, they cast off early in the morning and returned home well after dark. Hard work, long hours.

On one particular day, the catch was especially good. But, by mid-afternoon, a sudden squall blackened the sky and obscured the distant shoreline. While the three fishermen were groping for shore, tragedy broke out at home. The kitchen stove set the rustic cabin ablaze and, before neighbors could extinguish the flames, all the family's worldly possessions were consumed.

Eventually, the storm lifted enough for the father and sons to row, to shore. The fisherman's wife was waiting at the dock to tell him the sad news at home. "Karl," she wept, "fire has destroyed everything we own. We have nothing left." Unmoved by the dire news, the husband said nothing. "Karl, didn't you hear me? Our cottage is gone. All our earthly possessions are ashes," wailed the wife. "Oh, I heard you," Karl replied. "We've lost everything; but you don't understand.

"A few hours ago our boys and I were hopelessly lost at sea. We were certain we would perish. Then a miracle happened. Through the storm, I spotted a dim yellow glow. The faint light grew brighter and brighter. We turned the boat toward the light and safety. The same blaze that destroyed our home was the light that saved our lives."

None of us need go out in search of failure, but when it comes it may be the lesson that saves us. Many of the great successes of history resulted from people failing in the pursuit of one goal and finding another. When we rise above failure, or in spite of it, we become winners. Winning is experiencing failure and using it to prepare you for the next competition. When winning ceases, only character prevails.

Today we put a premium on the man who can make decisions quickly. One of my dearest friends used to argue against fast decisions. He was the late N.C. English of Thomasville, North Carolina. Mr. English said often, "When I'm in the dark, I stand still and wait for light unless I stumble in a hole."

Archibald Rutledge, poet laureate of South Carolina, studied the habits of the white-tailed deer for fifty years He discovered that, when in the presence of danger, the deer was disciplined to stand absolutely quiet until he could figure what to do. Maybe David, who was a shepherd and loved animals, learned from them so the Spirit of God could write through him, "Be still and know . . ."

Maybe even the late N.C. English had learned his business advice from his observations when enthusiastically hunting. Really, I think it was Mr. English's Quaker faith. He adhered faithfully to the Quaker discipline with strong emphasis on mysticism and meditation. This became his life-style.

Our difficulty is that we've placed glory on the activist. We greet each other, "You look tired; you must really be moving about; you're really working." We take that as a compliment. The "now" man is the one running up two steps at a time—but too out of breath to do anything when he gets to the top. We gulp our food or have a sandwich brought to our desk. We jump the traffic light before it changes. We walk back and forth when we could be sitting. We want every evening booked so home is where we drop into bed exhausted with a smile. "Boy, I'm a dynamo!"

We never slow down enough to measure our accomplishments. We never check our values. David said in Psalm 23: "He leadeth me beside the still waters" . . . and, in so doing, David says our souls are restored.

There is value in stillness. The flower bud blooms quietly. The tree grows silently. The stars shine noiselessly. Maybe we need less action and more accomplishment. Put down the ego blare. Drop the public relations trumpet. Sense what happens when each day, whether at work, play or church, is spent in glorifying God—a God you can meet in the quietness of meditation.

An oft-quoted prayer needs to be more than just a good arrangement of words: "Teach us, oh God, that in life as in music, the rests are just as important as the notes."

Cynicism, while not the best of traits, is better than being passive. And if our cynicism leads us to in-depth study, if our findings prompt us to work for solutions, if action results from our cynicism, then perhaps cynicism is a virtue. Could you have written this cynical lament?

My shattered financial situation is due to the federal laws, state laws, county laws, city laws, corporation laws, mothers-in-law, sisters-in-law, brothers-in-law, and out-laws.

Through laws I am compelled to pay business tax, amusement tax, head tax, bank tax, income tax, food tax, furniture tax, excise tax. I am required to get a business license, hunting license, and a dog license.

I am also required to contribute to every society and organization which the genius of man is capable of bringing, to give relief to the unemployed, the indisposed, plus the gold diggers relief; also to every hospital and charitable institution including the Red Cross, black cross and double cross.

For my own safety, I am required to carry life insurance, property insurance, liability insurance, burglary insurance, accident insurance, windstorm insurance and fire insurance.

My business is so governed that it is no easy matter to find out who owns what. I am expected, inspected, suspected, disrespected, examined, re-examined, informed, required, summoned, condemned and compelled, until I provide inexhaustible supply of money and reports for every known need, desire or hope of the human race.

And simply because I refuse to donate to something or other, I am boycotted, talked about, lied about, held up, held down, and robbed until I am almost ruined. This check I enclosed could not have happened but for a miracle. The wolf that comes to many doors nowadays had pups in my kitchen. I sold them and here is the money.

While taken to extremes, the letter might make us wonder how much encroachment on our freedom is needed until we say "no more"; until we force a political appraisal by those who, claiming to care about us, actually put us in a bind.

More and more books are being written about business and management practice. Despite the modern theory contained in these volumes, old-fashioned common-sense suggestions may still be the best guidelines for our working lives. Consider the following:

Poet Robert Frost wrote cynically, "By working faithfully eight hours a day, you may actually get to be a boss and work 12 hours a day."

An old saying states, "the man who gets ahead is the one who does more than is necessary . . . and keeps on doing it."

Charles R. Brown suggested, "We have too many people who live without working, and altogether too many who work without living."

There is a story about a young man who had been loafing on the job for most of the past year. As the time for his annual review by his supervisor neared, he anxiously asked a veteran employee, "Do you think that if I really work hard for the next two weeks, I might get a raise?" "Son," replied the seasoned veteran, "you make me think of a thermostat in a cold room. You can make it register higher by holding your hand over it, but you won't be warming the room."

Samuel Goldwyn, the movie mogul, once paid someone an obtuse compliment, saying, "You're overpaying him, but he's worth it."

That's the reverse of the executive who advised a young employee, "Your salary raise becomes effective when you do."

Larry Peter, author of "The Peter Principle," wrote, "Man cannot live by incompetence alone."

Herbert Procknow added another dimension, "Some are bent on toil, and some get crooked by trying to avoid it."

Finally, for those of us who guide others in their work, keep in mind these words: "A pat on the back is only a few vertebrae removed from a kick in the pants, but it is miles ahead in results.

Have you had a heavy week and even have a great deal to do right through the weekend? Let me see, then, if I can help us close the week with a smile.

Letter from a Mom to Her Son

Dear Son:

I'm writing this slow cause I know you can't read fast. We don't live where we did when you left. Your Dad read in the paper where most accidents happen within 20 miles of home, so we moved. I won't be able to send you the address as the last family that lived here took the numbers with them for their next house so they wouldn't have to change their address. . . .

The coat you wanted me to send you, your Aunt Sue said it would be a little too heavy to send in the mail with them heavy buttons, so we cut them off and put them in the pockets. . . .

About your sister, she had a baby this morning. I haven't found out whether it is a boy or a girl, so I don't know if you are an aunt or an uncle.

Your Uncle John fell in the whiskey vat. Some men tried to pull him out but he fought them off playfully, so he drowned. We cremated him. He burned for three days.

Three of your friends went off the bridge in a pick-up. One was driving, the other two were in the back. The driver got out. He rolled the window down and swam to safety. The other two drowned. They couldn't get the tailgate down.

We had quite a scare when a fire broke out in the den. I'd heard about the fire department so I called them. The fellow on the other end said, "Where is it?"

I told him, "Between the kitchen and the living room."

He then asked, "How do you get there?"

I said, "Well, you can come through the front door or the back door." Seemed like he was having trouble catching on.

Then he shouted, "How do I get from where I am to where you are?" And I asked him, "You mean you don't have one of those red trucks?"

Not much more news this time, nothing much has happened. Write more often.

Love,
Mom

P.S. Was going to send you some money but the envelope was already sealed.

What is your greatest source of security? Is it family or money, your job or your health? I take my greatest security from the knowledge that God does guide the destiny of men. My feelings are contained in a favorite poem by an unknown author:

> I asked God for strength, that I might achieve
> I was made weak, that I might learn humbly to obey . . .
> I asked for health, that I might do greater things
> I was given infirmity, that I might do better things . . .
> I asked for riches, that I might be happy
> I was given poverty, that I might be wise . . .
> I asked for power, that I might have the praise of men
> I was given weakness, that I might feel the need of God . . .
> I got nothing that I asked for, but everything I had hoped for
> Almost despite myself, my unspoken prayers were answered,
> I am among all, most richly blessed!

Another poem, also by an unknown author, further describes my feelings:

> My life is but a weaving between my God and me;
> I may not choose the colors, He knows what they should be.
> For He can view the pattern upon the upper side,
> While I can see it only on this, the underside.
>
> Sometime he weaveth sorrow, which seemeth strong to me;
> But I will trust His judgment and work on faithfully;
> 'Tis He who fills the shuttle, He knows just what is best;
> So I shall weave in earnest and leave with Him the rest.
>
> At last, when life is ended, with Him I shall abide,
> Then I may view the pattern upon the upper side;
> Then I shall know the reason why pain with joy entwined;
> Was woven in the fabric of life that God designed.

Faith in God's eternal purpose doesn't mean resignation. Rather, faith can actually motivate and push us. Or, as someone said so well long ago, "Pray like it all depends on God and work like it all depends on you."

Whether your Sabbath is Saturday or Sunday, it should be the most joyous day of the week. Here is a thought for everyone who claims that the Sabbath would be joyous if only they could find a church or synagogue they would be joyous if only they could find a church or synagogue they enjoyed:

If you want to have the kind of church
Like the kind of church you like,
You needn't slip your clothes in a grip,
And start on a long, long hike.
You'll find what you left behind,
For there's nothing really new
It's a knock at yourself when you knock the church;
It isn't the church—it's you.

When everything seems to be going wrong,
And trouble seems everywhere brewing;
When prayer-meeting, young people's meet and all,
Seems simmering, slowly stewing,
Just take a look at yourself and say,
"What's the use of being blue?"
Are you doing your bit to make things a hit?
It isn't the church—it's you.

It's really strange sometimes, don't you know,
That things go as well as they do,
When we think of the little—the very small mite—
We add to the work of few;
We sit, and stand around, and complain of what's done.
And do very little but fuss.
Are we bearing our share of the burden to bear?
It isn't the church—it's us.

So if you want to have the kind of church
Like the kind of a church you like,
Put off your guile and put on your smile,
And hike, my brother, just hike,
To the work in hand that has to be done—
The work of saving a few.
It isn't the church that is wrong, my boy;
It isn't the church—it's you.

Monday, Week Twenty

Life is a balance of good and bad news—you cannot escape disappointments. However, a positive attitude can help you cope with disappointments. Facing bad news with grace tells more about you than accepting good news with restraint.

Each of us probably knows someone we truly admire for having remained radiant in the face of unbelievable disappointments. Perhaps, like me, you have gone to comfort someone only to have that suffering person comfort you. Reaching such a high level of stability is not automatic, it comes from self-discipline.

Here are some practical suggestions to help you build the discipline to cope with the disappointments life dishes out:

1. Don't blame others when you are disappointed. You are not the cause of all your disappointments; others do let us down. But not much is gained by wasting time contemplating how bad others are. Try to understand their failings, or mark it down to human nature. If the other person has acted horribly wrong, be grateful you don't act that way; and if you have, use their behavior as an incentive to improve.
2. We create some of our own disappointments. If you feel unattractive or unloved, that is no one's fault except your own. Your lack of self-worth and self-esteem can only be corrected by you and God.
3. If you're disappointed, immediately spell it out and think of alternatives. Don't waste time complaining; consider the other solutions.
4. Prevent disappointment up front. It does no good to change your behavior once it is too late, expecting others to forget and forgive. Visualize the risks and pitfalls of your actions before you act.
5. Profit from disappointment. Some individuals have found their niche only after they were fired. Use a disappointment to enable you to say, "I hope I never go through that again, but I wouldn't have missed the experience for anything."

Bad news or disappointment is not the issue, but how we handle it. We can face each problem with negative thinking and guilt complexes and self-defeat, or we can see it as a test that lets us know we are strong.

We all admire those remarkable individuals who can recall a bushel-full of yesteryear, but are still excited about their plans for tomorrow. Fred H. Schomburg offers a humorous tribute titled "The Golden Years":

> How do I know that my youth has been spent? Because my "get up and go" got up and went.
>
> But in spite of it all, I am able to grin, when I think of where my "get up" has been.
>
> Old age is golden, I've heard it said, but sometimes I wonder as I go to bed.
>
> My ears in the drawer, my teeth in a cup, my eyes on the table until I wake up.
>
> As sleep dims my eyes, I say to myself: "Is there anything else I should lay on the shelf?"
>
> But I'm happy to say as I close my door that friends are the same as in days of yore.
>
> When I was young and my slippers were red, I could kick up my heels right over my head.
>
> When I grew older my slippers were blue, but still I could dance the whole night through.
>
> Now I am old and my slippers are black, I walk to the corner and puff my way back.
>
> Since I have retired from life's competition, I busy myself with complete repetition.
>
> I get up each morning, dust off my wits; pick up the paper and read the "Obits."
>
> If my name is missing I know I'm not dead, so I eat a good breakfast and go back to bed.

Such words as *glasnost* and *perestroika* were not even in our vocabulary a couple of years ago and now they are almost as common as the words *democracy* and *republic*. Even though we may have some reservations about Mr. Gorbachev and feel that there is far more public relations than there is substance, we wish for his goals to be achieved. However, his popularity outside of Russia might be greater than within his own country. We must not forget for a moment that there is a hard-core of Communists who have not waivered one bit from the "Communist Rules for Revolution" published first in 1919 when supposedly captured by Allied forces in Dusseldorf. Yes, there have been questions whether this document was authentic or whether or not the seven rules are consistent with the determined goals of the radical Communist. They are as much a threat to the Russian people themselves as to the United States:

1. Corrupt the young. Get them away from religion. Get them interested in sex. Make them superficial. Destroy their ruggedness.
2. Get control of all means of publicity and thereby get people's minds off their government by focusing attention on athletics, sexy books and plays, and other trivialities.
3. Divide the people's faith in their national leaders by holding the latter up to contempt and ridicule.
4. Always preach true democracy, but seize power as fast and as ruthlessly as necessary.
5. By encouraging government extravagance, destroy its credit, produce fear of inflation with rising prices and foster general discontent.
6. Foment unnecessary strikes in vital industries, encourage civil disorders, and foster a lenient and soft attitude on the part of government to such disorders.
7. By specious argument cause the breakdown of the traditional moral virtues: honesty, sobriety, continence, faith in the pledged word, and ruggedness.

There are those, including Zbigniew Brezinski, who believe the Cold War is over and we have won. I do not disagree, but I'm haunted by the fact that all Communism has ever needed is for the Free World to go to sleep or become too trusting. Our best answer is not to highlight the weaknesses of Russia as much as to exercise the spiritual, moral muscle of the United States.

Jack LaLanne is for real. He offers no magic formulas or easy systems for weight loss and beautiful bodies. Instead, Jack has dedicated his life—all seven decades of it—to helping us pay the strenuous price it takes to enjoy good health. He is a living example of his discipline, which begins first by challenging the mind and then the body. Here are some of his common sense tips:

1. Never eat between meals.
2. Eat slowly. Deliberately chew each bite a great number of times. This makes eating "more work" and more boring. The longer you take per bite, the less food you are likely to eat. Much of eating is psychological. If you use smaller plates, modest portions will look like more and in reality you'll be eating less.
3. Don't eat foods that contain white flour and white sugar, if possible.
4. Eat no fried foods.
5. Split your protein requirements into three meals, instead of trying to get all your proteins in just one or two meals. Proteins take four to five hours to digest, so if you get a third of your protein requirements at each meal, your appetite between meals will be decreased.
6. Don't use salt. Replace it with natural flavorings, or if you must use some salt, use sea salt.
7. At mealtime, limit your liquid intake to no more than half a glass. The more liquid you consume with a meal, the more diluted your digestive juices become, resulting in incomplete digestion. However, it is helpful to drink a full glass of water 15 minutes before meals. This will help decrease your appetite at mealtime. Drink eight full glasses of water daily.
8. Eat in a pleasant environment. When we eat in an unpleasant setting, we tend to overeat and overdrink.
9. Exercise vigorously each day.
10. A controlled vitamin and mineral supplement is recommended, as well as adding a half-cup of bran to daily consumption.

Raising teenagers is no small or easy task. Parents of troublesome teens have tried cajoling, begging, bribing, punishing—all to no avail. Many parents, in a futile attempt to cope with teenage difficulties, end up feeling guilty.

Faced with a similar challenge, David and Phyllis York, of Sellersville, Pennsylvania founded the TOUGH LOVE Foundation. The founders have said, "We know how helpless you feel when your kid is in trouble. You are not alone. Many parents in your community are having similar problems and also feel isolated, guilty and ashamed. We realize it is difficult for you to reach out at a time like this, but we have seen the lives of many who join a TOUGH LOVE parent support group change dramatically."

TOUGH LOVE, as defined by the Yorks, is a program to help parents who are troubled by the teenager's behavior in school, within the family, and their involvement with drugs, alcohol and the law.

TOUGH LOVE asks you to choose which road you will travel. Will it be confrontation, firm guidelines and mutual respect; or excuses, denials, helplessness, indulgence and bribery?

TOUGH LOVE teaches you to face the crisis, take a stand, demand cooperation and meet challenges.

TOUGH LOVE will help you develop new strength so you can give your young person a sense of direction and support.

Practicing the tenets of TOUGH LOVE can be difficult and stressful. But the rewards can mean a salvaged teenager and a return to a stable family life.

Love and softness have become wedded in our day. True love, call it "tough love," comes from God. And God will never let us off the hook, but He will also never let us down.

How curious are you? I remember taking a brilliant friend on a tour of a cloth printing plant. Suddenly I was aware that he was not with me. When I looked back he was down on his knees looking under a machine capable of printing a dozen colors at one time. No wonder my friend continues to grow. He's curious. How about you? Are you curious?

There is a fine line between being nosy and curious. The nosy person wants to know in order to flatter himself or gossip. The curious person wants to learn more to make himself knowledgeable and useful. It excited me that our son, Allan, asked questions constantly when he was a youngster. It told me he was growing; he was fascinated about the wonderment of knowledge.

We expect a child to be curious and hope he is not too shy to ask questions. As adults we become set in our routine. We become involved and busy and if not careful, use our busyness as an excuse not to grow. How pitiful when we rationalize and claim lack of time as our excuse for not growing.

What do you do with your leisure time? You might say you are so tired when you have a free moment that you just rest. I've found I'm as refreshed by reading or studying something as I am by idly resting. Nero's tutor said, "Illiterate leisure is a form of death, a living tomb."

Actually you may have had excellent formal education—or at least adequate—but our world moves so fast you must educate yourself at least six times during your lifetime to stay contemporary. Don't misunderstand. This doesn't mean reading only the latest publications. As our society becomes more complex, I find I'm going back more to the classic philosophies to gain strength to remain optimistic when so much seems to be coming loose.

Your curiosity level also can be called the true measurement of your age. The bonus? Curiosity is the cradle for creativity.

The greatest choice I made was when I chose my parents." If you've been in my audiences, you've heard me say that . . . and mean it. How good God was to me to give me such rich religious heritage and the security of abiding love.

My mother's maiden name was Steere—and most of the Steeres in America go back to the same English roots. My granddaddy was my pet and I guess I was his. He had one brother—my great-uncle Will Steere of Greater Boston where three of his sons are doctors in that area. Upon Uncle Will's death in 1941, they found among his papers his expressions of "What Religion Means To Me." He wrote:

> Religion means my relation to a Supreme Being, a Father who rules over the world and over the destinies of nations and individuals. He is called *God*.
>
> I trust Him under all conditions, though at times the way may seem dark and uncertain. I have confidence in Him to lead me in the way that is best for me. I believe in His Son, Jesus Christ, my Saviour.
>
> Each morning, upon awaking, I lift my thought to God, and thank Him for His kind care and protection, and ask Him for guidance for the day.
>
> Religion means attendance at public worship from time to time, joining with others to help and be helped. It means a kindly feeling toward those with whom I come in contact and a life of friendliness toward all races and religions. It means a curbing of passion and appetites, a control of temper, and a desire to help others.
>
> Religion means the uplifting of the thought to God in petition for strength and wisdom in special need or danger. Religion means to me that death is a continuation of life in a better world, a facing of the future with trust and confidence.

At times when I realize how blessed I've been with a good heritage, it scares me. After all, to whom much is given, much is expected.

How we deal with employees, just as how we treat our children, has changed dramatically in a single generation.

If your father was like mine, he was not autocratic as much by choice as by expectancy. He felt he should make decisions for the family and, in turn, our somewhat blind acceptance was a necessary discipline and sign of respect. As modern parents, we have not given up decision-making, but have come to feel our children deserve and expect an explanation.

The same principle holds true on the job, employing today's youth. A generation ago, employees accepted a job and blindly carried it out; any discontent was muttered under their breath. The contemporary employee expects an explanation.

When you ask people to do something, you benefit yourself by telling them why. Explanations can reveal your inner security. You gain the title of parent or boss by leading, not by commanding. On the job or in the home, an explanation removes the bossiness that people quickly resent.

In addition, an explanation serves as an automatic test of the logic of your request. If you cannot explain why and how a job is to be done, it may be that you are hiding a weak thought pattern behind your title.

People who see why they are doing a job make fewer errors and approach the task with greater enthusiasm. You want your children to sense that the house is their home, that they have a vested interest in helping with the chores, caring for their room, safeguarding their posses- sions. The perception changes from "mine and yours" to "ours." Likewise, on the job, it is no longer the aloof and arrogant manager demanding that employees become robots and do the supervisor's work. Now the team is doing "our" job, meeting "our" schedule, producing "our" profits—all because the time was taken for an explanation.

There are times when all parents and all bosses want to have their way, to speak without being challenged—but this only shrinks your world and your work. Explanation, however threatening, broadens your world and multiplies your thoughts and efforts.

The process of living is never an easy undertaking. Our relationships with others, through our roles as employees and friends and parents, take constant attention. You may be encouraged or rebuked, inspired or humbled by the following thoughts about our lifestyles and our children:

English novelist Margaret S. Jameson wrote, "Most of us spend 58 minutes an hour living in the past with regret for lost days or shame for things badly done (both utterly useless and weakening); or in a future which we either long for or dread. The only way to live is to accept each minute as a unrepeatable miracle, which is exactly what it is—a miracle and unrepeatable."

Carl Holmes, businessman and author, believes, "The older we get the more we realize that service to others is the only way to stay happy. If we do nothing to benefit others, we will do nothing to benefit ourselves."

Under the heading "Keeping Faith" in a trade publication: "If through all his days a man in business tells the truth as he sees it, keeps his word as he gives it, works for his company for its sake along with his own, he gets what is known as a good reputation."

Bishop Fulton J. Sheen says, "The greatest tragedy today is that parents themselves are so often without any convincing standards to offer for guidance of their children. They have the sextant but no fixed star; the material but no blueprints; the means but no ends."

Art Linkletter counsels, "We must persuade our children that getting everything they want with little effort does not build the kind of character needed to get through life."

Columnist Gloria Pitzer wrote, "We nourish the bodies of our children, but how seldom we nourish their self-esteem. We provide them with beef and potatoes, but neglect to give them words that would sing in their memories for years."

The poetry of Robert Frost has given us many inspirational moments, many thoughts and images to be savored. Equally inspiring is this wonderful poet's personal philosophy.

The Pulitzer Prize winner was surrounded by friends in celebration of the poet's 80th birthday. He graciously answered question after question until, in recognition of his lengthy life, someone asked the inevitable question: "Mr. Frost, in all your years and all your travels, what do you think is the most important thing you've learned about life?"

Despite the gaiety of the gathering, it was not a question to be answered lightly—and Mr. Frost didn't. He glanced away for a moment and then, turning back with a twinkle in his eye, replied, "In three words, I can sum up everything I've learned about life... it goes on. In all the confusion of today, with all our troubles, with politicians and people slinging the word 'fear' around, all of us become discouraged, tempted to say this is the end, the finish. But life... it goes on. It always has. It always will. Don't forget that."

Mr. Frost continued, "Just a little while back, at my farm near Ripton, Vermont, I planted a few more trees. You wonder why? Well, I'm like the Chinese man of 90 who did the same thing. When they asked him why, he said that the world wasn't a desert when he came into it and wouldn't be when he departed. Those trees will keep on growing after I'm gone and after you're gone.

"I don't hold with people who say, 'where do we go from here?' or 'what's the use?' I wouldn't get up in the morning if I thought we didn't have a direction to go in. What direction? I can't answer for it's different for each of us. The important thing to remember is that there is a direction and a continuity even if so often we think we're lost."

At 80, Robert Frost knew that life goes on. And so it does.

Happiness depends on happenings. The happy person may be the lucky recipient of good things such as a winning lottery ticket; or the happy person may be the one who uses a positive attitude to conquer everything life dishes out.

A British newspaper not long ago asked its readers the question, "Who are the happiest persons?" The four prize-winning answers were:

"A craftsman, worker, artist whistling over a job well done."

"A little child building sand castles."

"A mother, after a busy day, bathing her baby."

"A doctor who has finished a difficult and dangerous operation and saved a human life."

The list contains no entertainment personalities or rock stars, no kings or emperors, no business tycoons or heads of state. A child's sand castle can bring more happiness than a monarch's palace. Happiness is for the rich or the poor; happiness depends not on how one was born or what one has, but the attitude one possesses. Momentary happiness may come from a surprise gift, but constant happiness results from a disciplined positive attitude. The miserable individual views the happy one as lucky or dishonest, when the real difference is attitude. Each happy moment today may be the result of a healthy mental attitude yesterday.

Henry Van Dyke expressed the concept with these words:

Let me do my work from day to day
In the field or forest, desk or loom,
In the roaring market-place, or tranquil room.
Let me but find it in my heart to say,
When vagrant wishes beckon me astray,
This is my work, my blessing not my doom:
Of all who live, I am the one by whom
This work can best be done in my own way,
To suit my spirit and to prove my powers;
Then shall I cheerfully greet the laboring house
And cheerful turn when the long shadows fall
At eventide, to play, and love, and rest,
Because I know for me, my work is best.

True happiness—the good life we all seek—comes not from the spectacular, but from our attitudes as we work at our jobs, live in our homes, meditate in quietness.

From the minds and mouths of children often comes wisdom to guide us. We adults, growing cynical and jaded in our daily battle with doubts and fears, could recapture our innocence by looking at life through the eyes of the young.

Asked by her teacher to write about something she liked, an eight-year-old in Colorado listed the following:

Did you know there are many things in this world to be glad about?

Like I like to play with my frisbee and yo-yo. I like to go out camping with hot dogs. I like to go skate-boarding on the sidewalk, if the sidewalk is not bumpy. I like to make toast. I like writing poems because I am like a poet, because that's the way I feel inside. I wrote seven poems for my mother. I like to go in the wind and fly kites. I like to sunbathe and watch television cartoons and have a fire in the fireplace and play burning the witch. I like a spook house and ghosts and goblins. I like to ride a horse, a kind one. I like the zoo and the wild animals and to swing high on a swing. I like to watch movies at school and hold my guinea pig at the same time. I like to ride in our car and go buy bubble gum and candy at the store. I like to find money on the floor of the car ... and sometimes in the the seat. I like to read books and I love to jump in a big pile of leaves. I like to dress up in my pink dress with a long skirt and go to church. I like to play with my doll that wets and drinks. I like to play games and I like to pick flowers.

That's why I'm so glad I could burst.

L ittle League baseball is getting organized throughout the country for another summer. As soon as school is out, two million boys and girls between the ages of eight and fourteen will again don their uniforms and wait anxiously for the umpire to shout, "Play ball!" But is it all good?

Kids' parents have become a year around phenomena. During this past winter, some youngsters awakened at 4:00 A.M. in Massachusetts to play league hockey before school—and that 4:00 A.M. was with daylight savings time. Biddy league basketball, featuring kids no taller than five feet six inches, has an annual tournament with teams from five or six states. Gymnastics is the sport gathering girls both winter and summer. Indoor pools make swim club competitions year 'round. All told, four million of our thirty-six million kids between five and fourteen are involved in team competition.

All of this sounds good—unless it is overdone. The biggest danger is the ego of parents who want to be able to say proudly, "That's my son!" or, "That's my daughter!" Some years ago a friend of mine didn't eat for three days when his boy struck out three times in a crucial Little League game. We want our children to be competitive but not to be destroyed with a "failure complex" by the time they're fourteen.

Since I played sports throughout my school and college career, I know their value if kept in proper proportion.

Take these precautions:

1. Know the character and ability of the person coaching your child. His character is even more important than his ability at this time in your child's life. Be sure the coach, however, does know the sport well enough since this time in a child's life should be a learning experience. In fact, there ought to be at least three weeks of practice before the first game or event.
2. Before signing a permission slip for your child to participate, have a thorough examination scheduled for him/her, along with periodic check-ups. If it is a contact sport, insist a doctor be readily available during the games and practices. Substitution should be quickly made if a player is injured.
3. Of course, safety is a basic factor. The field, the rink, the gym, or pool should be in excellent condition. Equipment has to be constantly maintained.

How much we owe to so many adults who coach, officiate, and sponsor kid sports. It takes hours upon hours and often much generosity. Competition is healthy but, even when something is good, there still must be every effort to see that the good goals not be distorted.

For the first time in years, people are returning to traditional worship centers.

There is much I don't know, but two things I firmly believe: the earth will outlive the ecologists and the church will outlive the critics. Is the church effective? How do you measure the church?

Unfortunately our basic measuring rod for the church has been membership alone. Some religious leaders deny the church has lost numbers. They insist the computer age is doing a more efficient job, so we have just eliminated some of the dead wood. Still, the criteria most frequently used to measure a church are membership and budget. If both are large we automatically claim that church to be influential, effective, and spiritual.

Granted, membership increases do indicate activity. Yet, I'm familiar with churches that are comparatively small by design; but they are dynamic and by having rigid membership requirements, great demands are placed on the members.

A growing budget is a good barometer especially if there is increased giving to mission causes outside the church. Jesus put emphasis on man's use of material possessions.

However, using any kind of statistics can be unfair and give false impressions. The church that was once in a thriving community may now be in a rezoned area. As a neighborhood changes from homes to businesses, the church is almost certain to suffer heavy statistical losses.

The church may be in a racially changing area. Some shifts can be charted but often the shift comes quickly to a mixed congregation. No matter how the church may desire to take the Christian approach to racial relations, the ideal is never realized suddenly.

Another change is from rural to urban. The traditional country church, steeped in heritage and usually old, is suddenly caught up in a population boom as developments are carved out. On the surface the influx of new members looks great but people who go back two and three generations in a particular church are not always quick to relinquish or share the management of the church.

What I really want to say is that it is impossible to measure the church—that is, for man to measure. It is energized not by its size or the money it spends but by the Spirit of God. Its ultimate success is measured only by Him.

We are constantly changing, indeed, we are constantly aging. That aging process tends to highlight the acquisition of habits, the cementing of attitudes, a preoccupation with what we have done in the past. This is natural and only becomes detrimental if we lose our willingness and courage to try new methods.

Just as a pilot goes over a check-list prior to takeoff, here is a check-list to help maintain your innovativeness, your creativity, your adaptability, your openess, even your youthfulness. See if you possess each of these eight essentials:

1. Confidence in your ability, your company or store, the product you are selling, the service you are providing.
2. A positive attitude toward business, tempered with realism.
3. A pleasant appearance in front of your fellow employees or customers. You don't perform manual labor in your Sunday best, but neatness and cleanliness turn into efficiency.
4. A trustworthiness by your fellow employees or customers because you are as good as your word.
5. A good listener, not only hearing the words and nodding acceptance, but performing as you agree.
6. Constantly searching for new ways to do your work better, not only for your own satisfaction, but for the effectiveness of your company or store.
7. Genuine interest in all facets of your company and all employees, believing you are part of a team and cannot succeed in isolation.
8. Above all, an appreciation for the opportunity to work and to use your abilities; for a chance to earn an income to support your family; for recognition of your value. Such appreciation results in total honesty and enthusiasm.

True, we will all do basically the same things this week as last, and we will live much the same way. The difference is your dedication to making this the best week of your life.

This message is aimed at those of us over fifty, but anyone should find it intriguing, so here goes:

For All Those Born Prior to 1950

WE ARE SURVIVORS!! Consider the changes we've witnessed:

We were before television, before penicillin, before polio shots, frozen foods, Xerox, contact lenses, Frisbees, and the Pill.

We were before radar, credit cards, split atoms, laser beams, and ballpoint pens; before pantyhose, dishwashers, clothes dryers, electric blankets, air conditioners, drip-dry clothes—and before man walked on the moon.

We got married first and *then* lived together. How quaint can you be?

We thought fast food was what you ate during Lent, and Outer Space was the balcony of the Riviera Theatre.

We were before house-husbands, gay rights, computer dating, dual careers, and commuter marriages. We were before day care centers, group therapy, and nursing homes. We never heard of FM radio, word processors, yogurt, and guys wearing earrings. For us, time–sharing meant togetherness—not computers or condominiums. A chip meant a piece of wood. Hardware meant hardware and software wasn't even a word.

In 1940 "Made in Japan" meant junk, and the term "making out" referred to how you did on an exam. Pizzas, McDonalds, and instant coffee were unheard of.

We hit the scene when there were five and ten cent stores where you bought things for five and ten cents. For one nickel you could ride a streetcar, make a phone call, buy an ice cream cone, or enough stamps to mail one letter and two postcards. You could buy a new Chevy for six hundred dollars and a gallon of gas for eleven cents.

In our day cigarette smoking was fashionable, GRASS was mowed, COKE was a cold drink, and POT was something you cooked in. ROCK MUSIC was Grandma's lullaby and AIDS were helpers in the principal's office.

BUT WE SURVIVED!! In reality, we've had it much simpler than our children. Live life over? I'm not sure we're tough enough.

Wednesday, Week Twenty-Two

Success is all luck! If you doubt the truth of that statement, just ask any failure and he will be glad to verify it. In reality, the successful individual usually finds that luck increases with harder work and less scheming.

Over the years, whether we spell it out or not, all of us adopt a game plan for our lives. That may sound too long-range, but we certainly have our personal ideas and beliefs upon which we base our everyday decisions.

Let's think of ourselves in a team meeting just before the big game. Here's the game plan:

1. Your mind is where all success begins—and all success ends.
2. For every problem you face, there is a solution and the seeds of the solution are not from outside sources but your own mind.
3. To uncover a weakness is the first step to strength—for now you are no longer ducking and hoping, but you are now coping and planning. planning.
4. Whatever you focus your attention upon becomes the place where you use your strength.
5. Any fool can condemn, criticize, complain and most do—but we believe, with Dr. William James, that you can change your life by changing your attitude.
6. "Can't" means you won't try, and to lose your competitive fighting spirit is to lose all. There's nothing that can't be improved by a willing mind.
7. This week, like all weeks, you will meet and be part of one of three groups. You have three options: You can be like some people who will make things happen; or you can join the group who pride themselves on their patience as they wait for something to happen; or you can be part of the dismal crowd who view life going on about them and question, "What happened?"

If you had a tough day yesterday, or a tough week last week, resolve that this one will be better. It's not automatic, but neither is it beyond your control.

Here is a personal favorite of mine by Edna Massimilla titled, "Heaven's Very Special Child". It will be especially moving and meaningful to people with a special child in their life:

A meeting was held quite far from Earth.
"It's time again for another birth,"
Said the angels to the Lord above,
This special child will need much love.

Her progress may seem very slow,
Accomplishments she may not show;
And she'll require extra care
From folks she meets down there.

She may not run or laugh or play,
Her thoughts may seem quite far away.
In many ways she won't adapt,
And she'll be known as handicapped.

So let's be careful where she's sent
We want her life to be content,
Please, Lord, find the parents who
Will do a special job for you.

They will not realize right away
The leading role they're asked to play,
But with this child sent from above
Comes stronger faith and richer love.

And soon they'll know the privilege given
In caring for this gift from Heaven.
Their precious charge, so meek and mild,
Is Heaven's Very Special Child.

If you take one big family vacation every summer, it can seem like a long, long time until the next rolls around. An ideal solution might be to split your vacation and take half in the summer and half in the winter. However, if your type of work or particular company or family situation will not allow for doing so, then you have to find another solution.

We can all agree that a vacation is good for your health, both physically and mentally. So why not build a vacation into every week—even into every day? Every 24-hour period needs a built-in time to relax, to slow your pace or at least change your pace, in addition to getting the proper amount of sleep at night.

Most creative people claim that they get their best ideas when away from their offices or laboratories or studios. Even if you don't consider your job very creative, your mind and your body still need a daily pause. It might be the hour when you first get home from work or the hour just before bedtime when you let your mind float free, reflect or do some light reading.

We are all occasionally or daily burdened by problems, whether personal or business or family related. Rather than add to the problem by thinking you have to solve it today, just walk away from it for a time. Relax your brain; let your subconscious take over. You will find that your whole body will relax, your tension will melt away, the wrinkles on your brow will soften—you are enjoying a creative pause! By pausing to erase your mental blackboard, you can have a fresh start; by looking up from the problem, you have a fresh view.

So give yourself "the pause that refreshes"—take a mini-vacation; go outdoors and work in the yard; read a captivating novel; work on a hobby; take a walk; sit in a rocking chair or porch swing; even take a nap. Whatever it is, shift your mind and body into neutral gear and restore your poise and productivity.

Graduation is much earlier in most schools today than in my day. However, there are still a number of schools graduating this weekend and those who have finished still have it fresh on their minds.

As you graduate this year, we look at you with great hope in our eyes. We know the mess you are inheriting and we actually are putting pressure on you to redeem our times.

Father Daniel B. Ryan gave an eloquent graduation invocation which went like this:

Almighty God, we ask your blessings on our graduates tonight and always. We ask that their lives be honorable and rewarding to their country, to their families, and to you. We pray that these graduates find happiness and joy and optimistic dedication in a world in which too often they can experience only sadness, sorrow, and pessimism. Help them to find solutions to their problems, rather than just to criticize people and institutions and even themselves. Give them the willingness to listen to others as they expect others to listen to them; and let them use their wisdom to think through difficulties objectively and find solutions that are wise. Help them find meaning in their lives, not through pessimistic soul searching, not through interference in the rights of others, not through violent actions, for these never lead to true and permanent meaning. But let them find significance in their lives through active and unselfish concern for others; through positive, cooperative solutions, through a dedication to non-violence. Their challenges are many. Wars need to be halted permanently, inequalities in race, color and creed must cease, the problems of pollution, crime, and drugs need to be eradicated. So give these graduates the interest, the optimism, the fortitude and the courage to understand that these problems can be solved, and can be solved by them. But, most of all, we ask a re-birth to You if their love has died; a strengthening, if it should be wavering; an increase, if it hasn't been growing. Watch over these youth who graduate tonight. They need to love so desperately. Help them to realize that only in first knowing and loving You can this desire be satisfied completely. Amen.

Are we too ambitious for you? Are we expecting you to recover the ball we've fumbled? Probably so, but be flattered that we think you can correct many of our errors. I don't know whether you can, but I hope you'll try.

The next time you think it won't matter if your skip church or synagogue services once again, or turn down the call to serve on a committee or turn a deaf ear to appeals for needed funds, remember the following thought entitled, "This Is My Church":

This is my church.

It is composed of people like me. We make it what it is.

I want it to be a church that is a lamp to the path of pilgrims, leading them to Goodness, Truth, and Beauty. It will be if I am.

It will be friendly if I am.

Its pews will be filled if I help fill them.

It will make generous gifts to many causes, if I am a generous giver.

It will bring other people into worship and fellowship, if I bring them.

It will be a church of loyalty and love, of fearlessness and faith, and a church with a noble spirit—if, I who make it what it is, am filled with these.

Therefore, with the help of God, I shall dedicate myself to the task of being all things that I want my church to be.

We all live in stress, and we all love it," according to Dr. Ted L. Edwards, Jr., head of an Austin, Texas, stress management facility. "Stress is the catalyst that fuels productivity, and yet stress is also the single greatest threat to health."

Stress is simply a fact of life in modern America; without stress, we're not alive. When handled and harnessed effectively, stress can be a motivator that enhances health, satisfaction and personal growth. When allowed to get out of control, stress can lead to an alarming array of physical, emotional and mental problems.

Stress is hypnotic. It has the power to freeze our capacity for thinking, to impair our ability to concentrate, to cripple our productivity.

Stress is elusive and illusive. Identifying what causes us distress is half the battle. This discovery process is compounded because pride often prevents us from admitting that we are distressed by something others find only incidental or mildly annoying. We must keep in mind, however, that we are all individuals, and as such, we each have our own causes for stress and our own remedies.

When you feel stress building up, face the situation objectively and honestly. If you have difficulty bringing the problem into focus, talking it over with your spouse or clergyman may often help.

When you have isolated the cause of stress, concentrate on changes you can make to improve the situation and ease the conflict. Or admit to yourself that the particular situation cannot be altered, and learn to accept it as is.

Some people find the grip of stress can be broken by a change of pace—backing away gives a better view. Go fishing or take a day off. Do something completely different from your normal routine.

Some find comfort in reading, especially a biography. Reading about the obstacles another has overcome removes the tendency to be a martyr.

When I am under stress, my own practice is to do something for someone else. This is not generosity by any means; it is selfishness. I get involved in another's problems. I find that I cannot give attention to another and fret about myself at the same time.

But most important to me when I am distressed is to accept the Lord's invitation: "Come unto me all ye that labour and are heavy laden, and I will give you rest. Take my yoke upon you, and learn of me; for I am meek and lowly in heart; and ye shall find rest unto your souls. For my yoke is easy, and my burden is light."

Some time ago, reading an article entitled "A Full Life," I came across this thought—"The secret of a full life is found in the inner attitude of a man's life." It was one of the more profound passages in the article and I stopped to contemplate what was meant by an "inner attitude."

The Bible says it well, "As a man thinketh in his heart, so is he." A person's inner attitude determines their life, actions and deeds. It isn't the material things we accumulate and spend so much time trying to acquire, nor the spiritual philosophy we accept in this life, but our inner attitude toward these things that counts.

Someone is said to have lived a full life, and we sometimes feel deprived not having had their opportunities to travel or to be famous. We feel somehow cheated because others have been blessed with so much talent and opportunity, while we seem to have contributed so little to the world. We must understand, however, that a full life is one that realizes its own possibilities. And no two lives include the same possibilities.

We are all different. Some of us are made for seemingly big, important jobs, if we in fact know what is really big. Others of us are best suited to lives of quietness and smaller service. The fullness of life is determined not by the size of what we do, but by the contribution we have made to life and the happiness we have brought to others, and thus, to ourselves.

Good health, ample wealth, talent, background, and a successful career are fine—but they do not ensure a full life. Many have all these and still feel their lives are empty and unrewarding. The true secret to a full life lies in an individual's inner attitude toward life—the way we look at life and our ability to take what we find there. We must never take life for granted, for it is God's daily gift to each of us.

We can never have everything we want, for we have to say "no" to ourselves sometimes. But we can spend our time loving fully and well, giving unselfishly, and appreciating every moment given to us. That is a full life—not how long we lived, but how much we gave while living.

Most of us are involved in work that requires a minimum of 40 hours per week, and quite often much more. This lengthy workweek holds true whether our occupation involves selling insurance, retailing or business management.

In recent years, much attention has been given to the four-day/10-hour-a-day workweek. Employers receive the same number of productive hours and employees receive a longer weekend with more leisure time. On the face of it, this concept appears beneficial to all. There are, however, two major pitfalls.

First, studies indicate that man's productivity begins to wane after the sixth hour, so the 10-hour-day plan means four rather than two low-production hours each day. Secondly, we simply do not need more leisure time. History shows that many affluent civilizations, such as ancient Rome, have fallen because a bored populace could not manage their free time.

Dr. Charles Mayo, the eminent American surgeon and co-founder with his brother of the respected Mayo Clinic, was even more apprehensive of this trend, denouncing the shortening of the workweek to five days. "I know of no individual, no nation," he stated, "that ever did anything worthwhile in a five-day week."

America's hope to compete in the world market rests on more production per hour with better quality. Our wage scale prices us out of international competition unless we can offer extra quality. We cannot allow common people, who owe their jobs to the uncommon individuals who created those jobs, to shackle their providers and prevent the attainment of these twin goals.

We who work for others can lose job security by designing an employee lifestyle that completely frustrates management—frustration that can lead to more and more leaders opting for early retirement. The Dark Ages, in essence, resulted when frustrated leaders gave up, throwing the world into a period of eclipse and stagnation.

We cannot have employment protection with declining production. While we are a nation that prizes the "good life," our Constitution does not promise to provide happiness—to *pursue*, not to provide. That pursuit entails effort. And with that effort, we can heal the age of the neurotic—with harder work and less loafing, with more drive and less leisure.

Albert E. Day wrote, "Humble questioning is the recognition that one does not know it all. Sincere questioning is genuine hospitality to another's viewpoint. Brave questioning means a willingness to be disturbed mentally, morally, and spiritually. Intelligent questioning witnesses to a conviction that only in another's answers may lie salvation for absurdity."

When we question ourselves, the answers can be both revealing and rewarding. Often we find a drastic difference between image and reality, between how we see ourselves and how we really are. Facing ourselves for better or worse is the first step in turning the worse into better.

1. If you found a pocketbook containing one dollar, would you return it to the owner, provided no one would ever know you had found it?

2. If you could advance yourself by unfair methods, would you do so, provided no one would ever find out you were unfair?

3. If the bus driver failed to collect your fare, would you voluntarily pay it?

4. If there were no locks on any house, store or bank, would you take anything, provided no one would ever find out?

5. If your business partner died, would you pay his relatives their fair share, provided it was not mandatory that you pay them?

6. If you were an employer trying to hire an efficient, honest and competent employee, would you hire yourself at your salary?

7. If you were an employee, would you like to be working for yourself with the wages, hours and working conditions you provide?

8. If you are a parent, would you like to be the child of a parent just like yourself?

9. If you had a choice, would you like to live in a community where the people took the same interest as you do in civic, religious and community affairs?

10. If you had to live with someone just like yourself for the rest of your life, would you look forward to it as a wonderful opportunity and privilege?

My favorite free enterprise story does not detail the building of a colossal empire by a determined visionary. Rather, it is the simple story of how Bob Book, then an executive with Elanco in Indiana, taught his two sons what business was all about.

The summer his boys were 14 and 11, they were anxious to make some money, but were too young to get summer jobs around town. Instead, the pair leased five acres of the family farm from their dad for $120, the going rate for the area. And from the same source they borrowed funds for the purchase of seed, fertilizer and other materials.

On their small plot, the brothers planted Indian corn, gourds and three and a half acres of pumpkins. All that summer, while their friends went swimming and enjoyed the vacation from school, the two boys cultivated their five acres.

Around the beginning of October, they opened a produce stand—actually a wagon. To facilitate sales, customers were allowed to pick their own pumpkins. The innovative brothers cut six different-sized holes in a wide board so customers could determine the price of a pumpkin by the size hole it would fit through.

When the season was over and the need for Halloween pumpkins had passed, the pair turned the ground back to their father and calculated their expenses and sales. The two brothers had netted—not grossed—$1,200, an enviable income for two young boys. Inspired by their success, the fledgling entrepreneurs set their sights on the summer ahead and set a goal to net $2,000.

This story is a tribute to the two brothers, to their initiative and ambition, and to their proud parents who strongly believe in helping others help themselves—even their own boys. This simple account underscores the contention that free enterprise needs no defense, only practice.

Changing our language at times does us a disservice. Very seldom is someone called "a drunk"—now they're an alcoholic, which is more respectable. An alcoholic may be a sober person who is overcoming his problem, but when we say "drunk," we're speaking literally. As much as I love people, there are some of my friends who need to be sobered by being called a drunk.

Here are some "sobering" questions from the National Council on Alcoholism:

1. Do you try to get someone to buy liquor for you because you're ashamed to buy it yourself; or do you buy it at different places so no one will know how much you purchase?
2. Do you hide empties and dispose of them secretly?
3. Do you plan in advance to "reward" yourself with a little drinking bout after you've worked very hard in the house?
4. Do you have blackouts—periods about which you remember nothing?
5. Do you phone the host or hostess of a party the day after to see if you made a fool of yourself or do you find cigarette holes in your own clothing or furniture and can't remember when it happened?
6. Do you take a drink before leaving for the party where you know liquor will be served?
7. Do you wonder if people talk about how much you drink?
8. Do you feel wittier and more charming when you're drinking?
9. Do you panic when faced with non-drinking days, maybe caused by mother visiting from out of town?
10. Do you find yourself reading, or watching TV or movies about alcoholics?
11. Do you ever carry liquor in your purse or coat pocket?
12. Are you defensive when someone mentions your drinking?
13. Do you drink when under pressure or after an argument?
14. Do you cover up for breaking promises you can't remember making?
15. Do you drive while drinking, feeling certain you're in complete control?

If you recognize yourself in any of the above descriptions, seek professional help immediately. It could save your life—or someone else's.

Once a minister friend ordered some clothing from his favorite Hong Kong tailor. The reply from the tailor came addressed to: "The Owner—First Baptist Church." Who was qualified to open the letter? Who owns the church? Foolish question or one that needs some thinking?

Did you ever hear about the man who drove into a small county seat town looking for the Church of God? The stranger asked a man he found whittling on the courthouse steps. "Church of God, you want?" asked the whittler. "Well now, there's a big church over there sometimes called the Baptist Church but it really belongs to Mr. Jones. He runs it. There is a beautiful church on yonder corner some call Presbyterian but it belongs to Mr. McGregor. He runs it. There's a building around the corner I've heard called a synagogue but Mr. Stein calls the shots there. Then there's the cathedral but Mr. O'Murphy is the boss there. You know, stranger, I don't believe God has a church in this town."

Too often I'm afraid the little story is true. Ministers make the mistake of talking about "my church," "my staff," and "my official board."

Also I've known men who give generously and then think they can control the church by threatening to withhold their giving. I saw this happen and the year "Mr. Big" withheld his money, the church recorded a per capita giving record, so "Mr. Big" wasn't missed.

When I served as pastor, I welcomed people each Sunday in this language: "We cannot welcome you to this church for this church belongs to God and you are always loved by Him. However, we who regularly worship at this place are pleased to have fellowship with you and in turn we worship with all God's children around the world."

Here is why I know the church will endure. It is the creation of God. The church is not a democracy nor run by an individual. The church is a theocracy—to be operated by God whose will comes to the people seeking to know Him and His will.

Too often we say the church needs you. Really the church can survive without either you or me—but remember, God may not need us but God wants us—and He wants us to have fellowship with each other in worship.

Have you ever calculated how much time you spend listening? Either by choice or circumstance, we all do a lot of listening. But listening isn't necessarily hearing. All too often, we wish we could remember something that we recall being told, but we weren't listening.

Here are some suggestions on effective listening—listening to hear and remember:

1. Adopt the attitude that you can learn something from most of what you hear. Concentrate on the useful and interesting aspects of what is being said. Don't conclude that you're bored before you actually are.
2. Ineffective listening can result because of the person talking. Certain mannerisms or speech tones can be distracting. Forget how it is being said and concentrate on what is being said.
3. Don't be arrogant and start thinking you know more than the speaker. Often, when a conversation starts with knowledge you already have, you put your ears to sleep just about the time some new and useful information comes out.
4. Don't just pretend to listen—tell yourself you're going to listen. Looking the speaker straight in the eyes and nodding your head while your mind is 1,000 miles away is more than rude and offensive, it is dishonest.
5. Don't be afraid to ask questions. Questions add to your knowledge— the easiest way to learn is to exchange ideas. Questions also flatter the speaker and help the speaker clarify his or her presentation.
6. Don't allow emotional reactions to block your listening. Even if you violently disagree with what is being said, stubbornly refusing to listen accomplishes nothing.

Listening is much tougher than speaking. It is a sad fact that so much talking is done without listening. And without listening, we're soon talking only to ourselves.

Have you ever daydreamed about living your life over again and making major changes? Our Lady of Lourdes Church in Slidell, Louisiana, printed this thought on the subject:

Someone asked me the other day: If I had my life to live over, would I change anything? My answer was, "No." But after I thought about it, I changed my mind.

If I had my life to live over, I would have talked less and listened more.

Instead of wishing away nine months of pregnancy and complaining about the shadow over my feet, I'd have cherished every minute of it, and realized that the baby growing inside me was my only chance in life to assist God in a miracle.

I would have invited friends over for dinner even if the carpet was stained and the sofa faded.

I would have eaten popcorn in the "good" living room and worried less about the dirt when you lit the fireplace.

I would have taken the time to listen to my grandfather ramble about his youth.

I would have sat cross-legged on the lawn with my children and never worried about grass stains.

I would have cried and laughed less while watching TV... and more while watching real life.

I would have gone to bed when I was sick instead of pretending the Earth would go into a holding pattern if I weren't there for a day.

I would never have bought anything just because it was practical, wouldn't show soil, or was guaranteed to last a lifetime.

When my child kissed me impetuously, I would never have said, "Later. Now go get washed up for dinner."

There would have been more I-love-yous, more I'm-sorrys, more I'm-listenings. But mostly, given another shot at life, I would seize every minute of it. Look at it and really see it. Try it on, live it, exhaust it, and never give that minute back until there was nothing left of it.

None of us will ever get another shot at life. Resolve today to seize every minute and squeeze every last ounce of living out of it.

Those who do not learn from history are destined to repeat the mistakes of the past. If we believe that, we should be distressed to read polls that indicate our nation's young people are woefully ignorant of our history and out of touch with contemporary world affairs. But I wonder if we adults have a better understanding.

Does the United States still have a national purpose? The business community and social scientists, who seldom work in concert, seem to agree that we lack an overall sense of direction and mission. Our modern society is segmented into every self-seeking pressure group imaginable. We have always welcomed such groups, but we have also had an overriding sense of purpose. We have emerged from three decades of history-making prosperity, but it was built on a bankrupting national debt that indicates we are soft, flabby, undisciplined and unwilling to sacrifice today for a better tomorrow.

If we knew history well, we would have received the caution given by Charles Turner in Plymouth, Massachusetts, on December 22 in 1773:

> We trust in the God of all grace that North America will rise unto the noblest structure the sun has ever beheld; and which shall be a pattern and source of instruction and happiness to the rest of mankind. If God will grant that North America shall exceed Rome in its highest perfection, as much as our ancestry and our advantages exceed theirs, our highest expectations will be answered. *Is it impossible that there should once be a people wise enough to withstand the temptation of affluence?* . . . If you are found so immersed in worldly mindedness and sensuality, so dead to a sense of the importance of liberty, and so void of all religious and virtuous principles, as to be now ripe for squandering away the inheritance which we procured for you, we must beg leave to consider it as one of the most astonishing of all events.

If we could encapsulate our problem, it might be that we are so busy shouting for more and so busy trying to build a pseudo fail-safe society that we've excused ourselves from the responsibility and discipline of caring for the magnificent land we have. Just as a parent might insist that a child finish what was on the plate before dessert could be served, so are we being presumptuous to think we deserve more while wasting what we already have through our lack of morality and responsibility.

How did we ever function without all the handy, labor-saving gadgets that have been developed during our lifetime? How could we get along without adhesive tape, the ball-point pen, unbreakable containers? Perhaps the greatest of them all is the lowly, unheralded zipper.

What did we do before the zipper? The zipper has saved many a marriage by eliminating the lengthy ordeal of lacing up a dress. Today, the zipper is employed on everything from shoes to sleeping bags to purses to tent flaps.

The zipper isn't really new, but came into prominence during our life-time. In fact, the zipper was discovered about 1891 by a man who considered it useless. It seems that Whitcomb L. Judson had a business associate whose father suffered from crippling arthritis. His stiff fingers could not lace the clumsy hook-and-eye shoes of the period. So the son looked to Judson, known as a gadgeteer and tinkerer, to come up with a solution.

At the time, Judson was immersed in the development of a mass transit system in Chicago. But he took time to ponder a solution to his associate's request. In short order, he devised a crude, but workable, device that he labeled a "hookless fastener."

Judson thought his helpful gadget was insignificant, and not until two years later was he persuaded by friends to patent his hookless fastener. Together with a partner, he organized the Automatic Hook & Eye Company to market the new product. But few people were impressed with the novel device, including Judson himself. He eventually dropped out of the company and died in obscurity, believing to his dying day that there was little future or value for his hookless fastener that today we know as the zipper.

As the old saying goes, "Youth is wasted on the young." But more and more we see older adults who are youthful. Not narcissistic seekers of the fountain of youth, hiding behind a shield of exotic make-up, but those industrious, hard-working individuals who remain young because of the freshness of their ideas and the fertility of their minds.

Whenever the late General Douglas MacArthur set up command, he always hung pictures of Presidents Washington and Lincoln directly behind his desk. Between the portraits he had a framed creed which read:

> Youth is not a time of life. It's a state of mind. It's a test of the will, a quality of imagination, a vigor of emotions, a predominance of courage over timidity, of the appetite for adventure over love of ease. Nobody grows old by merely living a number of years. Years wrinkle the skin, but to give up enthusiasm wrinkles the soul. Worry, doubt, self-distrust, fear and despair...these are the quick equivalents of the long, long years that bow the head and turn the growing spirit back to dust. Whether 70 or 16 there is in every being's heart the love of wonder, the sweet amazement of the stars and the starlike things and thoughts, the undaunted challenge of events, the unfailing childlike appetite for "what next?" You are as young as your faith, as old as your doubt, as young as your self-confidence, as old as your fear, as young as your hope, as old as your despair. So long as your heart receives messages of beauty, cheer, courage, grandeur and power from the earth, from man and from the Infinite, so long are you young. When all the wires are down, and all the central places of your heart are covered with the snows of pessimism and the ice of cynicism, then, and only then, are you grown old indeed, and may God have mercy on your soul.

The general gave us perhaps the best offense for staying young. Discipline of thought keeps life flowing youthward. Or as someone once said, "Following the path of least resistance is what makes men and rivers erode. Men seldom drift to success."

Along the way I developed a speech titled "Chairman of the *Bored*." Our waste of human resources poses the biggest threat to our future welfare. When I speak of waste I'm not thinking of one person doing harm to another but the harm we do to ourselves through boredom. What is boredom? Are all people bored sometime?

Boredom is not a sickness but it has such an effect on the bored. Dr. Ralph R. Greenson of UCLA School of Medicine identifies boredom as "a signal, an indication that the conscious ego has lost contact with the deeper levels of structures of the mind." We laypeople think of boredom in terms of emptiness, frustration, and restlessness. We sometimes blame our boredom as being forced on us. We feel our talents or ideas have been rejected so we feel we're put on the shelf just to do the routines, but not much that challenges the mind. Others who have been highly successful gradually feel the world slipping by them. Soon they're saying, "I can't figure it out but I just can't seem to get with it. I feel I'm nowhere." This indicates boredom has dulled emotions and reactions.

Take comfort in the fact that all people are bored at one time or another. Sure, I've heard people brag that they're never bored, but such is "tommyrot." The person who has never been bored is yet to be born. The difference is how quickly you snap out of boredom. This reveals your discipline or your ability to keep challenging projects on the "back burner" to stimulate you when you feel the blahs. This is worthwhile escape as opposed to harmful escape. Harmful escape from boredom is kids using drugs or adults taking tranquilizers to eliminate feelings.

Some of the possible ways to fight boredom are to associate with stimulating people—even those who completely challenge you. If your principle work is boring, find a challenging hobby, if change of employment is not merited. Some people need to change jobs while others know they have the best job for their abilities and need outside activities to help their daily routine.

As in any human problem, identifying the problem is a step toward the cure. Don't be bored to tears. That's a waste. Seek the avenues of stimuli that work for you.

"Have a good week." This phrase is commonly used. It's pleasant to hear "have a good week." It makes you think the greeter is sure he'll have a good week and wants you to have the same, but what can we do to assure a good week?

Dr. William James is considered the father of American psychology. He felt the greatest discovery of his generation was that man can alter his life by altering his feelings. Sounds so simple! You can alter your life by altering your feelings.

The poem we've used so often says:

> If you think you are beaten, you are; if you think you dare not, you don't. If you'd like to win but think you can't, it's a cinch you won't. If you think you'll lose, you're lost, for out in the world we find success begins with a fellow's will, it's all in the state of mind.

What am I saying? Let me give you a simple exercise. On the first day of the week, take a piece of paper and write in one sentence or two the type of person you'd like to be this week.

We get our lives so messed up that we add to our woe by becoming hopelessly complex. Go back to your grade school days. Remember Nathaniel Hawthorne's "The Great Stone Face"? It is really a bit of an autobiography. He tells of the boy who is fascinated by the great stone face in the mountains. Every day he stares at the stone face until gradually the little boy begins to look like the great stone face.

Solomon knew years ago that as a man thinketh in his heart, so is he.

Several years ago a young bride joined her husband at an Army base at the edge of the desert. The one-room apartment was dilapidated—the heat smothering—the wind scourging. The bride finally wrote home and told her mother to expect her—she couldn't take it any longer. The wise mom wrote back: "Two men looked out from prison bars. One saw mud, the other saw stars."

The daughter got the message and started helping the Indians nearby as well as making her apartment a miniature palace.

Need I say more about your attitude toward your job?

It is important to me that I have a good week, and I want you to have one. Write the type of week you want on a piece of paper—think about it—and watch it come true.

Ask any five people what they want out of life, and see if any of the answers match John Stuart Mills' prescription for happiness: "Those only are happy who have their minds on some object other than their own happiness...on the happiness of others...on the improvement of mankind...even on some art or pursuit, followed not as a means, but as itself an 'ideal end'."

Ask the same five people what they expect from their work and the answers, while varying according to priority, would probably include: money—for basic needs as well as status; security—the confidence that working well will mean having a job as long as they want it; satisfaction—the feeling that work is part of a greater whole, providing a sense of purpose, a feeling of being part of a team; status—the pride that comes from working at a prestigious company, performing a valuable service; recognition—the acknowledgement of their value by their employers.

If people expect money, security, satisfaction, status and recognition from their jobs, what does an employer have a right to expect from employees? Employers should be able to anticipate good performance and increased productivity and more. The "more" is what Dean Briggs described when he stated, "Do your work but not just your work and more. Do a little more for the lavishing sake."

That little extra effort raises you from working as a self-indulgence to working for an objective greater than your own happiness. Good quality comes from putting your heart into your work. The following formula can help you do more than merely work and exist:

1. First, be a quality worker. Sloppy work pulls the rug out from under any later possibilities.
2. Set goals that are challenging to you. Be a professional. Learn to do your work faster and make it easier. Strive to identify ways to accomplish greater production or improve the climate of the workplace or attitudes about yourself. And your attitude toward others will make working conditions better for them.
3. From your work, envision what you can do in your home, community, church or synagogue to make life better. Only when you work and respect yourself can you move out of yourself to assist others.

For each of us, our job is our ticket to accomplishment, to recognition, to satisfaction, to freedom. With the independence our work gives, we can be contributors to better living.

Living is filled with experiences or, as the saying goes, "Experience is what you get when you were expecting something else." Our lives are filled with expectations, and yet the best of life can be the unexpected, the unanticipated. The unknown, rather than to be feared, may be the most exciting door you have ever entered.

The following, among my favorite quotations, give some unique views of life and living:

The late Sam Rayburn, a man of unusual common sense, presided over the U.S. House of Representatives with a blend of savvy and few words. One of "Mr. Sam's" most pithy statements was, "Any donkey can kick down a barn, but it takes a good carpenter to build one."

Helen Hayes, the first lady of American theater, recalls that her mother drew a distinction between achievement and success. "Achievement is the knowledge that you have studied and worked hard and done the best that is in you," her mother advised. "Success is being praised by others, and that's nice too, but not important or satisfying. Always aim for achievement and forget about success."

Stephen Grellet, a French-born Quaker who died in New Jersey in 1855, would be unknown except for a few lines that made him immortal: "I shall pass through this world but once. Any good that I can do, or any kindness that I can show any human being, let me do it now and not defer it. For I shall not pass this way again."

Lastly, we can all benefit from the sage advice Supreme Court Justice Louis Brandeis gave his daughter, "My dear, if you would only recognize that life is hard, things would be much easier for you."

If we were to judge by popular expressions, we could assume there is nothing free in this world. "There is no such thing as a free lunch" and "If it's free, how much is it going to cost me?"

And yet if you are bored or in need of a change, just consider the things you can do right in your own community that are free or relatively inexpensive:

1. Visit a museum. It doesn't have to be the Smithsonian or the New York Museum of Natural Science. Most communities have museums, as well as many colleges. You've probably never visited them, and if so, not recently; new exhibitions and collections are always being added.
2. Entertain yourself at the public library. Most public libraries have not only a selection of books to loan out, but educational films to view and research volumes to study while you are there. Books, more than travel, are the key to the world.
3. Watch a Little League baseball game. If you want to see a serious, exciting, action-packed ball game, forget the televised game of the week and watch the kids in your own neighborhood dreaming of being big leaguers. The only thing missing is the traditional chewing tobacco— it's been replaced by a wad of bubble gum.
4. Pack a picnic basket and get together with neighbors or visit a local park with your family. Often we travel so far we miss the parks and scenery right at home. Spread that picnic basket in a farmer's field by a rippling stream or on a hillside abloom with wildflowers. Or how about homemade ice cream right in your own backyard?
5. Then there's the shopping mall where you usually rush in to make a purchase and rush back as fast. Malls are designed for leisurely window shopping—take the time to enjoy it.
6. There's no better way to greet your neighbors than a slow walk through the community; then make it a brisk walk home to get some exercise.

We all yearn for the simpler days gone by, but they demand a little creativity and effort. Perhaps we have all become too used to being entertained rather than entertaining ourselves. When we find our own amusement, we slow down enough to discover the real values in our own communities.

Companies have personalities—whether big corporations or a single retail store, multi-national conglomerates or small partnerships. In essence, companies reflect their leadership; the personality of a company is usually a representation of the attitudes and style of the executive.

What is it that determines why some companies are consistently successful, others cycle up and down, and still others never quite fulfill their promise? What are the ingredients that set some companies apart? The successful companies:

- Are people-minded. The successful retail store owner, for instance, does not consider the public to be his customers—instead, the public are the customers of his employees. So his employees, in a manner of speaking, become his customers. Knowing he cannot accomplish his goals alone, he places emphasis on helping his employees establish a feeling of self-worth and on making effective employees feel secure.

- Are action-oriented. While some companies fall victim to the paralysis of analysis, tearing up one plan after another in search of the perfect plan, the successful company moves ahead. While highly important, planning can become an excuse of inactivity; it can reveal a reluctance to dare.

- Are customer-thoughtful. Whether dealing with products, goods or services, the successful company wants the customer to be satisfied. This means understanding the customer's wants and needs, not allowing the customer to be unreasonable.

- Are idea-encouragers. Good executives know they don't have all the answers, so they encourage their employees to offer ideas and suggestions. This gives the successful company an element of freshness and creativity, and gives the employees a sense of belonging.

- Are consistency-proud. Change is necessary for survival if you intend to remain up-to-date, but the successful company doesn't change merely for the sake of change. To the contrary, if current operations are working, change is conscientiously avoided. Maintaining quality is the key.

- Are simple. Successful companies tend to do even complicated tasks with simple ideas and simple attitudes, ideas and attitudes that work, that produce results, that lead to success.

One of our greatest problems as a nation—if not our gravest problem— is loneliness. The more we crowd together, the more isolated we feel. A major cause of depression, loneliness is the voice whispering in the dark that no one cares.

Loneliness has many descriptions and fits into many categories:

1. Loneliness is feeling unloved. Love is our basic source of strength, stability and security. So when we feel alienated, we are lonely. We may feel unloved because we believe we are unattractive and doubt whether anyone wants our friendship; we may feel unloved because we realize we have developed a negative, unpleasant personality; or we may feel unloved because we believe we haven't measured up aca- demically or athletically.
2. Loneliness is feeling socially alienated. No matter how hard we try, we feel we will never be accepted. We may blame this social alienation on race, education or economic background. Perhaps we are aspiring to a level that doesn't exist or is too far above or below us.
3. Loneliness is feeling that there is no one we can talk to.
4. Loneliness is a sudden change in style or location. Loneliness is being fired, ashamed to face friends. Loneliness is a new job in a distant city and, despite the excitement, feeling isolated and without friends.

Loneliness, whatever the description or category, reveals that you don't like yourself. You have not become a friend to yourself; you are alienated within yourself. Being surrounded by people cannot cure loneliness, any more than merely being by yourself can create loneliness. Moments alone can be rewarding and fulfilling.

When loneliness does set in, don't mope around, but become more active; don't wait for people to come to you, but reach out to assist them. Lose your loneliness through your involvement with others.

M any modern educationists are reinforcing the meaninglessness felt by youth, reducing man to the level of 'nothing but an animal.'" This is the accusation of Dr. Victor Frankl, Professor of Psychiatry and Neurology at the University of Vienna—and one of my favorite authors.

Dr. Frankl, before accusing many educators of failure, said, "Pornography, crimes and violence, drug taking, alcoholism, and the growing suicide rate among young persons are symptoms of a much deeper sickness in the modern soul . . . the sense of inner void and frustration, particularly among the young, is spreading."

Dr. Frankl suggests the problem is what *Fortune* magazine described as "the first generation born without optimism." Dr. Frankl said, "As a psychiatrist and a neurologist, I know to what extent we are not free. But as a survivor of the German concentration camps, I want to bear witness to the incredible and un-expected extent to which a man can brave the worst conditions man can ever face and triumph over them . . . those prisoners most oriented toward the future, those who clung to some shred of meaning were the most likely to pull through." Dr. Frankl's observations came from living through Auschwitz and three other Nazi death camps.

You would think that our age of learning and enlightenment would produce an accompanying sense of freedom and peace and mental satisfaction. Instead we have a mounting sense of despair climaxed in suicides—one of the top killers among students.

The nineteenth century looked forward to our affluent times with complete optimism. Reade said, "Hunger and thirst will be unknown, and the earth will be a garden." But Bertrand Russell sounded the death knell and disillusionment with Utopia when he wrote, "Only on the firm foundation of unyielding despair can the soul's habitation henceforth be safely built." The affluent society sacri-fices the discipline to stay afloat, so we sink in despair.

Rather than being computerized facts, education must be returned to the teacher/philosopher who teaches standards of right and wrong—and condemns the wrong. Students must be led by example to do right, think right, and be right in character and goals in life.

Facts and figures, no matter how intriguing, do not prepare the student for living. The teacher is the craftsman, applying truth and giving the student a sense of direction in life.

H e sauntered into the Holiday Inn South in Lubbock, Texas, ten minutes ahead of his breakfast appointment. He always arrived earlier than promised. I saw him before he spotted me. I hadn't seen him in a decade, but he had changed so little. John Lott, though he was 75, could have passed for 60. There was no mistaking that he's a West Texan: wiry, quick-stepping, fast-moving, with a twinkling eye and an engaging grin.

He fascinated me because he was a rancher. John's grandfather established Slaughter Ranch in Post, Texas, in 1901, before it was even a town.

John was born in Kansas City and built a successful career there in international business. He finally moved back to the family ranch when his grandmother insisted that it was "high time" for him and his wife, Ryla, to bring their children back to West Texas, "where real life begins."

In 1963 John turned the ranch over to *his* son, John, and moved to Lubbock. There he and Ryla were instrumental in developing the West Texas Museum Association and the Cowboy Museum at Texas Tech. They donated the John B. Slaughter carriage house from the U Lazy S Ranch to the museum's Ranching Heritage Center. They also donated numerous paintings and artifacts collected from their world travels. The Lotts established scholarships and gave additional financial support to the art department of the university.

As we talked over breakfast, I reminded John that, on one particular visit years ago, he had shown me his secret of looking younger than his years—"The Round House" in his back yard. Inside, this very successful rancher and businessman had built a scale model of the Panhandle and Santa Fe Railroad. He commissioned Dr. Clarence Kincaid of the Texas Tech art department to paint the backdrop. Then John meticulously laid out the countryside to a scale representing thirty-two miles. We watched his trains move across the "plains," and I soon found myself caught up with him in dreams of yesteryear.

You may be saying, "The difference between the man and the boy is how much he pays for his toy." But youth is not a time of life; it is a state of mind. I'm convinced that people who maintain their youthfulness have some way of keeping their lives bridged to the good things from their childhood. We are to lose our *childishness* and to mature, but we are not to lose our *childlikeness*—it is the source of our vigor, our hope, our dreams of better tomorrows. Jesus said that unless a person become as a little child, he would not see the kingdom of heaven.

Some dreams turn into nightmares, but we must never be afraid to dream—for our dreamers become our deliverers.

Give your dreams a chance and you will be surprised how many good things can happen. Don't become disillusioned; recycle your dreams and work to bring them true with action and effort.

When we lose our dreams, we tend to lose our goals. Our dreams become a self-imposed nightmare; we aim at nothing and we hit it. We don't have to live that way. One of life's most powerful forces is the person who dreams and awakens with the confidence to capture the dream.

The dividing line that separates those who are successful and those who fold their tents and run is nothing more than a powerful, two-word sentence— "I can." Truly amazing results have come to people who realistically say, "I can", people who accomplish what they truly believe they can do.

Give yourself a chance. You cannot win the race unless you start running; you gain nothing without having ventured. Pity the poor soul who nurses a dream, who builds an ambition, always wishing, always hoping— but never taking the risk to begin.

What is your hidden dream? What do you want but are afraid to try for? Take the challenge; start this week. Grasp onto the excitement of your dream, not the excuses why it can't be done. Don't stifle your dream, give it a chance.

If you have a flame burning in you, or even a spark, don't smother it. Nurture it, thank God for it, run out and act on it. You better than anyone else can fulfill your own dreams.

Music is the universal language—we find it somehow easier to sing our innermost thoughts than to speak the language of our souls. Annie Johnson Flint was one of those who expressed themselves in rhyme and music as a release of their own emotions.

Annie Johnson Flint spent half her life as an invalid. Her parents died before she reached the age of 6, and she and her sister were adopted by a childless couple. At 9, the young girl discovered she could put words to rhyme and rhythm. Her first poem described frost pictures on a winter window. She was so thrilled to uncover her talent that everything became a poem—her school lessons, letters, dreams.

At 17, Annie was stricken with arthritis and within five years she was destined never again to walk. She went to Clifton Falls, New York, in search of a reported "miracle cure" for her affliction, but her condition was too advanced. Yet she so enjoyed the town and the people at the sanitorium that she remained there until her death.

Her hope of putting music to her poems was denied by the arthritis that prevented her from playing. But over the years, others have done it for her. Throughout her life, Annie Johnson Flint saw her poems as her way to help others who also shared adversity. Her strong faith formed the foundation of her poetry:

God hath not promised skies always blue,
Flower-strewn pathways all our lives through;
God hath not promised sun without rain,
Joy without sorrow, peace without pain.

God hath not promised we shall not know
Toil and temptation, trouble and woe;
He hath not told us we shall not bear
Many a burden, many a care.

God hath not promised smooth road and wide
Swift easy travel needing no guide;
Never a mountain rocky and steep,
Never a river troubled and deep.

But God hath promised strength for the day,
Rest for thy labor, light for the way,
Grace for the trials, help from above
Unfailing sympathy, undying love.

What is the biggest problem facing American business today? There are many, many types of businesses in different industries serving different customers, but they all share the same common problem—how to encourage employees to take pride in their work.

My concern is for the employee. When an employee does shoddy work, it isn't a character flaw, it is a sign of weakness, it is a wrong against the company. Shoddy work usually indicates that people do not like themselves, that they don't respect their abilities. Shoddy work is an indication that the worker is putting himself or herself down.

The workers may feel that their jobs are insignificant and unchallenging. I remember what my father always told me: "Son, whatever you do, do well, no matter how small a job, for you never know when God is measuring you for a larger opportunity."

Every job has significance. I cannot do what you do, so I automatically admire your skills. The president of a company cannot perform each job in the firm. Stung by a comment that it doesn't take much to make a suit, the clothing factory worker responded, "Just skilled cutters, talented sewers, cloth from five countries and a feeling for fashion." A parking garage attendant who kept track of the vacant spots in order to guide arriving customers placed no special significance on this small courtesy—until a woman commented, "Of all the fellows on this job, you are the only one who tells the customers where to find a spot, and I appreciate your doing that."

A loss of self-respect makes doing a good job impossible. Poor workmanship and poor service reflect badly on the company or store or organization but, more importantly, show that you have lost your self-respect. Respect yourself enough today to do a good job; like yourself enough to do it well.

A joker once said that the most outspoken evangelist in our society is a tie between the person who has quit smoking and the person who has lost weight.

Dieting is not easy. I've tried any number of fad diets, and they all worked. But as soon as I stopped, I regained each pound and found it had been drawing interest while it was away! What has worked is a disciplined, patient but steady weight loss using some of the following rules:

1. I weigh myself each morning. We have all been told this leads to discouragement, but I use it as a daily reminder.
2. I made my weight a matter of daily prayer. I feel that my religious life should have an effect on me spiritually, of course, but also mentally and physically.
3. Evenings at home are the danger moments, so I plan an evening of activity. If I do watch television, I select a program that absorbs my total interest and keep papers by my side to read during commercial breaks rather than head for the refrigerator.
4. We all snack. Like Gary Coleman, when he was told by his stepsister on "Different Strokes" to eat a balanced diet, he replied, "I do have a balanced diet . . . 50 percent junk food and 50 percent good food." The snacks I keep around are low-calorie.
5. Losing weight has to be a family matter. My wife helps by protecting me from overdoing fried foods and teaching me what a potato tastes like by substituting a little salt and pepper for butter and sour cream.
6. It takes exercise every day. I abhor calisthenics, but I've found that a stationary bike with a reading stand lets me ride away the pounds and inches while I catch up on my reading.
7. I have had to fight to learn to eat slower. Once accused of being a human vacuum cleaner, now I try to pause a little between bites.

Do I feel better; is it worth it? When I receive compliments about my weight loss, I feel great; at the same time, I enjoy eating. So it's a tough battle—especially for someone whose idea of heaven is not streets paved with gold, but a pond of butter pecan ice cream and swimming in it for 100 years without gaining a pound.

One million children run away from home each year. This national problem is brought sharply into focus by children's pictures on milk cartons and grocery bags and television. There is a danger of our becoming preoccupied with this national tragedy at the neglect of those who occupy our own homes. The recurring pattern in this country is to make headlines of a problem, but too soon America becomes impatient and takes them for granted.

The breakdown of the family is rooted in the loosening of our moral values. Parent-child relationships are built on respect. When we accept unmarried people living together, children out of wedlock, celebrity indiscretions and immorality, we wipe out the foundation of trust and confidence needed by our youth toward the older generation.

All the laws of the land, all the in-vogue social cures are not going to help children who are subjected to a poor parental example. Inquisitive youngsters will still want to know why a soft drink spoils their dinner while a martini helps their parents'; they will still be puzzled why marijuana will send them to jail while parents use high-powered uppers to lose weight.

Still another force that confuses our youth is parental indecision and inconsistency. We parents blame it on the shifting morals of our age—or is it more our cowardice to take a firm stand? We cannot be so insecure that we think giving in to our children is our only hope for popularity. Respect is only reserved for the parents who are decisive and lovingly firm. Our children may disagree, but will still feel part of a strong, caring home.

On a short TWA flight from St. Louis to Paducah, I had sitting next to me a fellow who had enjoyed his cocktails and was determined to monopolize my attention. When he saw me doing my usual on-plane reading, he proceeded to give me a slurring oration on how lucky we are to read. I completely agreed and only wished he would give me the chance. There are some things, especially poetry, that are good repetitive reading.

We all have favorite poems—some short, others long—some funny, others serious—some religious, others secular—but all of us have been touched by poems. For over twenty years I've carried a miniature copy of Rudyard Kipling's classic "If" in my wallet. You can almost quote it with me.

IF you can keep your head when all about you are losing theirs and blaming it on you;

IF you can trust yourself when all men doubt you, but make allowance for their doubting too;

IF you can wait and not be tired by waiting, or, being lied about, don't deal in lies, or being hated don't give way to hating, and yet don't look too good, nor talk too wise;

IF you can dream—and not make dreams your master;

IF you can think—and not make thoughts your aim;

IF you can meet with Triumph and Disaster and treat those two imposters just the same;

IF you can bear to hear the truth you've spoken twisted by knaves to make a trap for fools, or watch the things you gave your life to, broken, and stoop and build 'em up with worn-out tools;

IF you can make one heap of all your winnings and risk it on one turn of pitch-and-toss, and lose, and start again at your beginnings, and never breathe a word about your loss;

IF you can force your heart and nerve and sinew to serve your turn long after they are gone, and so hold on when there is nothing in you except the Will which says to them: "Hold on!"

IF you can talk with crowds and keep your virtue, or walk with Kings—nor lose the common touch;

IF neither foes nor loving friends can hurt you;

IF all men count with you, but none too much;

IF you can fill the unforgiving minute with sixty seconds' worth of distance run, Yours is the Earth and everything that's in it.

AND—which is more—you'll be a Man, my son!

Talk about security—the goals of this poem describe a man who is at peace with himself. It's good reading—only wish I could qualify, but let's keep trying.

The Bible speaks of the wisdom of children, and that came to mind when reading an essay penned by a twelve-year-old girl of Perry, Alabama. She was reflecting on the joys of her courageous and determined people, despite their meager possessions:

A person can never get true greatness by trying for it. It's nice to have good clothes, it makes it a lot easier to act decent, but it's a sign of true greatness to act when you have not got them just as good as if you had.

Once there was a woman who had done a big washing and hung it on the line. The line broke and let it down in the mud, but she didn't say a word, only did it over again and this time she spread it over the grass, where it could not fall. But that night a dog with dirty feet ran over it. When she saw what was done, she didn't cry a bit. All she said was, "Ain't it queer he didn't miss nothing." That was true greatness, but it is only people who have done washings that know it.

Once there was a woman that lived near a pig-pen, and when the wind blew that way it was very smelly. At first when she went there she could not smell anything but pigs, but when she lived there a while, she learned to smell the clover blossoms through it. That was true greatness.

The child sounds like Seneca of Old: "Great is he who enjoys his earthenware as if it were plate, and not less great is the man to whom all his plate is no more than earthenware."

For a company to survive, every employee must sell. The clean-up crew at night sells the company just as much as the vice-president of sales. No one person makes the company succeed—we all have the excitement of sharing.

One of our best writers, Wilferd Peterson, put it this way:

When everybody sells, goods, services and ideas move faster and prosperity is achieved. Selling is not limited to people called salesmen, for we all have something to sell, and that includes you! When everybody sells, we create a mental and emotional climate of friendliness and goodwill that makes buying a joyous, happy adventure. Customers are won and held through a multitude of acts and attitudes. Here are some of the things that represent the art of selling at its best:

COURTEOUS WORDS instead of sharp retorts.
SMILES instead of blank looks.
ENTHUSIASM instead of dullness.
RESPONSE instead of indifference.
WARMTH instead of coldness.
UNDERSTANDING instead of a closed mind.
ATTENTION instead of neglect.
PATIENCE instead of irritation.
SINCERITY instead of sham.
CONSIDERATION instead of annoyance.
REMEMBERING people instead of forgetting them.
FACTS instead of arguments.
CREATIVE ideas instead of the humdrum.
HELPFULNESS instead of hinderance.
GIVING instead of getting.
ACTION instead of delay.
APPRECIATION instead of apathy.

Everyone selling together blends hearts and minds and spirits, as the musicians in an orchestra harmonize musical tones, to create a mighty symphony of prosperity. Let's earn more business by deserving the business we have. Let's roll out the red carpet for the most important person in the world . . . the customer. Let's everybody sell!

For a great many years, this poem has been a special favorite of mine. I hope that you, too, get a special feeling from the "The Secret," by an anoymous author:

I met God in the morning,
When my day was at its best
And His presence came like sunrise,
Like a glory in my breast.

All day long the Presence lingered;
All day long He stayed with me;
And we sailed in perfect calmness
O'er a very troubled sea.

Other ships were blown and battered,
Other ships were sore distressed.
But the winds that seemed to drive them
Brought to us a peace and rest.

Then I thought of other mornings,
With a keen remorse of mind.
When I, too, had loosed the moorings
With the Presence left behind.

So I think I know the secret,
Learned from many a troubled way;
You must seek Him in the morning
If you want Him through the day.

The end of the day is time for contemplation, for retrospection. It is a time for self-evaluation, for self-analysis. This is the thrust of "Can You Say," by an unknown author:

Can you say in parting with the day that's slipping fast
That you helped a single person of the many you have passed?
In a single life, rejoicing o'er what you did or said,
Did one whose hopes were fading now with courage look ahead?
Did you waste the day, or lose it? Was it well or poorly spent?
Did you leave a tread of kindness—or a scar of discontent?
As you close your eyes in slumber, do you think that God would say:
"You have made the world much better for the life you have lived today."

Understanding the unique problems of the aged requires a special sensitivity and awareness and feeling. The following poem by Esther Mary Walker titled, "Beatitudes for Friends of the Aged" never fails to touch my heart:

Blessed are they who understand
My faltering step and palsied hand.
Blessed are they who know that my ears today
Must strain to hear the things they say
Blessed are they who seem to know
That my eyes are dim and my wits are slow.
Blessed are they who look away
When coffee spilled at the table today.
Blessed are they with a cheery smile
Who stop to chat for a little while.
Blessed are they who never say
"You've told that story twice today."
Blessed are they who know the ways
To bring back memories of yesterday.
Blessed are they who make it known
That I'm loved, respected, and not alone.
Blessed are they who know I'm at a loss
To find the strength to carry the cross.
Blessed are they who ease the day
On my journey Home in loving ways.

A fellow was bothered with a continual ringing in his ears, bulging of his eyes, and a flushed face. He went to doctor after doctor to diagnose his difficulties. One doctor took out his tonsils, but his ears kept ringing, eyes bulging, and his face remained flushed. Another doctor took out his appendix, feeling it was about ready to burst, poisoning his system. Still the symptoms persisted. A third doctor thought the problem was much simpler—bad wisdom teeth, so he removed them. But you guessed it. The ears were still ringing, eyes bulging, and the face flushed. The fellow even tried to find out if there wasn't some exotic treatment that could be given in one of those celebrity health centers of Switzerland, for he knew at the rate he was going, he didn't have long to live.

Finally he gave up. He figured that if they couldn't cure him, he was going to enjoy the last days of his life. He quit his job, sold his belongings, and planned for extensive travel. In preparation for his journey he went to his clothing store, ordered several suits and shirts. The owner of his haberdashery waited on him personally, picked out suits that looked like they were tailored for him then measured his neck for his shirts. He said, "Let me see what I have in 16½." The fellow said, "No, no. Not 16½, I wear 15½." The haberdasher measured again and said, "No—it's 16½." The fellow replied, "It's always been 15½." "Well," said the supplier, "I guess the customer has to be right, but I'll tell you, with a neck your size, if I were to wear a 15½ shirt my ears would ring, my eyes would bulge, and my face would flush."

Everytime I've heard my good friend Ken Goodson tell that story, I've laughed. First, because of the humor and then I've laughed at myself, for I'm reminded of how many times I've applied respected solutions to the wrong problems. So, the number one question when we face a challenge is . . . "What is really the problem?"

Before you and your family attend worship services this week, take time to consider these thoughts by Harvey Williams entitled, "Before Worship":

These few moments before the service begins are important ones—important for you. Use them to realize the ways in which we tend to behave as though there was no God.

- Our bitterness at misfortunes, even at small inconveniences.
- Our lack of friendly interest in persons we meet, some of whom may be lonely or hurt.
- Our preoccupation with ourselves and anxiety about impressions we make on others.
- Our hesitation to take a stand for the "hard right against the easy wrong," both personally and in groups.

Where is thy God, my soul: Is He within my heart,
Or ruler of a distant realm in which thou hast no part?

Come, Creator, and show us ourselves and Thee. Help us see our pettiness and Thy greatness. Show us our self-concern and Thy loving care for all the world. Reveal to us our many standards and Thy straight and narrow way. Make us more like Thee. Amen.

Narcissism came from the Greeks—the myth of a youth who fell in love with his own image reflected in a pool and who, after eventually wasting away from unsatisfied desire, was transformed into a flower.

Narcissism may have shifted generations when it is we, not youth, who are hypnotized by our own image. Joe Clark, president of Ball Consumer Products Division, wrote the following to a group of his associates:

> In this age of insider trading, greenmailing, leveraged buyouts, and corporate sellouts, it is easy to forget that—despite what the "me generation" believes—wealth and happiness are not synonymous.
>
> A German high performance car will not give you inner peace. Armani suits won't make you feel more likeable. A beautiful 33-room villa on the Mediterranean coast won't build character in your children. And gold, diamonds, furs and Aspen weekends pale in comparison to the priceless gift of time spent with your mate.
>
> A local minister said, "No man ever raised up on his deathbed and uttered these words, *If only I'd spent more time at the office.*"
>
> There's nothing wrong with hard work. Our jobs depend on it, and heaven knows this country could stand more of it. But when our need for a good job and necessary means are replaced by an obsessive, voracious desire to accumulate material wealth at all costs, we have fallen victim to the cruelest of all deceptions.
>
> As always, the Scripture says it best, "For what shall it profit a man if he gain the whole world and lose his own soul."

Peggy Lee sang some years ago: "Is that all there is?"

It is strange that truly great men seem to share a common kinship of inner strength and wisdom that transcends time and supersedes nationality.

Confucius, the celebrated Chinese philosopher who lived in the fifth century B.C., is credited with a great many observations and maxims, among them his "Rules of Life":

> The rule of life is to be found within yourself. Ask yourself constantly, "What is the right thing to do?" Beware of doing that which you are likely, sooner or later, to repent of having done. It is better to live in peace than in bitterness and strife. It is better to believe in your neighbors than to fear and distrust them.
>
> The superior man does not wrangle. He is firm but not quarrelsome. He is sociable but not clannish. The superior man sets a good example for his neighbors. He is considerate of their feelings and their property. Consideration for others is the basis of a good life, a good society. Feel kindly toward everyone. Be friendly and pleasant among yourselves. Be generous and fair.

Abraham Lincoln, with his blend of folk wisdom and common sense, expressed similar thinking on the basic rules of life in his "10 Cannotments":

> (1) You cannot bring about prosperity by discontinuing thrift. (2) You cannot help the small man by tearing down the big man. (3) You cannot strengthen the weak by weakening the strong. (4) You cannot lift the wage earner by pulling down the wage payer. (5) You cannot help the poor man by destroying the rich. (6) You cannot keep out of trouble by spending more than your income. (7) You cannot further the brotherhood of man by inciting class hatred. (9) You cannot build character and courage by taking away man's initiative and independence. (10) You cannot help men permanently by doing for them what they could and should be doing for themselves.

These two great thinkers, separated by time and vastly different cultures, are surprisingly linked in their philosophies. And their rules of life are just as appropriate for us today.

The earth will outlive the ecologists!" This seemingly cold-hearted battle cry is more an objection to the critics than a rejection of the problem. We have grown weary of condemnation. The environment, in particular, has become an arena for self-styled do-gooders and self-serving activists to grab the spotlight and the headlines.

I am infinitely more impressed by the quiet, earnest efforts of many groups, such as the Boy Scouts. While many give only lip service to our national pollution problem, thousands of Scouts across the country are actively doing something about it, cleaning up streams and turning vacant lots into playgrounds.

Our sincere environmental concerns can best be guided by the philosophy contained in the "Ten Commandments of the New Earth" prepared by Milwaukee's Environmental Teach-In Committee:

1. You shall live in harmony with all the earth and with every living thing.
2. You shall return to the earth all the organic treasures she freely gives you.
3. You shall not put greed above duty, nor wealth above wonder.
4. You shall not demand useless or unnecessary things.
5. You shall have your fair share of the earth and no more than that.
6. You shall fight to protect the earth; it is your home.
7. You shall be masters of technology and not its slaves.
8. You shall make beautiful and enduring whatever is to be made.
9. You shall keep faith with future generations and be wise guardians of their inheritance.
10. When all this is done, come together with all your brothers and sing the joy of earth.

We are stewards of a miraculous planet. We have been its corrupters, and now we face the challenge of being its correctors.

Some years back, Kenneth A. Carlson called for the institution of a national "Decency Day." His pipe dream never came to pass; yet his intentions can fuel the desire in each of us for decent behavior. His vision never became reality; yet his outline for "Decency Day" can give each of us something to think about:

Militants would declare a 24-hour moratorium on hurling obscenities and foul language at the police or at anyone else who disagreed with them. Meaningful dialogue could take the place of acts of violence.

No one would tell a dirty story—even for a laugh at a men's smoker or at a service club.

Bosses would not cuss out their employees, and employees would not mutter under their breath at employers.

Producers of suggestive, sexy motion pictures would close up for the day and go fishing. Purveyors of pornography could stay home and read a good book.

Everyone would respect the other fellow's property—not throw rocks through windshields nor steal car stereos.

Mothers would refrain from screaming at their youngsters, and fathers would cease knocking their children around.

Talk would center upon some creative thing we could do in the name of decency: matters relating to housing, jobs, and pay for those existing on the poverty level; to bettering schools; to achieving a decent environment for everybody.

Everyone would go into church or to some other quiet place and take at least five minutes to ask the good Lord to help keep them decent.

How far is an hour?" queried the headline in the in-flight airline magazine. An intriguing question deserving of some discussion. In a bygone era, traveling by horse and buggy, an hour was about four miles. Today, an automobile traveling on a highway can legally cover 55 miles in an hour. Commercial aircraft cruise at 700 miles an hour, military fighters many times faster.

So, how far is an hour? It depends upon the age in which we live and the method of travel available.

And how far is a lifetime? Lifetimes vary in the distance covered and the things accomplished. Some of us get off to a slow start and end our days in a blaze of glory. Others begin with a glow and somehow become lost and disoriented along the way. And many just seem to be headed nowhere at all.

How far have you traveled thus far in your lifetime? Have you walked down the road of self-awareness and understanding? If you have, you are willing to accept the bad things about yourself as well as the good. You are willing to change those things about yourself which cause you shame.

Have you traveled down the road to forgiveness? If so, you have surrendered feelings of resentment and revenge. Each mile traveled along this road is difficult, yet a rare and beautiful spirit awaits at the end of the journey.

Have you avoided the detour of shallow values? If so, you treasure values far beyond money and material objects. You cherish the smile of a small child, the morning dew on a rose, the whistle of the wind in the pine trees, and the hand of someone who has walked beside you through the years.

If you are well along your lifetime journey, keep on going. Look around you at all those people going nowhere in particular and invite them to share your journey.

How far is a lifetime? It is not the distance you must travel, but the manner in which you travel that determines how far it is. Take with you an open mind, a loving heart, a willing spirit and a generous nature. You will discover that your lifetime can be as far as eternity when you go with God.

The mercurial mixture of ingredients we call a boy has been captured in the whimsical essay, "What is a Boy":

> After a male baby has grown out of long clothes and triangles and has acquired pants and freckles and so much dirt that relatives do not dare to kiss it between meals, it becomes a boy! A boy can swim like a fish, run like a deer, climb like a squirrel, balk like a mule, or bellow like a bull, according to climatic condition. A boy is a piece of skin stretched over an appetite—an uproar, covered with smudges. He is called a tornado because he comes at the most unexpected times, hits the most unexpected places, and leaves everything a wreck behind him.
>
> A boy is a growing animal of superlative promise, to be fed and watered and kept warm. He is a joy forever, the despair of his elders, the problem of our time, and the hope of a nation. Every boy is evidence that God is not discouraged by man. Were it not for boys, there would be no Boy Scouts, no Boys' Clubs, no Little League. Boys are useful in running errands. A boy can easily do the family errands with the aid of only five or six adults. The zest with which a boy does an errand is equaled only by the speed of a turtle on a July day.
>
> A boy is a natural spectator. He watches parades, fires, fights, automobiles, and airplanes with equal fervor, but not the clock! Boys faithfully imitate their dads in spite of all efforts to teach them good manners. A boy, if not washed too often, and if kept in a cool, quiet place after each accident, will survive broken bones, hornets, swimming holes, neighborhood fights, and nine helpings of pie at supper, some of the ingredients that go into the making of a boy.

Often our children annoy us and try our patience, displease us and cause us concern. But the years pass. And childhood gives way to adulthood. And their mischief grows sweeter in the recollection of it. God bless boys everywhere!

Hanging Loose" was the solution for stress in the 1970s. It was an update of "cool." It was based on the theory that whatever you do is alright as long as you hurt no one—except yourself.

"Hanging loose" included fascinating and contradictory concepts that may be worth revisiting:

1. When a problem gets rough, "hang loose" and walk away from it.
2. Don't try to think your way out of a mess, "feel" your way through it.
3. Accept people the way they are, pimples and all.
4. Abandon absolute standards; they only hang you up.
5. Never exploit another person; never be cruel.
6. Turn the volume high. Don't listen to music, feel it.
7. Grow your own tree! Which means studying the subject that you want to study, obeying the home rules that you want to obey—like running your whole life, man, guided only by your quivering senses.
8. Distrust tradition and institutions, but have faith in people.
9. Carry your life in your hand or in a gunny sack or a duffle bag. Accumulate no property and don't worry about bread. Making time payments, reducing a mortgage, or paying a church pledge are a drag.

"Hanging loose" sounds cool and good in this time of pressures, but there is no way of just walking away from life.

Dr. Frank Crane would advise patients, "Responsibility is the thing people dread most of all. Yet it is the one thing in the world that develops us, gives us manhood or womanhood fiber."

Sunday, Week Twenty-Eight

You often hear the phrase "old-fashioned honesty," but we forget there is also old-fashioned corruption. Corruption is one of the basic reasons pollster Louis Harris found for a total lack of confidence in all branches of government. Politicians of local, state, and national levels can't equal the respect given to the garbage collector. This may mean that Jonathan Winters has done more for garbage than Mike Mansfield has done for the Senate. Seriously, it is time for alarm.

Scandals have not only swept Washington and the big cities, but also the county seats.

With bad news comes good news. Recent revelations of corruption have done more for the conservative cause than all the dreams of a Bill Buckley. As people have lost confidence in government, they've realized we have been too dependent. As painful a rupture as Watergate or Jim Wright's indiscretions, it tells us neither the President nor Congress can solve our problems. Our affluent society has made it clear that money alone doesn't mean "the good life." A democracy is not constructed to leave good government to the politicians—no matter what they promise.

Here are some questions we need to ask, beginning on the local level:

Do I know the man running for public office? Am I concerned solely about what he'll do, or do I want to know who he is? Do I elect a balance in government or do I tend to elect only one group—lawyers because they have been trained in law, forgetting that doesn't automatically make them knowledgeable about people and business? My lawyer friends are embarrassed that so many of their profession have used their skill to bend the law instead of upholding it.

Do I wink at illegal gambling or abuse the liquor laws in my community? Do I care if minors are sold alcohol illegally?

Who is apprehended for crime in my area? The minor offender who smokes pot or the pusher who may have ties with people in high places?

Is jury duty easily avoided and left to almost "professional jurors"?

Are traffic tickets easily "fixed"?

Is my local government open to the public and do I read the reports of the business? Are committees held accountable and not allowed to be a "closet government"?

Am I willing to be involved if called upon to witness?

A republic using a democratic government only stays as clean as we want it. We don't have to be personally corrupt to have corrupt government. All we have to do is not care and let "them" run it for us.

An optimist builds castles in the sky. A dreamer lives there. A realist collects rent from both of them." This writer clearly understood that achievement is an inside action, the meshing of ambition, preparation and vision.

Being an achiever takes a little bit of the optimist, a little of the dreamer, and a little of the realist. Being an achiever means progressing, not just surviving; it means contributing, not just existing.

Achievers think their way to the top, not just work their way to the top. The incubator of ideas open to all of us is reading. We all read trade magazines and professional journals related to our industry or field. While that is important, our reading needs to be more eclectic. We should read a little each day just for pleasure—even if it means getting up half an hour earlier or staying up a bit later or turning off the television. Some of the best ideas will come from pleasure reading totally unrelated to your career.

Achievers look for better ways to do their jobs, and have the courage to do it in a way they've never seen done.

Achievers associate with people they admire, who are fresh and enthusiastic about their work, whether in similar jobs or not. Admiration leads to emulation. Just as athletes challenge each other, good workers stimulate each other.

Achievers are able to keep themselves in perspective. They develop a good sense of humor to insulate and condition themselves for the minor or major setbacks that are bound to come along.

Achievers have an inner drive and, quite often, an inner faith that is even stronger than their drive.

If you see yourself as an achiever, first measure your abilities, both used and unused, as best you can. Count what you have done to prepare yourself for a better job or greater opportunity. Ask yourself if you are willing to assume the responsibilities and decision-making that accompany the better job. Or are you just looking for more pay and prestige?

Many of us have difficulty changing, difficulty distinguishing that fine line separating strong convictions from pure stubbornness. We may wonder if changes on the job are necessary or merely the whims of a new supervisor trying to prove his power. The increasing demands of our technological society seem to make it impossible to plant our feet in the same spot two days in a row.

A Chicago minister named Frank Gunsaulus was once introduced to a large crowd as "the man with the backbone." The master of ceremonies interspersed all the appropriate biographical details with additional references to "the man with a backbone," stressing that the speaker was an individual who proclaimed strong convictions and lived by them.

Once the introduction was concluded and the applause died down, Dr. Gunsaulus began his speech by responding to the introduction. "The master of ceremonies told you several times that I have a strong backbone. I hope that I have a backbone, but I also hope that it has some joints in it so that I may be able to bend. If it hasn't, then it isn't a backbone, but a crowbar."

Pausing to let the visual imagery sink in, he continued, "A great many people mistake their prejudices for convictions and take credit for being very strong-minded when in reality they are just stubborn. They proceed on the assumption that to see one's mistakes and to acknowledge them is a sign of weakness. Nothing of the sort! Strength of mind and sweetness of spirit usually go hand in hand. It is the small being who refuses to give in. They who boast that they never change their minds love themselves more than they love truth! By all means let us 'have backbone,' but backbones with joints in them!"

As Dr. Gunsaulus wisely perceived, criticism of change may tell more about our stubbornness than our rightness. There are people who feel they are accomplishing something if they are creating change. Others think accepting change without complaint is weakness instead of progress and cooperation.

We find it easy to accept certain national problems, such as declining productivity, but we never see ourselves as part of the problem. We don't think people generally work as hard as they used to, but we feel we work harder ourselves. We know there is a decrease in overall productivity, but we feel we are more productive.

Check your own personal productivity quotient according to the following demanding definitions:

- Productivity is doing your job—not wishing you could do it, or dreaming you could do it, or wondering if you could do it.
- Productivity is the power to learn how to do a job by doing it, like learning to walk by walking.
- Productivity is turning what might be a temporary defeat into experience and using it to achieve success.
- Productivity is the ability to control your personality, even when things are unpleasant, and to keep on doing your job.
- Productivity is using every experience from the past to make you efficient in the future.
- Productivity is eliminating these pests—regret, worry and fear.
- Productivity is self-reliance, but clothed in modesty, not cockiness.
- Productivity is persistence—keeping on at the point others give up.
- Productivity is alertness, presence of mind and readiness to change and try new methods.
- Productivity is sacrificing personal feelings for the good of all employees.
- Productivity is not counting on luck or succumbing to fate or giving way to prejudice.
- Productivity is the measure of yourself and the dependability of your character.
- Productivity is self-mastery, concentration, purpose, practice, patience.
- Productivity is the ability to use your passions, likes, dislikes, habits, experience, education, mind, body and heart to achieve your goals.
- Productivity is using the sum total of you.

If you are using less than the sum total of yourself, then you must judge how productive you are.

I cringed as I heard one of America's so-called superstars boast that he owed nothing to any man. At first, I was irritated at the arrogance of the individual, then I became embarassed at his ignorance. Each of us are debtors for what we have received from so many others.

The superstar felt he owed no man; I feel I owe almost every person. The best part of my life and the finest part of my personality is the part others have invested in me.

In its series of editorial ads, United Technologies touched on this idea with a statement titled, "Do You Remember Who Gave You Your First Break?":

> Someone saw something in you once. That's partly why you are where you are today. It could have been a thoughtful parent, a perceptive teacher, a demanding drill sergeant, an appreciative employer, or just a friend who dug down in his pocket and came up with a few bucks. Whoever it was had the kindness and the foresight to bet on your future. Those are two beautiful qualities that separate the human being from the orangutan. In the next 24 hours, take 10 minutes to write a grateful note to the person who helped you. You'll keep a wonderful friendship alive. Matter of fact, take another 10 minutes to give somebody else a break. Who knows? Someday you might get a nice letter. It could be one of the most gratifying messages you ever read.

When did you last go out of your way to write a letter of appreciation or take time to pick up the phone and chat a few minutes with an old friend? Such demonstrations of gratitude not only lift the spirits of the recipients, but have a way of lifting your own spirits and bringing a positive reaction.

Who came to mind as you read about gratitude? Write or call that person right now—it will make their day, and your own!

In every room of every Hilton Hotel around the world is a copy of "Be My Guest," the biography of Conrad Hilton. In one chapter, Conrad Hilton offers his suggestions for successful living, comparing his guide to the checklist a pilot uses before take-off:

1. Find your own particular talent. Don't lament or worry about something you can't do, or don't have a special skill for doing. Find what you can do and do it with all your might, building positively on such.
2. Be big. Think big, dream big, act big. Thereby you fashion a mold into which your self is fitted. It can be of great and vast dimensions, or it can be very, very restricted.
3. Be honest. Honesty means more than not cheating, lying or stealing. Honesty means standing for truth and integrity.
4. Live with enthusiasm. The test run is if you can do your job with enthusiasm. If you're not enthusiastic about your job, you have the wrong job or the wrong attitude.
5. Possess your possessions . . . never let them possess you. Things are nice to have . . . enjoy . . . share with others, but if you have something you feel you can't do without, get rid of it immediately lest it possess you.
6. Don't worry. Worry is like a tight cord choking you around the neck. Worry strangles your better self.
7. Don't cling to the past. Build on yesterday's experience. Profit by past mistakes and successes, but don't let the past conquer you. Otherwise you've stopped forward motion.
8. Look up to people whenever you can . . . but never look down on them. Be slow to criticize people but quick to appreciate them.
9. Assume your full share of responsibility for a world in which you live—do not be a "buck-passer" when problems confront your community.
10. Pray consistently, confidently, constantly.

Conrad Hilton's checklist is easy to read, but difficult to practice. Make your own checklist for living successfully—better still, live by it.

The Tarant County Medical Society bulletin in Texas asks these questions:

Do you remember when attending college was a privilege rather than a right?

Do you remember when taxes were a nuisance rather than a burden?

Do you remember when charity or giving was a virtue instead of big business?

Do you remember when the aged were cared for by their children?

Do you remember when a life sentence didn't mean possible parole in ten years?

Do you remember when a parent went on welfare only out of desperation and got off it as soon as any type of job could be found?

Do you remember when U.S. Grant was the name of a president and a general rather than a federal handout?

And do you remember when we were safe on the streets and especially in our homes?

Ten years ago when principals were asked their top concerns in high schools, drugs never made the list. Now they put drugs and alcohol abuse second on the list. What is number one? They still say that young people must do better in writing, computing, and other basic skills.

We do live in complex, constantly changing times; but is the present really a great deal different than years long passed? Not to give us any comfort, but to remind us that the problem is not new, hear these lines that were written in the fifth century B.C. by Socrates:

Our youth now love luxury. They have bad manners, contempt for authority; they show disrespect for their elders and love chatter in place of exercise. They no longer rise when others enter the room. They contradict their parents; chatter before company, gobble their food and tyrannize their teachers . . .

Yes, the problems are old, but the need to address them is urgent.

In a land of plenty, our biggest sin is still covetousness and selfishness. Jesus told a powerful story of a rich farmer who thought he could reap enough and hoard enough so he didn't need anyone else, including God. If you want to refresh your memory, turn to Luke, chapter 12, verses 13–21.

How do we become covetous? It begins with *authority*. Who governs your life? The rich farmer used the singular first person pronoun exclusively. His sentences consisted of *I . . . my . . .* and *mine.* His conversation was a monologue of what he had done on his farm. It takes a heap of bragging to swoon a man into believing he is self-sufficient. Too often in recent years we have had leadership training that tends to encourage man to embellish his own image. The big *I*. The biblical view affirms that our lives are under the authority of God. We are stewards; He is the owner. The Christian feels he was purchased at Calvary. When he speaks, he speaks of *we . . . ours . . . us,* indicating a vital relationship with the indwelling Holy Spirit. When we bow our selfishness before God, we get the security of His partnership.

The rich farmer also practiced one-man administration. He would make the decisions. He was the master of his fate. He was the sole administrator of his affairs. A child of God wants God's advice in all of his life. He relies on God for help in business and social decisions. Paul had this in mind when he wrote the Philippians: "For it is God which worketh in you both to will and do of His good pleasure." Commitment to God settles continuously the management of one's life.

The last comment about the rich farmer deals with appraisal. He said, "Soul, thou hast much goods laid up for many years; take thine ease, eat, drink and be merry." This is a logical appraisal. Since the rich farmer was turned on by things, then his appraisal of heaven was having enough things to celebrate by eating, drinking, and merry-making. The beginning and end of his life had to be things.

The question is, which is better—being thing–centered or following the injunction of Jesus, "But seek ye first the kingdom of God, and His righteousness; and all these things shall be added unto you"? Maybe all of life simply means "thing-centered vs. God-centered."

The key word to living must be *choice*. Our free will gives us options daily and moment by moment. Everything we call living depends on these choices.

A great job is the result of great expectations being fulfilled. But just what should and could employees expect from their job opportunities? What should all of us be able to expect from our work?

1. *A necessary job that puts demands upon us.* At times when business is bad, we might be underemployed; when things are tight, we might be called upon to do more than our normal share. For most of us, expecting more from us is better than making us feel we're just hanging around. We want a job that stretches us or gives us a genuine sense of accomplishment at the end of the day.
2. *Authority to do our jobs.* The surest and finest way to show respect is to call upon us to perform and then let us do our jobs—even giving us the right to make a mistake or fail. Plaques and "employee of the week" awards won't make us feel respected if we're not trusted.
3. *Security and training.* We don't want or expect to feel so secure that we become soft or careless. Yet we expect that if we do an acceptable job, there will be a tomorrow. Training is the best way to give us security, to make us positive and not fearful. When employers invest in us with additional training, we feel we're becoming more and more a part of the company.
4. *A voice in company affairs that pertain to us.* If our opinion is asked, we expect our recommendations to be heard and weighed. We don't want to be patronized by an employer going through the motions. If our opinion is valued, the sharing of that opinion obligates us to perform on our suggestions—the pride of authorship contains a performance clause.
5. *Judgment and appraisal that are fair and consistent.* We should be measured, not by how our employer feels today, but with standards not prejudiced by his headache or ulcer. We should be appraised on standards we could impart, not on conditions beyond our control.

Fortunately, we have progressed in our society to the point where we don't think work and fun must be divorced. We can be serious and still enjoy a happy work experience. And we all benefit, employer and employee alike.

Picture pioneering America and the days of the trailblazers and frontiersmen and consumer activists. Consumer activists? No, they weren't around in those days. If there had been consumer activists in the 1800's, our forefathers never would have made it across the plains to the Pacific. No one would have moved a covered wagon because the wheels weren't safe and the roads weren't secure. If my father had waited for a safe ship, he would never have escaped the Near East for the freedom of the United States. The same is true of many of our immigrant parents and their grandparents before them. Our growing attempt to build a risk-free society may be more decadence than progress.

As a nation, we continue to falter in our attempts to come to grips with the nuclear age. Certainly, no one wants an accident; no one wants the spectre of catastrophe hanging over our heads. At the same time, if we commit ourselves to a risk-free society we will lose our creativity and inventiveness. Mankind has made progress on the heels of risk. There is a fine line separating risk-free progress and the desire to play so safely that we become neutralized and retrogressive.

What a society dedicates itself to becoming risk-free, it loses its momentum and finally goes soft protecting itself. Risk-free discourages scientists from reaching for the stars; risk-free creates a cease-fire with our destiny; risk-free means we no longer reach out, but use our hands to pat ourselves on the back.

Just look at the world around us. America remains ahead because of technology, but is being challenged by Japan, Germany and others; while we are being brainwashed into becoming soft and safe, they are taking the risk to pass us on the curve. Greatness comes from sweat, tears, agony, pain. Eliminate the tears and you take away the need of laughter's relief. We end up safe and bored, but most of all, scared.

Bernard Baruch was a poor Jewish boy from South Carolina who grew up to become a multimillionaire and the personal advisor to four presidents of the United States. Once, when asked the secret of his great success, he replied simply, "I buy my straw hats in the fall." There is a far deeper significance to his disclosure than the obvious money-saving tactic of buying clothing in the off-season.

What the titan of industry suggested was that to achieve success, one had only to observe what everyone else was doing and then do the opposite. Writing to his friends in Rome, the Apostle Paul expressed a similar idea, "Don't let the world squeeze you into its mold." This advice is in direct opposition to the pleadings parents hear every day—"All the other kids are doing it" or "That's what everybody is wearing."

Frederick Herzberg, one of our most controversial and respected behavioral scientists and author of *Motivation to Work*, claims that man performs by one of two standards: the animalistic nature to survive and the human nature to achieve. In a sort of twisted irony, we Americans have debased ourselves in the process of becoming more affluent, falling from the level of God's highest creation to the level of animalistic survival. Our animal-like nature seeks to avoid hunger and pain, to be comfortable. So we have become a nation of docile sheep, working enough to have what every other person has, but satisfied simply to exist. As a result, we are not as happy as we were during the Great Depression. Certainly, we were unhappy with our plight in that era, but we were motivated to overcome our poorness. We not only wanted tomorrow to be better, we worked to make it so.

Our affluence has weakened us. Everything comes so easily; we are satisfied to look alike and think alike. Ancient Rome reached such a peak in her day, became soft and soon was dominated by a series of conquerers—not because the enemy was stronger, but because Rome had allowed itself to grow weak and soft and complacent.

We have in America what the rest of the world dreams of attaining. We are vulnerable unless we respond to the challenge to continue our improvement rather than lull ourselves with our sameness, tameness and lameness. We must be willing to be different, willing to go against the mainstream, willing to do more than just survive.

One of the pioneers of southern merchandising was W. H. Belk. He earned a well-deserved reputation for being unusually generous toward the communities where he had stores. His philanthropy was linked to his business philosophy, which he often expressed—"That's a good, generous thing you're doing . . . and it ain't bad for the Belk Stores either."

With his own brand of simple wisdom, W. H. Belk had found that goodness and profitability can be companions that become lasting friends. This same discovery has been made by small retail stores and giant corporations alike. We *can* do right and still have profits. Over the long haul, a business that cares about its customers will retain its customers and add more.

No finer example exists than Johnson & Johnson's handling of the Tylenol crisis. Through no fault of their own, company management faced catastrophes and were forced to make a monumental decision. By placing customers ahead of costs, by placing people ahead of profits, they earned the praise and loyalty of millions.

Regardless of your business, you need to keep examining your heart and testing your motives. You want to beat the competition, but you want to do right by people, whether or not it gives the greatest growth. You can care about people while caring about profits and, in the end, the two will lead to success.

We all seem to be afraid of aging. We never even use the word "aging" until we reach that nebulous plateau termed "middle age." We attempt to mentally escape the aging process with such time-worn slogans as "life begins at 40," usually uttered half-heartedly. Even as we try to bolster our resolve to accept the inevitable passing of time, we feel the grip of panic as we watch life rushing by and witness the first shadows of old age creeping upon us.

According to Ogden Nash, "Middle age is when you've met so many people that every new person you meet reminds you of somebody else." Middle age has been defined in a Royal Canadian Bank publication as that period "when policemen start looking young to you, and you find yourself in the midst of a party wishing you were home in bed. It's when you can't recall the name of the girl or boy you once loved madly, and when you meet young grown-ups you knew as babies. It's when you conclude, like George Bernard Shaw, that youth is wasted on the young."

Frankly, I believe that it is better to admit middle age and enjoy it youthfully, than to be dragged screaming to your next birthday party. Age is more an attitude than a calendar.

Middle age is the first time you sense that you have to command your body to be healthy. Pains and groans reveal your body has some mileage on it; but like an engine with many miles, you can reach a comfortable groove.

Middle age is when you sense that you cannot put off difficult decisions because you're no longer a kid. The buck stops here, you realize, especially if you have lost your parents.

Middle age is when you begin to see a shadow of the end and, without fighting it, make sure no time or effort is wasted. Middle age finds you defining priorities. Most people are most handsome and beautiful in their middle years, as character lines of strength appear on their faces. They play a better game, not running after shots but making the shots count.

Middle age is the smooth air after the climb through the turbulence. And I wouldn't go back for anything, nor would I reach forward faster than a day at a time.

Martha Patton of the Chicago Tribune wrote a helpful article for parents titled, "How to Teach Your Child to Save":

You're pretty much on your own when it comes to teaching a child to save his money. In an instant world—instant coffee, instant gratification—there are no TV commercials to tout the pleasures of postponement. And it's too bad. Because if your child's going to succeed with a savings program, he needs to know that he can get satisfaction from waiting as well as from getting.

But there has to be something at the end of the wait. Saving for saving's sake may work for some adults, but a child will need a more tangible, more immediate, reward. This is why a piggy bank alone won't teach a child to save. There is little reason for putting money in it other than to hear it jingle. And while a jingle may satisfy a toddler, it's not enough for a nine year old. Which is probably the age he should start to save in the first place. Most experts agree that few children learn from a savings program before the fourth grade level. Even then, saving will be more successful when it's for a definite, short-range goal—say, a bike or the price of a school trip.

After your child has several such accomplishments to his credit, he will be far better prepared to save for a more distant, future need. And it's not hard to find one. With college costs what they are, everyone in the family should begin early to plan how they will be met. But even the high school student, accumulating college tuition, needs frequent encouragement, just as the younger saver gets from his more immediate reward. This can be accomplished in part by simply letting him know you're proud of him. Routinely review his savings record and give him a pat on the back.

Go with him to visit a bank or a savings and loan association, and ask questions. Investigate mutual funds, the stock market, government savings bonds. Find out which savings are insured, look into interest rates and dividend records, explore the advantages of saving a regular small amount over an occasional larger one. This kind of saving habit may mean more than just a faster-growing balance. Such a record could help establish credit for an education loan or even the securing of a mortgage in later years.

Don't let your child think of this training as a restriction of his freedom. Having money in the bank doesn't limit freedom, it increases. A sound savings program doesn't mean giving up, it means getting.

Once your child understands this—that he can get what he wants by saving—chances are he'll be a saver the rest of his life.

A lovely coed wrote it: "People are puppets of society. They pull each other's strings. We do what others want us to. Why don't we try to pull our own strings? Why even consider it? In doing so, we might and probably would not cave in to society. We would be ourselves for once."

Does it seem odd to you that with all of our prosperity and creature comforts we are a frightened people? A recent newspaper cartoon pictured a couple reading the newspaper headlines with bold print about crime, political corruption, and confusion in foreign affairs without one headline of good news. The caption of the cartoon read, "Pretty soon we'll have nothing left to believe in but ourselves."

Maybe this is good. Maybe we've been hiding behind all the events of our time and escaped facing ourselves. Would it be bad if this became the year Americans rediscovered individuality? We have become an institutionalized people. We talk about the Rotary not the Rotarians. We talk about the Protestant or Catholic Church, we don't speak about the individual members. We talk about Democrats and Republicans as a Party, not the individual citizens. Our schools have grown so large that we receive computerized report sheets rather than report cards. Now Americans have lost confidence in our institutions; but you can't turn back to yourself unless you are comfortable with yourself.

In my mind there are two basic requirements in accepting yourself and feeling secure. You must be free from guilt and you must feel loved.

If you sense your faults, you lose confidence in yourself because the bottom line reads, "guilt." Confession of sin to God then is not to make God feel good but to allow you to feel cleansed.

The love you and I need comes from two sources. Our faith is the only one which has God saying, "I love you." In the spirit of Divine Love, we get love by giving love. As we give love to family, neighbors and friends, it comes back to envelop us in warmth and security.

As our institutions stumble, we've lost our security blanket. Good—this may lead to maturity. We break the puppet strings and become whole people who don't bathe in egotism but, through forgiveness and love, find our identity.

U nless a man is given more than he can possibly do, he will never do all that he can," said Samuel McClure. Industrial surveys bear out this contention—people are more likely to quit their jobs when they have it easy than when they have it tough. People want to be challenged.

One of the gravest problems facing business today is not a lack of discipline, but a lack of motivation. When employees are sufficiently motivated and challenged, discipline takes care of itself. Surprisingly, companies often perform at their best when a crisis hits. The crisis becomes a motivating force and people feel they can contribute, they feel needed, they feel essential.

Of course, this doesn't mean you should create a crisis within your company or department or store and try to operate from crisis to crisis. Crying "wolf" too often will become a counterproductive demotivator. But you should not hesitate to ask employees for extra effort; don't underestimate the willingness and desire of people to be called upon to go the extra mile.

Julian Dyke quit his highly respected, well-paying job in the aerospace industry for the strangest reason. He was extremely satisfied with his salary and benefits; he liked working in Washington D.C., he had no unusual pressures on him. His family was contented; his employer was satisfied with his work. And yet he quit his job and took a cut in pay because his employer was not making him work hard enough. By midmorning each day, he had cleared his desk of work and was looking for more to do. He felt underemployed and underutilized and, in the end, his integrity forced him to quit. Today, Julian Dyke guides relationships and memberships for the Boy Scouts of America. It pays less, but he is satisfied that his talents and abilities are being fully utilized and stretched.

C. Northcote Parkinson gave his name to a law that states, "Work expands so as to fill the time available for its completion." However, good employees such as Julian Dyke won't buy wasting time. As a result, their potentially greater contribution is lost when they go elsewhere in search of greater challenge.

People need challenge as much as they need pay. Like the milk company that used the slogan, "Our cows are not contented, they are anxious to do better," people feel the same way and want to do better.

Time is the only commodity that cannot be replenished. Time spent cannot be recovered, and so becomes more valuable than any precious gem. But time is also the great equalizer—regardless of how powerful or influential a person may be, we each have only the same 24 hours in a day.

Although we cannot recover time lost, we can redeem the time we have before us. The Apostle Paul spoke of redeeming time. He felt that he had wasted much time with misplaced priorities before he met Jesus. So he resolved to make each remaining minute count for two, each hour count for two, each day count for two. By doing so, he redeemed the time remaining to him.

Have you heard of the man who didn't have time?
He hadn't time to greet the day, he hadn't time to laugh or play;
He hadn't time to wait a while, he hadn't time to glean the news, he
hadn't time to dream or muse;
He hadn't time to train his mind; he hadn't time to see a joke, he
hadn't time to write his folk;
He hadn't time to eat a meal, he hadn't time to deeply feel,
He hadn't time to take a rest, he hadn't time to do his best;
He hadn't time to help a cause, he hadn't time to make a pause;
He hadn't time to pen a note, he hadn't time to cast a vote;
He hadn't time to sing a song, he hadn't time to right a wrong;
He hadn't time to send a gift, he hadn't time to practice thrift;
He hadn't time to exercise, he hadn't time to say goodbye;
He hadn't time to study poise, he hadn't time to repress noise;
He hadn't time to serve his God;
He hadn't time to lend or give, he hadn't time to really live;
He hadn't time to read this verse,
He hadn't time—he's in a hearse—he's dead.

Using time wisely is not a display of energy. Redeeming time is inexorably linked to the depth of our need and the dedication of our effort.

Here is a favorite of my late mother, who was unabashedly patriotic, entitled "Hello, Remember Me?":

Some people call me Old Glory, others call me the Star-Spangled Banner, but whatever they call me, I am your flag, the flag of the United States of America...something has been bothering me... because it is about you and me.

I remember some time ago people lined up on both sides of the street to watch the parade and naturally I was leading every parade. Proudly waving in the breeze. When your daddy saw me coming, he immediately removed his hat and placed it against his left shoulder so that his hand was directly over his heart...remember?

And you, I remember you. Standing there straight as a soldier. You didn't have a hat, but you were giving the right salute. Remember little sister? With her right hand over her heart...remember?

What happened? I'm still the same old flag. Oh, I have a few more stars since you were a boy. A lot more blood has been shed since those parades of long ago.

But now I don't feel as proud as I used to. When I come down your street and you just stand there with your hands in your pockets and I may get a small glance and then you look away.

Then I see children running around and shouting...they don't seem to know who I am...I saw one man take his hat off and then look around. He didn't see anybody else with their's off so he quickly put his back on.

Is it a sin to be patriotic anymore? Have you forgotten what I stand for and where I've been?...Anzio...Guadalcanal...Korea ...and Vietnam. Take a look at the memorial honor rolls sometime, of those who never came back to keep this republic free...one nation under God...when you salute me, you are actually saluting them.

Well, it won't be long until I'll be coming down your street again. So when you see me, stand straight, place your right hand over your heart...and I'll salute you, by waving back...and I'll know you remember.

Each day of our lives, we face the challenge of deciding what is urgent and what is important. At first glance, we might believe they are one and the same. In fact, accepting these terms as synoymous has filled our lives with panic and pressure.

Once we can distinguish and acknowledge the difference, we can begin to free our lives of much stress. Frustration, tension, uptightness, nervousness and fatigue have become common words in our vocabularies today. Much worse, they accurately describe our hectic lifestyles. The calm and peace we seek in our lives can begin when we effectively differentiate between urgency and importance.

In our scurried quest for action, we have actually adopted a crisis mentality founded on urgency. We hurt, rather than help, our children when we overreact to their every demand or problem. In too many homes, the whine of a child becomes a command for parental action. An entire evening can be ruined by the trifling demand of a spoiled child, allowed to rule over adults.

In business, too many managers create a crisis if one doesn't already exist. They delude themselves into thinking they are only working effectively when they work under pressure.

On the opposite side, truly important matters are often silent, voiceless and easily overlooked. Important tasks can be pacified and put aside with a promise to think the issue through at some later date. Important affairs can be detoured without shocking us; superficial affairs are more visible because we see all there is to see.

Important matters are more like an iceberg. We only get a glimpse of the top; much, much more remains unseen and often its importance is discovered too late.

We all believe we are too busy. We are, but perhaps it is because we spend too much time on insignificant matters and waste too much time on trivial pursuits. We don't need more time—we only need to separate the truly important things from the urgent things that pester us.

A child drops out of school by the fourth grade. He just makes it official when he's 16." This is the distressing prognosis of the superintendent of schools in a major urban city. It is revealing to think that man's destiny, for good or bad, is locked in so early in life.

Leaders such as George Washington are not born, but are developed early in life. He is a striking example of how quickly the course of a child is determined, although it might not be apparent for years. Washington had the following rules of conduct:

> Sleep not when others speak, sit not when others stand, speak not when you should hold your peace, walk not when others stop.
>
> Let your countenance be pleasant, but in serious matters let it be somewhat grave.
>
> Show not yourself glad at the misfortune of another, though he were your enemy.
>
> Let your discourse with men of business always be short and comprehensive.
>
> Strive not with your superiors in argument, but always submit your judgment to others with modesty.
>
> When a man does all he can, though it succeeds not well, blame not him that did it.
>
> Associate yourself with men of good quality if you esteem your own reputation, for it is better to be alone than in bad company.
>
> Be not forward, but friendly and courteous; the first to salute, hear and answer; and be not pensive when it is time to converse.
>
> Think before you speak; pronounce not imperfectly, nor bring out words too hastily, but orderly and distinctly.
>
> Be not curious to know the affairs of others, neither approach to those that speak in private.
>
> Undertake not what you cannot perform, but be careful to keep your promise.
>
> Speak not evil of the absent, for it is unjust.
>
> Labor to keep alive in your breast that little spark of celestial fire called conscience.

You've heard about the two small boys standing on the corner when a very pretty little girl walked by. One of the boys said, "When I stop hating girls, she's the one I'll stop hating first."

Some of us are that way about our contemporaries. We want to make new friends but are afraid we'll fail so we shy away from people we really want to know.

It is possible to dislike people from afar because we're afraid of rejection up close. Insecurity is a detriment to making friends. Yet, without question I know friendships are my greatest asset and I take pride that I retain friends through the years—which is probably a tribute to the friends who endure me.

To make a friend you must genuinely meet people. When I'm in Washington, D.C., I especially note how people so often look over my shoulder. I used to think they were checking for dandruff but soon learned politicians have a habit of shaking one hand while looking beyond that person to see another. To say the least, that isn't the way to make friends. The handshake must be accompanied by genuine concern and interest in the person you're meeting.

Dr. Leonard Zunin suggests three P's: positive, personal, pertinent. A positive approach is a magnet. People gravitate and feel strength from a positive individual. It gives intimacy when you cover the handshake with your other hand—or an arm around the shoulders. JoAnn Castle who used to appear with Lawrence Welk talks of Mr. Welk's friendship. At the moment the doctors told JoAnn her daughter was retarded, she said Mr. Welk didn't say a word—there wasn't anything to say—he just put his arm around her shoulders and she felt strength.

Pertinent refers to conversation. Talk about subjects you think are of mutual interest, and not about yourself. Ask questions to see if your partner is interested. Place value upon the answers.

Friendships often start by sharing a common emotion or even a tragedy. We become attached to those with whom we share life.

The door opener to friendship is a warm smile. A smile puts the other person at ease. A smile brings warmth. A smile is the window for friendship to shine through.

Who is rich? We could have answered the question easier in the past. Today we know money is not the single answer. We are finding money can't buy everything.

You and I have grown up in a society where you are measured by what you have and, even worse, by what you show. Such riches are subject to economic and political conditions. In turn, we all admire people who seem to successfully live above the storms. Their attitude and personalities are not dictated by the stock market. How does someone reach such stability?

I imagine they fill their minds constantly with rich thoughts. They are curious about people and history. They escape hysteria because they know their forebears braved problems greater than theirs. Usually I find balanced people see wealth in nature, appreciate the beauty of music, share the sensitivity of the poet. We say such people have simple tastes so they don't even yearn for rich things. Such people have sublime tastes—simple is our immature world.

People of true security have rich feelings. They obey their impulses to help. They are willing to selflessly give themselves in friendship. Another's tears they dry—not by laughing but aiding.

We have been so busy in our pursuit of riches that we've passed them by. We miss the blush of the rose, the bite of the apple, and the warmth of the breeze.

Mrs. Glenn Burgdorf of St. Louis put it poetically:

Take the Time

Is time so dear we can't afford to stop our day's routine,
To think about our purpose here, our debt to those unseen?

Is life so hard we cannot stop to smile at those in need,
To speak a warm "hello" to them? To cheer by some small deed?

The time we take to meditate on things that we believe
Is worth the extra effort for the blessings we receive.

Who is rich? You can be! Real wealth is beyond the limits of possessions.

We humans are funny creatures. We seem to always find a reason, or at least an excuse, for failing. It is as if we shy away from success, avoiding it at all costs. Some people, of course, fumble opportunity because it frequently comes disguised as hard work.

Here's an iron-clad, guaranteed formula for failure:

1. Wake up in the morning and, even before getting out of bed, begin thinking of yourself and what you want for yourself.
2. Because you are thinking only of yourself, get irritated with your spouse and children because they keep interrupting your selfish thoughts. Make sure you made the kids unhappy before they leave for school; and throw a couple of nasty barbs in your mate's direction.
3. Whatever the weather, find something bad about it. If it is sunny, think of the growing grass and having to mow it. If its rainy, think of the gloomy atmosphere and how difficult it is to stay neat in wet weather.
4. Let your irritations sour your disposition until you are rude as you drive to work, impolite as you park your car, and grumpy toward your fellow employees as you enter. Make certain you have banished pleasantness for the day.
5. Undertake the easy, non-productive tasks first, saying that they have to be done. Keep telling yourself that you are getting routine matters out of the way so you can tackle the difficult assignments with a clear day tomorrow, or maybe the next day.
6. Convince yourself that everyone around you has an easier job than yours. Attribute your lack of work and their ambition to the fact that they have better and easier jobs.
7. At lunch, be sure to eat too much. This will ensure that you are drowsy and sluggish all afternoon.
8. Don't waste any time learning to do your job better—you might inadvertently get excited about your work.
9. If you fall behind on a task, don't catch up. Instead, leave it unfinished and go on to something else.
10. Be certain to gather all the negative comments you hear and pass them on.

A famous professor—philosopher—psychologist once said, "The greatest discovery of my generation is that human beings can alter their life by their attitudes. As you think, so shall you be."

What is a true friend? Real friends in life don't require frequent contact, calls or visiting. Friends remain constant and supportive whether seen or not for lengthy intervals.

A British publication offered a prize for the best definition of a friend. Among the thousands of responses were these. A friend is:

One who multiplies joys, divides grief and whose honesty is inviolable.

One who understands our silence.

A volume of sympathy bound in cloth.

A watch which beats true for all time and never runs down.

The winning definition was this one: "A friend is one who comes in when the whole world has gone out."

Well over a century ago, a visitor to the White House asked President Abraham Lincoln for his definition of a friend. "My definition of a friend?" he repeated slowly. "One who has the same enemies you have."

Over the years, there have been any number of classic definitions of a friend and descriptions of friendship:

True friendship is like sound health; the value of it is seldom known until it be lost.

You can make more friends in two months by becoming interested in other people than you can in two years by trying to get other people interested in you.

A true friend is somebody who can make us do what we can.

Friendship consists in forgetting what one gives and remembering what one receives.

A friend is 'one who knows all about you and loves you just the same.'

Silences make the real conversations between friends. Not the saying but the never needing to say is what counts.

All the definitions, both vintage and modern, are good but inadequate in describing a friend. Throughout our lifetime, we are fortunate if we have half a dozen true friends. We can afford to lose almost anything before losing a friend.

The consumer movement of recent years has made people demand better product quality and better product information. The old axiom of "sell the sizzle, not the steak" might have worked in the '40s and '50s, but not today. Not with today's aware consumers.

Manufacturers and retailers need to adopt the reverse policy—sell the steak and let the customer make it sizzle. Savvy consumers want a product for what it will do for them. We no longer sell merchandise or things, per se, we sell the satisfaction of people's needs. The following essay, titled "Don't Sell Me Things," illustrates the point:

> Don't sell me shoes. Sell me comfort, economy and the pleasure of walking in the open air.
>
> Don't sell me furniture. Sell me a room full of fashion in a home that has comfort, cleanliness and contentment.
>
> Don't sell me toys. Sell me playthings to keep my children happy and active.
>
> Don't sell me tires. Sell me freedom from worry, low cost-per-mile and safety.
>
> Don't sell me clothes. Sell me a neat appearance, style, attractiveness and pride in the way I look to others.
>
> Don't sell me things. Sell me ideals, feelings, self-respect and happiness, but . . . please do not sell me things.

Selling to today's consumer means more than taking an order—it means getting acquainted with customers and using your ingenuity and imagination to help them gain satisfaction. In the end, everyone benefits when there is pride by the seller and pride by the buyer.

Self-improvement is not selfish—self-improvement is enlightened self-interest. When we work to improve ourselves, we are making ourselves more valuable and more useful.

Setting a goal of self-improvement, you begin a journey to know yourself better. When you attempt to improve, you undertake a study of your personal strengths and weaknesses, good habits and bad.

As a first step toward self-improvement, glean good ideas from others. Watch for traits in others that you admire; make note of suggestions and ideas you gather from reading or listening to others.

Next, face yourself honestly. Don't be afraid of asking yourself some difficult questions: Am I worth what I'm paid? Would I hire myself? Am I doing the best job I can? Do I leave work each day with pride?

Then, design a course of self-improvement. Take correspondence courses; read books about your vocation. Apply yourself to your routine job just as you would expect a physician to do his or her job. Also, seek to improve your knowledge of people. Constantly widen your horizons.

Also, improve your hobby or avocation skills as a way of improving your job skills. As odd as it sounds, becoming good at a hobby rubs off on your work. Get involved in some pastime; get involved in community or charitable activities.

Finally, if you want to improve yourself, help others in your family or on the job to improve themselves. When you lift others, you always step up to a higher plateau yourself.

Friday, Week Thirty-Two

Being a parent is no easy task, considering all the options faced by our children today. We feel threatened by and in competition with influences invading our homes. Compared with today's youth, we were protected and sheltered.

Dr. Thomas P. Johnson, a San Diego psychiatrist, offers the following suggested guidelines for modern parents:

1. Don't disapprove of what a child is . . . disapprove of what he does.
2. Give attention and praise for good behavior . . . not bad behavior.
3. Encourage and allow discussion, but remember it's the parents who should make the final decision.
4. Punishment should be swift, reasonable, related to the offense and absolutely certain to occur . . . it need not be severe.
5. Throw out all rules you are unwilling to enforce and be willing to change the rules if and when you think they need changing.
6. Don't lecture and don't warn . . . youngsters will remember what they think is important to remember.
7. Don't feel you have to justify rules, although you should try to explain them.
8. As your youngsters grow older, many rules may be subject to discussion and compromise. The few rules you really feel strongly about should be enforced no matter what rules other parents have.
9. Allow a child to assume responsibility for his decisions as he shows the ability to do so.
10. Don't expect children to demonstrate more self control than you do.
11. Be honest with your youngster . . . hypocrisy shows.
12. The most important factor in your youngster's self image is what he thinks you think of him. His self image is a major factor in how he conducts himself.

Do you judge people when you shake hands? I'm afraid I do. Somehow I've never been able to accept a weak handshake. At the same time, when the handshake is firm and the wrist is kept rigid, I get the feeling the person is trying too hard to impress. Still, there is a bond in handshaking, no matter the style.

Tradition tells us the handshake originated as a symbol of peace. The open hand was the expression of openness. It was a revelation of no weapon and a pledge of trust and friendship. As children we were told to meet a strange dog with the open hand and the palm turned up.

Now with the emphasis on Oriental defense—karate, etc.—the handshake can be turned into a weapon, but basically it is a worldwide symbol of goodwill.

We do need to touch each other. Although I reject the "touch groups," I admit there is value in physical contact. Strength comes as you feel the vibrancy of fellowman. You no longer feel alone.

The handshake also became a symbol of integrity. Many a big deal has been transacted on the basis of a handshake.

To the contrary, a handshake can also be the agreement of ground rules for disagreement. We find there are strong differences of opinion but we are shaking hands to say we will not be disagreeable in our disagreeing. We will not violate the rights of each other even though we may be competitors. We are promising to play fair. So the boxers shake hands before the fight and the team captains shake before the kick-off, pitch, or toss-up.

Still, the hand can't be separated from the rest of the body. The first impression comes from the grasp but immediately we search the eyes to see if hand and eyes are conveying the same thing. Also we listen to the tone of the voice as the greeting is made.

Unfortunately we've substituted legal contracts for handshakes. Hypocrisy or dishonesty has made us draw up more binding contracts.

The handshake is usually the greeting of equals. At times it is reaching down to pull someone up—the grasp of rescue. I'm grateful for the strong hands that have reached out to me throughout my lifetime. Our hands are tools of communication.

Lost, stolen, or missing—how often we hear these words. We use them in print, a plea for help in getting something valuable returned to its owner. Sometimes the object is missed immediately. In other instances, no matter how much value the owner places on it, he does not know when it was lost because he did not miss it for some time." This is the introduction to some good paragraphs written by a friend, Dr. John Roberts.

Dr. Roberts continues:

Some intangible things as well as pieces of property are lost or missing . . . probably stolen . . . from many a home. Their loss may go undetected for some time but at some point in the future a frantic effort will be made for their recovery.

One thing lost by some people is integrity. Personal relationships and business transactions hinge not on right and justice but whatever is to the individual's advantage. Truth is not an unknown word to such people. We encounter this attitude with such frequency that one is tempted to respond in kind. If we do, we suffer the loss of our own integrity.

Regular prayer and Bible study have never been known by many. But they have been lost by others who once had a time of meditation each day. The tragedy is that as problems develop or domestic difficulties mount, such individuals have increasing difficulty finding the solution they once had.

Love and family togetherness have been lost to many and threatened to most by the steadily increasing tempo of life. Things beckon for leisure time until it becomes not leisure but mad pursuit of entertainment. Disenchantment in marriage may be only boredom where there is no new place to go and the television is broken.

Loss of church attendance leaves an individual poorer than he would be otherwise. It can easily be reclaimed. Unfortunately, those who need it may not notice the loss. Spasmodic visits to various churches will not suffice. Nor will viewing worship services on television adequately substitute for a church home and regular worship.

Loss of friendship and communication is a universal problem of any busy and complex society. These are not reclaimed by accident. Conscious effort is necessary. Some people find this extremely difficult. A stable Christian life and involvement in church work greatly help in preventing or regaining this loss.

Good things in life have a way of disappearing, if we do not guard them carefully.

I am certain that you know people, as I do, who can make you feel good just by being in their presence. These special individuals seem to radiate a warmth and friendliness that draw others to them wherever they go. This magnetic characteristic is not a gift bestowed only on the beautiful or famous or wealthy—anyone can have it. Those who do are truly blessed and long remembered for their special ability to give of themselves.

One of my favorite poems by Frank B. Whitney may help you, as it does me, to face each day with a fresh, exhilarating outlook:

Begin the day with friendliness, and only friends you'll find.
Yes, greet the dawn with happiness; keep happy thoughts
   in mind.
Salute the day with peaceful thoughts, and peace will fill
   your heart;
Begin the day with joyful soul, and joy will be your part.
Begin the day with friendliness. Keep friendly all day long.
Keep in your soul a friendly thought, your heart a
   friendly song.
Have in your mind a word of cheer for all who come
   your way.
And they will bless you, too, in turn, and wish you
   "Happy day."
Begin each day with friendly thoughts, and as the day
   goes on,
Keep friendly, loving, good and kind, just as you were
   at dawn.
The day will be a friendly one, and then at night you'll find
That you were happy all day long—through friendly thoughts
   in mind.

What a wonderful way to greet each new day! And what a challenge to so many of us who have a difficult time getting our bodily motors running in the morning! Commit yourself today to adding one more outgoing, warm and friendly person to this world—yourself.

Nothing is quite so exhilarating as the moment we first understand a principle we memorized in childhood. A truth accepted as a child because it came from a trusted parent becomes all the greater when we discover the truth for ourselves.

Something old becomes new when we first grasp the wisdom and meaning of a concept already existing in our minds by memorization. Knowledge, philosophy and truth are ageless, but become new when we begin to comprehend and apply them.

One such ageless, universal truth is the Golden Rule—"Do unto others as you would have others do unto you"—which appears in one version or another in nearly all the philosophies and religions of the world. Beyond recognition of the Golden Rule, beyond memorization, must come an understanding of the power of this principle. Within this simple declaration is an avenue for finding personal power, peace of mind, freedom from guilt, mental health, happiness, success and fulfilling relationships with others.

Think what could happen if we truly understood the logic of the Golden Rule, which nurtures self-interest while appearing generous. Treat others well, for you want to be treated well by them.

Think how an unkind remark cuts you, so don't make one about another.

Think how you are crushed by someone shouting at you, so don't shout at others.

Think how you wilt under constant criticism, so be careful that any criticism of others is justified and constructive.

Think how dishonesty or deception makes you feel like a fool, so be honest with others even if it hurts.

Think how a slight makes you feel lonely and insecure, so always make others feel wanted.

The Golden Rule guarantees no instant results, but provides long-range rewards. The Golden Rule gives no immunity from this world's pains, but offers peace of mind. The practice must precede the results.

We must ask ourselves if we merely recite a Sunday school truth or if we fully understand a sound principle necessary for human survival. We must ask ourselves if more than 100 languages can be wrong. In that many languages, in one form or another, exists the principle, "Do unto others as you would have others do unto you." All the languages are unimportant unless my tongue and yours not only repeat the Golden Rule, but our minds dictate to us the true meaning of it, as well.

The prominent British author and historian H.G. Wells always believed in Utopia. He dreamed of a world perfect in every respect; a world of equal opportunity for all its citizens to achieve their ambitions; a world with food enough for all to eat. Mr. Wells did more than merely dream of his Utopia, he suggested that this world could evolve in any given generation when the young people utilize their talents to the fullest.

In light of daily headlines and newscasts, we may find it difficult to agree with Mr. Wells that our troubled world could ever become perfect. Each day we appear to slip farther backward. Nevertheless, we must realize that the utilization of our God-given abilities is basic stewardship and the true purpose of living.

In achieving this purpose, I strongly believe that the free enterprise system is the finest avenue of expression for the abilities we have. Free enterprise is based on a simple premise—supply and demand. Under this system, we have a global need for each other; we are interdependent inhabitants of this tiny planet.

This interdependency is so great, in fact, that there has never been a war during which enemies did not have to trade with one another in order to survive. Even today, we trade everything from wheat to technology with our ideological enemies around the globe.

The underlying principle of free enterprise is that we make demands on each other. You can do something for me that I cannot do for myself and, likewise, there are some things that I can do for you that you cannot do for yourself. The demand then gives us the opportunity to be the "supply answer." In answering or supplying the demand, we perform a service or provide a product. This payment is not based on some arbitrary rule stating that all services and products are worth the same price. And more than one person can supply the demand, giving us competition.

Competition becomes the regulator of the price we can charge for the service we render or the product we produce. When one person is able to provide better service or come up with a better idea, then that person not only gets the job, but perhaps can realize an even greater profit.

While our free enterprise system is a far cry from the Utopian ideal of H. G. Wells, it is still the best arena for exercising our God-given talents and abilities.

Arnold A. Bennett was a poverty-stricken young clerk in a London law office. He was frustrated; he saw his life as aimless. He took stock of himself and came to the realization that his most precious possession was *time*—a resource that must not be wasted. He resolved to budget his time wisely and, in the process, turned his dreams into reality. He details his unusual philosophy in his famous book, "How to Live Twenty-Four Hours a Day":

> Time is the inexplicable raw material of everything. With it, all is possible; without it, nothing. The supply of time is truly a daily miracle, an affair genuinely astonishing when one examines it.
>
> You wake up in the morning, and lo, your purse is magically filled with 24 hours of the unmanufactured tissue of the universe of your life! It is yours. It is the most precious of possessions; no one can take it from you. It is unstealable. And no one receives either more or less than you receive.
>
> In the realm of time there is no aristocracy of wealth, and no aristocracy of intellect. Genius is never rewarded by even an extra hour a day. And there is no punishment. Waste your infinitely precious commodity as much as you will and the supply will never be withheld from you. Moreover, you cannot draw on the future. Impossible to get into debt! You can only waste the passing moment. You cannot waste tomorrow; it is kept for you. You cannot waste the next hour; it is kept for you.
>
> I have said the affair was a miracle. Is it not?
>
> You have to live on this 24 hours of daily time. Out of it you have to spin health, pleasure, money, content, respect, and the evolution of your immortal soul. Its right use, its most effective use, is a matter of the highest urgency and of the most thrilling actuality. All depends on that. Your happiness—the elusive prize that you are all clutching for, my friends—depends on that.
>
> If one cannot arrange that an income of 24 hours a day shall exactly cover all proper items of expenditure, one does muddle one's whole life indefinitely.
>
> We never shall have any more time. We have, and we have always had, all the time there is.

With our busy, on-the-go lifestyles, we rarely find time for the truly important things—we have to *make* time. Make time today!

Thank God for the "generation gap"! Though only labeled in recent years, this curious animosity between generations has existed throughout history—since Saul's put-down of David or Socrates' condemnation of youth in the fifth century B.C., terming them "tyrants" and denouncing their "bad manners, contempt for authority, disrespect for elders."

Discontent between generations is healthy and good. A rejection of one generation's actions gives the next generation something to think about. As each generation ages, it loses its audacity and defends its accomplishments with self-serving braggadocio or criticism of the succeeding generation. All of us seek fulfillment and resent being replaced. We give lip service to preparing the world for the next generation, but we are reluctant to turn it over. And so it should be.

Youth, in turn, looks only at the surface. They judge us by what they see, with limited regard for history. Youthful energy, combined with cocky vanity undiminished by living, makes the young feel they can do better if they can only wrestle leadership from the adults.

This normal competition equals survival! In the animal kingdom, the older animals paw and snarl at the young, creating in them the desire for independence and the strength to survive.

So, the generation gap must not be erased, merely understood. Youth should feel they can make the world better—but with restraint and respect for what has gone before. Adults should welcome the hot breath on their heels from the herd of galloping youth—the challenge of youth revitalizes the flow of adrenalin.

Thank God for the generation gap, it is the hope for tomorrow!

W e're constantly having an update of how many of our citizens will be sixty-five or older when we usher in the twenty-first Century. Even being aware of these statistics, we are doing a pitiful job giving a sense of meaning, purpose, and dignity to the last half of a person's life. We need to completely change our mental images and destroy some myths.

One of my best friends recently retired as CEO of a large corporation. He took the company from a staggering position to leader in its field. He has never been seriously ill—he enjoys robust health—he had no desire to retire but it was company policy. Now I worry about him. The most dangerous time is the first two years after retirement. The fatality rate of people suddenly slowing down at the arbitrary age of sixty-five has been a shame. When will we learn as a nation we can't afford the loss of such talent just because a person is sixty-five?

I'm all for a person being able to retire if they choose at age sixty-five or even younger, but I also support that person staying on if they so choose. Why does it have to be one way?

The rocking chair is not designed for most of my friends sixty-five years of age. They are in good health and that health will only get better if they feel needed and remain active.

We seem to be hung up on senility. Ninety-five percent of all older persons are alert. Their ability to think, it is proven, is as good as at age thirty, plus they have the bonus of the maturity and wisdom that comes by living.

We even have a mistaken myth about potency. When you see Senator Strom Thurmond fathering three children after age sixty-eight, or the late William Henry Belk having six children after age fifty-five, you have to redefine the junk thinking we've had forced on us.

We fear the burdens of older people, then we take from them their means of self-support. Despite this, the below-poverty level of older people has diminished and most I know would like to work if possible.

When I look at the good causes of my city and nation, I find older people are the most valued volunteers. They care about this land. Subversive activity is foreign to our older citizens. They unashamedly love America.

We've had too many pictures of sour older people. I find them involved, alert, loving life and most anxious to do more if we'll take away the curse of sixty-five plus.

From England comes the story about an incident at a railroad station in London. A train was about to pull out of the station when the shrill voice of a lady called out to her husband, "Wait! We've forgotten our non-entity cards." Of course, what she meant to say was "identity cards." As workers in a factory, they had to have them clipped to their garments in order to be admitted to the plant.

We may smile at the lady's mistake but it does relate to a problem we face, or a feeling that we have—our society has become impersonal. The help the computer gives on one side is balanced by the nagging feeling that we have fast become a number rather than a name. The signature at the bottom of my check is important but not nearly as important as the twenty-five-digit number. Believe it or not, the picture on my driver's license does resemble me a bit, but more important to the person asking for it is the number. When I fill up with gas, they only want to know two things—the expiration date on the card and the number. My plane tickets are charged by number, as well as my hotel bills. The worst insult of number use is the one I'm given when buying a hamburger or an ice cream cone.

Quite a contrast to the Sovereign of the Universe who says through the mouth of Isaiah the Prophet that our names are written on the palms of His hands; or as suggested in the New Testament that the hairs on our head are numbered.

We grew up with the idea that we had a family name and then we had a given name. The family name had already started us on a road to identity but there could be many Joneses and Smiths, and in some parts of the world, even a great number of Haggais. So the given name gave us distinction. We may, in our desire for efficiency, reduce the importance of the name but never the value of the name. A good name is to be chosen among riches and that's why God promises that when we go to our "eternal home" we will be given a "new name." Thank goodness, not a new number.

In moments of despair we may feel as a nobody, but the genius of faith in God is that to Him we're always a somebody.

Are you prepared to face today with a fresh outlook? Too many of us, unfortunately, measure our lives on productivity, on what we can do. Our worth is not what we do, but who we are. The following sentences can help you change your life and create a better you:

1. *I am sorry.* An uncaring apology can only amplify your error; an honest apology will almost always be accepted. Saying "I am sorry" indicates an awareness of your error and an awareness that others have been hurt by your actions. Offering an apology builds companionship; it takes away any pretense of superiority and indicates your security. An apology shows you are strong enough to be honest with yourself and confess an error; it shows you don't live in the shadows but can face the mirror.

2. *I appreciate you.* We often get so busy that we forget we cannot do it alone. None of us is conditioned to be a hermit; we need one another. We are debtors to each other and saying "I appreciate you" verbalizes this debt. All of us stand taller knowing we are not taken for granted. The person you appreciate is built up by your esteem.

3. *What do you think?* There is no easier way to learn than by picking the brain of a friend or associate, instantly receiving the worth of another's thinking. Companies that use the suggestion box are indicating a willingness to improve and a respect for employees' abilities and ideas. Think of the proverb that says, "He that knoweth not and knoweth not that he knoweth not is a fool, shun him."

4. *I need help.* In her book *I'll Cry Tomorrow*, Lillian Roth revealed that she never began to conquer her destructive personal problems until she uttered the three hardest words she ever formed—"I need help." Whether your plea is to a friend or to your God, help begins with the request.

These four simple sentences—I am sorry; I appreciate you; What do you think; I need help—can help you greatly throughout your life. Why not start using them today?

Sympathy can only be extended by people who believe the same misfortune could befall them, people who feel that "there but for the grace of God go I." Honest sympathy cannot grow out of smug, secure, benevolent feelings. Many of the problems nagging our society could be solved with sympathetic kindness.

True kindness is not a soft answer for hard problems. Kindness is not to be mistaken for sentimentality. Kindness may mean your having the courage to be candid, truthful, demanding and tough. Letting a friend off the hook is not kindness; instead it contributes to the problem. A fine line exists between condemning to destroy or condemning to draw attention to a problem and help.

True kindness is not given by those who want credit for helping others. Professional do-gooders are only as kind as the credit lines they receive.

True kindness does not depend on the dramatic; it is more a question of timing and sincerity than the size of the act. A favorite story of Dr. Leslie Weatherhead concerns a nurse in his congregation who lost her favorite patient. "Dr. Weatherhead," she said, "I don't know what to say to the grieving husband. All I could think to do was make him a cup of tea." To which Dr. Weatherhead replied, "What could be more eloquent than a quiet cup of hot tea!"

There is an old saying—"Remember every home has a sorrow and every man carries a burden." So often we never know the burdens that others bear. Some of us just conceal our heartaches better than others; some of us build protective walls of defense. The heavier the problem, the less likely we are to talk about it and the more prone we are to hide it. Some things just hurt too much to discuss with others.

True kindness on your part could change a life today. You could help a discouraged person hang on a bit longer; you could help a sad individual know there is still goodness in this world; you could help a lonely person know that someone else cares.

We have become a nation of split personalities. We have become the people of the Working Life and the folk of the Leisure Life. We experiment with various types of working hours in an effort to promote and protect leisure time.

Throughout the history of our country, our forebears had a singular life—everything centered around their work. Vacations came just once a year and were savored as a luxury. Only the most wealthy populated the playgrounds of the rich—Newport, Palm Beach and Palm Springs.

Today, we have evolved into a nation of split personalities, placing as much emphasis on our leisure life as our working life. As far back as a decade ago, "U.S. News and World Report" claimed that our nation would spend $130 billion on leisure—at that time "exceeding national defense costs. It's more than the outlay for construction of new homes. It surpasses the total of corporate profits. It is far larger than the aggregate income of U.S. farmers. It tops the overall value of the country's exports."

Such emphasis on leisure means big business. "Standard and Poor's Index" wrote a decade ago that "leisure stocks as a group were among the best performers . . . devotion to leisure remains intact."

I, perhaps, stand alone in wondering if this concentration on more and more leisure time and activity is healthy. I am not a total captive of the "Puritan work ethic" nor do I believe that leisure smacks of sin and guilt, nor do I think leisure equates to "idle hands of mischief," for much leisure activity is strenuous and athletic.

It is a question of priorities. We need to have time for recreation; we need to rid ourselves of tension; we need to get away from daily problems and take the long view; we need time for refueling and rededication.

But leisure well spent depends on work well done. This means more than merely working to afford leisure. Ancient Rome began to crumble when leisure became an end in itself instead of a recreational experience for better achievement. Leisure, if it is honest recreation, can stimulate a tired nation—leisure as an end-all can break our fiber.

Are you ever late for work? Often? Many totally honest people, who wouldn't think of stealing even a penny, somehow don't consider their tardiness as stealing from their employer. Here are some suggestions for correcting the problem of chronic tardiness:

Tardiness may simply result from hating to get up early. If so, use at least two alarm clocks and even a clock radio, and set them 10 minutes apart. I used this trick in college, even putting one clock in a metal washbasin. It didn't always work, but it woke up all my neighboring classmates and their hollering soon aroused me.

When you go to bed at night, open the shades. Then, except during the winter months, the sun will be shining warmly into your bedroom when you wake up in the morning.

Plan your schedule to be at work 15 minutes ahead of time. This will allow for interruptions and traffic jams and other unexpected delays. If there are no delays, you will arrive early, get a more convenient parking place, and have a chance to settle down before work.

Reward yourself for overcoming tardiness. Plan something special at the end of the week when you have been to work on time everyday.

Look for any hidden reasons for your being late often. Perhaps you are dissatisfied with your job, annoyed by someone you have to work with, or resent having to work and feel sorry for yourself. Perhaps you are influenced by the tardiness of others, following their example rather than setting the example.

Like habitual tardiness, consistently leaving work early indicates a lack of respect and integrity. But both shortcomings can be corrected with sincere effort.

We tend to place a great deal of emphasis on the problems faced by our teenagers. The teen years, despite all their problems and pressures, are really offshoots of the formative ages during childhood and adolescence when a child's personality is developed and a child's character is cemented. Consider the following story:

Once there was a little boy. When he was three weeks old, his parents turned him over to a babysitter.

When he was two years old, they dressed him up like a cowboy and gave him a gun.

When he was six, his father occasionally dropped him off at church school on his way to the golf course.

When he was eight, his parents bought him a BB gun and taught him to shoot birds. He learned to shoot windshields by himself.

When he was 10, he spent his afternoons kneeling at the drugstore newsstand reading comic books. His mother wasn't home, and his father was very busy.

When he was 13, he told his parents other boys stayed out as late as they wanted, so they said he could too. It was easier that way.

When he was 15, the police called his home one midnight. "We have your boy at the station," they said, "he's in trouble."

"In trouble?" yelled the father. "It can't be my boy!"

It is sadly odd that we train our household pets and stake our backyard plants, yet somehow expect our children to train themselves. By the time we realize our failures, children have grown into teenagers and, for all practical purposes, beyond our reach or help.

I am reminded of a story that sums it all up. A 5-year-old boy was given a marvelous cassette library of fairy tales by his father. One night, the youngster left the audio equipment in his bedroom and crawled up into his dad's den chair. "Is something wrong with your tape recorder?" asked the father. "Yes, sir," answered the young lad, "the tape recorder doesn't have a soft lap."

How do you build a successful work force? Why do some companies function so much better than others? The answer is always people—how they're hired—how they're motivated.

Mal Braesicke, an insurance executive with American General Life, gave me his thoughts back in 1974:

Several weeks ago while flying home from a business meeting, I met an interesting gentleman. He was the owner of a very successful real estate firm. Since we were both in the sales field, our conversation came quite easily for our fields are closely related. We naturally got around to discussing how to build a sales organization.

What would be the top priorities? After several minutes we agreed on the following: integrity, loyalty, successful atmosphere, and desire.

First and foremost is integrity. The Scriptures say where there is no vision, people perish. To paraphrase, I would say where there is no integrity, an agency perishes, or at best barely survives. With a lack of integrity, distrust quickly moves in; and then a lack of confidence; and then below par sales.

Secondly, I would put loyalty. Loyalty is in as great a demand today as it was yesterday. It has always been in short supply. Loyalty between a manager and his associates is born out of a mutual trust and respect, and can survive only in this kind of atmosphere.

Now let's look at a successful atmosphere. There is an old saying, "Success breeds success." That is to say that once you have the momentum of a successful operation going, it seems to maintain itself, provided the atmosphere stays healthy and positive. By this I mean we continue to do the things that bring success and do them with a positive attitude.

Next, we come to desire. Webster says it is a strong craving that amounts to a need or hunger. To me, this is inadequate. Studies show that for most people, 85 percent of success in life is due to a personal sense of values and 15 percent is ability. The effectiveness of a person is directly related to his sense of values—his priorities in life—what things are most important to him. In other words, isn't it his desires that determine his degree of success and happiness in life? Emerson once said, "One of man's greatest desires in life is to find someone who will make him do what he is capable of doing."

What Mal Braesicke shared with us today applies to your job and mine—to all of us who work and are the least bit conscientious about our work.

Armchair psychiatry is a hazard of our times. I don't plan to join the ranks of those who analyze people. Still, I think helping people is dependent upon some basic ability to spot people's problems and sympathetically assist. As I've written previously, my mission is not to see through people but to see people through.

Before criticizing people we must try to walk in our neighbor's shoes. He needs help if he displays:

- *Belligerence*—walking around continuously with a chip on the shoulder, ready to argue or quarrel at the slightest excuse, or even without cause.
- *Excessive moodiness*—signifies "the blues" or "feeling down in the dumps," that "nothing is worthwhile or really matters."
- *Exaggerated worry*—continuous anxiety about nothing at all or entirely out of proportion to the cause.
- *Suspiciousness and mistrust*—a persistent feeling that the world is full of dishonest, conniving people; that "everyone is trying to take advantage of me."
- *Selfishness and greediness*—lack of consideration of the needs of others; a "what's in it for me" attitude.
- *Helplessness and dependency*—the tendency to let others carry the burden; difficulty in making decisions.
- *Poor emotional control*—emotional outbursts out of proportion to the cause and at inappropriate times.
- *Daydreaming and fantasy*—spending a good part of the time imagining how things could be rather than dealing with them the way they are.
- *Hypochondria*—worrying a great deal about minor physical ailments, experiencing imaginary symptoms of illness.

As I've identified our weaknesses, don't let me alarm you. All of us probably have most of these weaknesses at one time or another. The question is the degree. Also, if we can see ourselves at the beginning of the problem, we can, with discipline, correct ourselves. There, too, we can help each other when we see these problems.

Working together day in and day out with the same group of people takes a special kind of ability. Merely doing your job, speaking when spoken to and avoiding concern over fellow employees is as far off base as digging into everyone's private lives. For the company to succeed, it takes teamwork, and teamwork means communication between employees.

The key to all successful relationships—person to person, family to family, supervisor to worker, employee to employee—is communication. You may not owe the company good relations with your fellow employees, but your owe it to yourself and to them. Even if you prefer keeping to yourself, the individual next to you needs a feeling of belonging rather than isolation.

Even if you don't care to talk, then listen. About the nicest thing you can do for your fellow employee is to listen. Mortimer Adler once said, "If you ask me what is the most important requirement for successful communication, my answer is the ability to listen well, to hear what the other fellow says. This is much more difficult than any of us realize."

We all have to work for our very survival, to pay our bills and care for our families. So, let's make it as pleasant as possible. Make room in your life to accept your fellow employees. Even if your co-workers are difficult to know, sound them out, learn their feelings; reach out to communicate. Many of us work in small areas and have to rub shoulders whether we want to or not—the key is making such contact a touch of harmony rather than a rub of friction.

We, as a people, are frustrated—frustration that stems from what we cannot control. We can produce the computer to put accurate facts and figures at our fingertips, yet we cannot find the wisdom to live by. We are a generation of limitless knowledge, but we possess limited wisdom—we have endless data, but not the ability to use it.

We can send man to the moon, but we cannot explain how this improves mankind.

We can develop nuclear warheads, but we cannot devise a safe system to harness nuclear energy, one guaranteed to protect man and protect our environment.

We have the scientific capability to give man external comfort, but science has proven incapable of solving man's inner turmoil and restlessness.

The major forces in our world are religion, science, education and government. And yet, from all appearances, religion is failing to make man happy. Science is failing to make man safe. Education is failing to provide answers to the questions we ask, while offering abundant answers to questions never raised. Government is failing to provide stability and leadership, and as a result, overthrow is a regular occurrence. Where do we turn; where do we go?

We don't! We stop! We ask ourselves why are we here? What do we believe? Who are we? Do we have a value system? Does our community, our nation? Could we put down in a few sentences our creed and reason for living? What is life all about anyway?

I begin with God, and then seek His will through me. By so doing, my fragmented life has a center and circumference so that mankind's improvement becomes my true business no matter what I do for a living.

Think of the signers of our Declaration of Independence and the creators of our Constitution. You can probably name several of these historic figures, but do you know what they did for a living? Their business was founding a new republic; their purpose overwhelmed their daily living. Where are such Americans today? Where are the leaders to ease our frustration?

My hero corps is made up of all those who volunteer their time so generously for community benefit. We are busy people, yet one out of every seven of us is engaged in some kind of community service.

Several years ago, the Christophers made a study of volunteerism in America. The most common motives for volunteering, according to author Martin Glaser, are: "A tradition of mutual helpfulness . . . increased leisure . . . the changed status of women . . . disappearance of the self-sufficient family and its internal satisfaction . . . call to service as promoted by many major religions . . . need to belong, to be associated with a group . . . desire to gain special knowledge and competence . . . opportunity to put dormant skills to work . . . desire for status and community recognition for further social, professional or political contacts . . . desire to say 'yes' rather than 'no'."

It is easy and natural to be selfish. Receiving has a way of making us want more. We need to monitor ourselves, perhaps by asking ourselves, "What have I done today for someone that was totally unexpected and in no way was I obligated?" We all engage in backscratching—you help me with my project and I'll help you with yours. While that is good, we need to feel there are moments when we are responding to the compassion of our hearts.

We all want more out of life than existence or even property. We want something that outlives us. A little caring goes a long way and, when we sincerely help, we are just as rewarded as the recipient.

As the old saying goes, "When the going gets tough, the tough get going." This thought came to mind not long ago while I was enroute from Canada and changing planes in Pittsburgh.

The stopover in Pittsburgh came in the late afternoon when I was tired from a long day of traveling at the end of several demanding days. I wearily approached the ticket counter and found two check-in desks side-by-side, with four flights posted, and only one agent on duty—and he was at the other counter. It was about an hour before departure time so I said, "I guess the agent for flight 981 isn't here yet." With an ear-to-ear grin, the lone agent cheerfully replied, "I'm here and I will check you in." "Working all four flights?" I quizzed. "Well, we've had to cut corners anyway we can," he explained, "and we've cut our manpower to the bone, but I'm fortunate to have a job and a payday every two weeks. If they requested, I'd work four more gates in order to retain my job."

By this time, the young man's attitude had perked me up and brought me back to life. I moved to a spot where I could sit and observe this committed individual in action. It was totally refreshing to hear someone so grateful for a job.

All too often we hear complaints from the supposedly overworked—the waitress who complains when the hostess has to add another table to her station or the service station attendant who is too lazy to wash the windshield and just wipes enough to make it worse.

Even in the worst of times, there are many jobs left vacant because people are not willing to go the extra mile—to get tough and get going. A welfare check can seem more tantalizing than taking a menial job that would at least offer self-respect. We can sympathize with anyone who has lost their job, but that sympathy turns sour when they do little to look for another opportunity.

Praise can often put us to sleep, but criticism startles us awake. We can get carried away with ourselves on the wings of compliments, but we are brought back to earth by criticism. Praise may motivate us to grow, but criticism makes us determined to grow.

We may be temporarily wounded by criticism, but usually it only cuts away some rotten, poisonous flesh. Taking ourselves too seriously is a by-product of success; criticism lets us know that we've only just begun. Look at criticism with an open mind; consider the following:

1. Criticism is a compliment. In our hurried, impersonal society, criticism is a sign that you are noticed. Your actions matter to someone if they take the time to criticize. Better to be looked at with a critical eye, than overlooked entirely.
2. Criticism is a sound teacher. The artist needs the critic to view and judge the canvas. Even if criticism is unjustified, it has made you examine your action or position enough to know the difference.
3. Criticism is an observation of the outer person. There is a difference between who you are and how you perform. Though your flaws are criticized, you have the inner ability to improve and the willingness to correct yourself.
4. Criticism doesn't mean the critic is right. It costs nothing to listen; then, in the quietness of your privacy, you can judge whether the criticism is justified.
5. Criticism teaches us to laugh at ourselves. Don't make light of criticism, but don't let it tie you in knots. Laugh at your blunder, while determining not to make the same mistake in the future.

Tomorrow is merely an extension of today—no better and no worse unless we do things differently. Criticism, no matter how painful, can give us a fighting chance for a better tomorrow.

My heart went out to the teenager. She was pretty when I looked into her face but she had sad eyes. The problem seemed to be more than fifty pounds of excess weight that made her feel conspicuous and "put down." What could be done in her behalf?

I felt sorry for the fat teenager, not only at that moment but for the future. A prominent pediatrician, Dr. James B. Sigbury declares, "Eighty percent of fat children end up as fat adults." Dr. Sidbury says further, "Doctors often tell parents that an obese child will just grow out of it . . . but the truth is that most don't grow out of it."

It isn't pleasant to be a fat boy but even more unacceptable to be a fat girl. Many medical authorities consider fat as our most common health hazard. Actually I guess the child is fortunate who is overweight because it is now a treatable medical problem. A visit to the family doctor can correct the condition.

Unfortunate is the child who is fat because of poor eating habits or parents who encourage overeating. When our incomes are low, starchy diets often result because they are inexpensive, but careful nutritional balance can be achieved if parents are made knowledgeable.

Dr. Sidbury suggests such steps as not letting your child watch TV in the afternoon upon arriving home from school. Too often the routine is being glued to TV with potato chips or candy to munch on.

Children must be encouraged to exercise. It may be an interest in team sports, such as baseball, football, or basketball. Now single sports like tennis and golf interest a child. There is no better exercise than riding the bike or walking to the store for mom.

Oversimplification would be to say "no snacks" but this is impractical. Better still to have a plan. Maybe forget planning a dessert on week days but allow a snack later in the evening.

A crash diet such as we adults keep trying can be bad for the child. Better to control the amounts or portions. Children need potatoes as well as lettuce.

Most of all, parents need to explain to children what foods are most fattening and the danger involved in obesity.

The best weight control is example. Buren did this well for our children while I only demonstrate the constant battle of the bulge and the misery of having to refuse my favorite dessert, ice cream. Pounds are easier to keep off as a child than fight as an adult.

Think of all of your old favorite songs. When were they written? Am I right? Most of your old favorite music was written in the depression or the war years. This seems ironic, but it often takes suffering to bring out the brightest and best in people.

A prime example of such music writing was my favorite, Oscar Hammerstein. The lyrics of Hammerstein had a way of making you wish you had written them. You knew they were written by a man of high ideals. Oscar Hammerstein believed it was important to sing about the beautiful things in life despite the immediate circumstance. He could not write a song without hope in it.

Oscar Hammerstein didn't close his eyes. He knew as we do that life is not all beauty and some days, there's very little beauty. Here is the hook. We cannot rid the world of ugliness by letting the ugliness plunge us into despair. The ability to see beautiful dreams where ugliness now exists is the first step in making the dreams come true. Hope is our inspiration to achieve our goals. Hope is the basis of happy music.

I have heard people talk about the slums, moan about inequities, cry over injustices, and not do one thing to alleviate the problems. We don't need people to paint our misery. We need to sing about potential rose gardens in our misery.

Victor Frankl, the Viennese Jewish psychiatrist, was one of a few to come out of Hitler's concentration camps. There he saw beauty amidst man's hatred. He wrote: "We who lived in concentration camps can remember the men who walked through the huts comforting others, giving away their last piece of bread. They may have been few in number, but they offered sufficient proof that everything can be taken from a man but one thing: the last of the human freedoms—to choose one's attitude in any given set of circumstances, to choose one's own way."

Might we be encouraged to whistle a joyful tune as we seek to remedy man's misery. Hope makes life beautiful. Oscar Hammerstein had Mary Martin sing, "I'm stuck like a dope with a thing called hope. I can't get it out of my heart." Of such, great music is made.

I recall seeing a picture of a dilapidated old barn leaning precariously in an overgrown field. The barn's roofing was virtually gone and much of the siding was torn loose; the siding that remained was weathered and worn. The fact that the barn still stood at all was a tribute to its original construction. Evident in the picture were sturdy, rough-hewn supporting beams and a solid rock foundation. But the barn was in ruins.

Beneath the bleak and depressing picture was a quotation taken from Francis Bacon: "That which man altereth not for the better, time altereth for the worse."

We all need to develop habit patterns that will help us alter our lives for the better and prevent us from becoming like the barn. Here are some ideas:

1. Picture your specific goals in life, both personal and business. See yourself, not as you are now, no matter how good, but rather how you would like to be.

2. Keep your goals on center stage until they generate a burning desire for achievement. Willpower then becomes growth power.

3. Share your goals with your employees and together map practical steps to accomplish your goals. Spell out what you want to accomplish this week, next month, next year.

4. Actually graph your goals so you and your employees can check the program. There will be days of disappointment but these days will make for a better tomorrow. Or, as Frank Tyger said, "In every triumph there's a lot of try."

"If you work for a man, in heaven's name work for him. If he pays the wages that supply you your bread and butter, work for him . . . speak well of him, think well of him, stand by him and the institution he represents," wrote Elbert Hubbard in the early part of this century. His advice is even more appropriate today.

Today, we hear a common complaint that workers are being used by their employers. They are absolutely correct! If an employer is any good, he is using his employees. But I am certain that the unemployed would quickly change places if they could.

For a business to succeed today, it takes more than employees who put in their eight hours and leave the job behind at quitting time. Some psychologists might say this is a healthy attitude, to separate the pressures of the workplace from our leisure time and home life. However, I take a differing view. I find the happiest people are those who truly feel a part of the company; who gladly work overtime; who brag about the company and its products at social gatherings; who know with confidence the product is good because they helped make it.

One of the saddest occurrences is when we see capable employees get careless; when they reach a personal comfort zone. They have allowed themselves to flatten out to mediocrity. Such employees have traded excellence for being only average; they mistakenly think seniority automatically equates to value. Such employees feel they are working hard enough even if the business is suffering; they let down at the very time their efforts are needed most—and they will be the first to blame management when business is bad and the last to understand why they were laid off.

Be proud of your company; work hard for your company. The gain will be twofold—the company will grow and so will you.

Bread so dear and life so cheap," wrote a British philosopher. Death and accidents have become so prevalent that we regard them callously unless there is a great loss of life in some headlinemaking calamity.

Today, someone working with you will have an accident—and it never should have happened. About half of on-the-job accidents result from personal factors and personal problems. There are other reasons, as well.

To stay competitive, a company has to embrace constant change. This can mean adding new machinery and, with new machinery, usually a training program. If we let our egos get in the way, having used similar machines for years, we might claim to know the new process before we're ready. An accident results and it's too late.

Accidents also result from carelessness with what knowledge we do possess, from familiar everyday tasks. Serious accidents frequently occur from the simplest mistakes. A pilot goes through an extensive checklist before takeoff—though our jobs are less technical, perhaps we should go through a mental checklist before we turn the switch.

But, by far the biggest cause of accidents is personal factors—you're hopelessly in debt, your teenager is troubling you, your marriage is on shaky ground, your boss makes you feel insecure on the job, you're worried about your health. All of these feelings can cause you turmoil and preoccupation at work. When your mind is 1,000 miles away, an accident happens right where you're standing.

We cannot escape personal problems or eliminate them from our lives. But instead of running to your job, flustered and preoccupied, take a few minutes to bring things into perspective. Plan to arrive at work a few minutes early and take those moments to talk to yourself before you enter. Say to yourself, "I can't do one thing about my problems during the next 8 hours, but I can add to my problems if I carelessly have an accident; so my job is to operate my machine carefully and safely today." A brief moment to clear your head before starting your job may prevent a tragic accident that would only compound your problems. Take a moment to care about yourself.

We all enjoy the enthusiastic person. But, have you ever noticed that sometimes the higher one can fly, the farther one can fall? Mood swings can carry an individual from the heights of joy to the depths of depression.

There is no question about moods. Even nature has moods, why else do we have summer and fall, winter and spring? Without varying moods, life would be boringly bland. While we admire the stability and control of the Bjorn Borgs of this world, we find them a bit colorless; and while we denounce the antics and tantrums of the John McEnroes, we enjoy the spice they add.

The question is not whether we have moods, but if we control them. Let's look at the causes of our moods:

1. Personal Temperament—We have all seen families with children miles apart in behavior. Moods may reflect the intellectual level of the individual or circumstances of birth. Our minds may determine whether we are ruled by fact or feeling. The discipline we received as children may establish how controlled or wild we are.

2. Physical Causes—Perhaps you have noticed drastic changes in someone you've known for years and remarked that he or she is not the person you used to know. Sometimes we notice change in a person before they are aware of it themselves. Or perhaps, the individual is aware of their illness, but tries to cover it up and ends up falling into the pit of irritability and despondency. The YMCA views man as a combination of body, mind and spirit. If these are out of harmony with one another, trouble results.

3. Failure—Despair is incubated by defeat and self-condemnation. Failure causes us to feel isolated, believing that we and we alone have had to cross this particular bridge. Failure, while not to be taken lightly, should not destroy the individual.

We cannot be blamed for our basic nature and dominant attitudes. But, we can strive to rise above them and learn to control our moods.

I never promised you a rose garden." We have all heard that verse from a popular song.

Roses are my favorite flower. I will make up almost any excuse to send some to my wife, so I can enjoy them as well. Even a gardening neophyte like myself knows that to grow roses you first have to select a variety compatible with your locale and climate. Then you have to plant the bushes, water them, feed them, spray them and tend them. There are beautiful wildflowers, but roses take effort.

The same is true of our lives. Many things happen automatically or accidentally, but others take effort. There is so much good about America, we can lull ourselves into thinking that good jobs, good business, good incomes happen automatically. But the good life we have come to expect takes effort. Groping our way, as a nation, out of periods of inflation or recession or unemployment takes effort; it takes effort to work smarter; it takes effort to produce more; it takes effort to increase quality. With effort, we can preserve the flower of our way of life.

My immigrant father let me know early in life that America promised me not a rose garden, but the privilege of planting roses—and that is the excitement of work.

I helped build the cathedral! I helped build the cathedral!", was the cry of a little girl crushed in the throng for the dedication of the Cathedral of Milan. One of the guards standing by in a handsome uniform, irritated by her shouts demanded, "Show me what you did." She replied with pride, "I carried the dinner bucket to my father while he worked on the spires."

The little girl taking credit for building the Cathedral of Milan because she carried her dad's dinner bucket is a little farfetched. It goes under the heading of "We killed a bear." Still I guess it is good to find a child knowing there are responsibilities that must be assumed.

We do have a "responsibility crisis." A few years back I thought the crisis was people refusing responsibility, and there is much of that. However, I believe the crisis today is more people not giving each other credit for the responsibility they do assume. Really I can't understand our insecurity, but it seems we need recognition to such an extent we can't share credit with others or give accolades that are richly deserved. We are card carrying grandstand members who yell loudly in victory, but in losses, we harshly second guess as Monday morning quarterbacks.

When we fail to turn loose of responsibility we compound our problems. We must take the weight of potential failures for performances others did. It is much safer to give responsibility and corresponding authority. The authority gives incentive to the person you're counting on. Yet, it is an indication of trust. To always look over the other person's shoulder keeps you from doing your work, plus it gives you a headache from tired eyes. People, fellow workers, our children, will let us down but I believe they will let us down less when they have the responsibility of trust.

Also, I question the attitude of "He let me down." Maybe the one given responsibility doesn't let down anymore than the one giving responsibility. There is the old adage, "If you're going to complain about the way the ball bounces, don't drop it."

A fail-safe operation is only an idealist's dream. The human equation is fraught with failures no matter how conscientious. I believe failures are minimized in direct proportion as we trust in the competence of others and realize that carrying the dinner bucket is a responsibility to be appreciated and rewarded.

The way you praise others tells what you think of yourself. Whether you praise or criticize your fellowman, it is a reflector telling how you evaluate yourself. The self-centered can't praise sincerely for they are too wrapped up in themselves to observe the praise-worthy qualities of others. Any compliment from the self-centered is an effort to bait for praise of one's self.

The "put-down" comes naturally. Most of us have to fight being critical while praise has a cleansing and uplifting effect. Praise can awaken the sleeping. Praise can cause the careless to be concerned. Praise can make a winner out of a habitual loser. Praise moves the dissatisfied worker into a happy performer. Praise helps children to be well-adjusted, teenagers to feel secure, and adults to be worthwhile.

Praise is not only for those who accomplish the good but also for those who sincerely try with all they have.

Dr. Thomas Tutko of San Jose State University tells of a fascinating experiment. He took five groups of twenty-five boys, ages thirteen and fourteen. Each of the hundred twenty-five lads was asked to run a fifty-yard dash a number of times over several days. He reports group one was the control group: "I didn't say anything to them. Group two was criticized constructively. Group three was criticized and then told they did well. Group four was told they did well and then criticized. Group five was not criticized at all—they were only told they did well and were praised.

"Group five that was only praised did the best. The more they were praised, the better they ran. The groups we criticized—even mixing it with praise—actually became discouraged and ran slower."

What works on children usually works on us. As adults we can take constructive criticism, but it must be smothered with praise.

Let's look for good things in others to praise. Let's praise the honest effort even if it leaves a little to be desired. About the time we get ready to criticize, let's stop and ask, "Have I praised this person in the past?"

Believe me, I've witnessed companies turned around by praise. I've seen employees who were previously at each other's throats work in harmony when one began to praise the other. Best of all, praise given has a cleansing and uplifting effect on the one doing the praising.

Are you successful? Being able to answer "yes" should not lessen our desire to be better, nor diminish our commitment to do things better today than we did yesterday. Here are several tongue-in-cheek rules for maximizing your effectiveness and efficiency:

1. Do the easy thing first. Don't face a problem when you can spend your time reading the latest publication. After all, you do want to be well read. If we keep doing the easy things, the day will be gone before we have to sweat out the tough ones. Remember, it's not how much you accomplish, but how busy you look.

2. Use the phone. The telephone is very personal, so be sure to ask about the family. Idle conversation is especially effective if you're calling long distance. After all, what's a few dollars between friends? Remember, all the time you spend on the phone keeps you from tackling your other work.

3. Be a paper shuffler. Never answer a letter, just move them from one pile to another, and never read a negative one. Maintain a clean desk by piling all the papers in a drawer at five o'clock and forgetting them. If someone pushes you for an answer, feel sorry for yourself and complain about the big pile of paperwork overwhelming you.

4. Delegate in order to escape. Delegation should carry authority, but it's better if you retain the possibility of "second guessing." If someone fails, blow the whistle; if they succeed, take credit for picking them for the job. That way, you either protect yourself or take the bows.

5. Write memos. When you're mad, but cowardly, when you're afraid of the unpleasant, write a memo and leave it on the person's desk after they leave for the day.

6. Be suspicious. Spend a lot of time wondering whether the employees like you or not. Read something negative into every gesture or re-action. Make the good employee ineffective by withdrawing your support.

7. Survive. Play it safe. If you don't make waves, you'll eventually outlast all the others and get a better job.

If you saw the humor in this reverse list of rules and vow not to follow any of them, there may be hope for you.

There is a bit of wit and wisdom in the warning that if we don't judge ourselves, we'll be left for others to judge. While partially true, others will probably judge us no matter what we do. Yet, judging ourselves can become preventive medicine—the best defense is a good offense, if we don't let it make us offensive.

How do we go about judging ourselves and adopting a plan of self-improvement? If you begin by making yourself more likeable to yourself, then it follows that others will like you better. I am not advocating vanity, but here are some suggestions for self-evaluation:

1. Take a moment and actually write down what you consider to be your strengths. What do you do best on the job? Why should management consider you valuable? Why should people enjoy working with you? How interested are you in others; how complimentary; how supportive? What can and do you contribute to another employee's life?

2. Just as honestly, list your weaknesses. Don't be afraid of them; they won't go away by ignoring them. List the areas of your life where you feel insecure. Spell out your embarrassments and list your hurts—you will see how ridiculous some now appear and laugh at yourself for being so oversensitive. Do you talk too much and have trouble listening? Are you too self-centered to be sympathetic? Do you feel mistreated at work; does the boss put you down? Do other employees receive more favorable treatment? Do you feel guilty because you've gossiped about someone?

3. Having honestly worked through your strengths and weaknesses, now is the time to adopt some immediate and short-term goals. One goal may be to get more sleep each night so that you're more rested, in turn improving your disposition. Another goal may be to turn that person you haven't liked into a warm friend. You may want to begin a new hobby to give yourself better relaxation on the job. You may decide to spend more time with your children and, surprisingly, be nurtured by their love.

We won't improve ourselves overnight or without effort, but an honest and aggressive plan will lead to a better tomorrow and a better you. You be the judge.

Can one single person make a difference in this world? If we doubt this, it is not so much a matter of not caring, as it is honestly feeling there is nothing we alone can do.

Historian Arnold Toynbee claims, "Apathy can only be overcome by enthusiasm, and enthusiasm can only be aroused by two things: First, an ideal that takes the imagination by storm; second, a definite intelligible plan for carrying that ideal into practice."

The ideal that takes your imagination by storm, hopefully, will be an acceptance whereby you begin a process of living a good life before family, fellow employee, community. That is the heart of the ideal. The hands of the ideal are implemented when you think of one person—a fellow worker, a teenager on your block—but zero in on one person.

You may feel your place of work lacks warmth and happiness or the employees aren't producing as much as they could be. You can change this for the better. Go to work with a smile; be pleasant to the worst grouch. Most of all, set the example of good, honest work.

You can make a difference. William James, the father of American psychology, suggested, "If you want quality, act as if you already had it." This works on you personally, it works on the friend or neighbor you want to help, it works at your place of work.

You can make a difference. Robert P. Spitzer said, "Individual excellence and enterprise are America's greatest strengths. Too often, in this day of centralization, uniformity and conformity, the power of the individual has been overlooked."

Don't overlook your own power to make a difference—in your life and the lives of others.

Reprimanding someone can be the most difficult task we face in our jobs. As managers and supervisors, we cannot escape this unpleasant chore, but there are right ways to go about it.

Dr. George S. Odiorne, in his book "How Managers Make Things Happen," lists his "seven deadly sins of reprimanding" which might be useful guidelines in your own organization:

1. Failing to get the facts. Never reprimand an employee before you have all the facts. And make sure you have facts, not rumors, hearsay, or general impressions.
2. Acting while angry. If you reprimand while angry you'll lose perspective, objectivity and, thus, effectiveness. Always ask yourself, "Could it be my fault that this problem occurred?"
3. Being unclear about the offense. It is not enough to allude generally to the charge. Be specific and be prepared to provide details.
4. Failing to get the other side of the story. There may be mitigating circumstances underlying the problem. You'll never get the full story unless you are able to listen to what the other person has to say.
5. Backing down when you are right. Just as bad as jumping to false conclusions is not sticking to your guns once you have examined dispassionately and concluded you are right to reprimand. You'll lose your effectiveness if you go against your own principles.
6. Failing to keep records. You'll want to keep a record of all reprimands so that you can document the employee's work history if the problems continue and dismissal proves necessary.
7. Harboring a grudge. Once the reprimand is given, let it go. Holding on to your displeasure will benefit neither you nor your employee.

These cautions should help you with the unpleasant task of reprimanding someone. If reprimanding doesn't bother you, then you've really got trouble.

Being married to a success-oriented business executive is no easy job. Some view the situation as a husband-wife-job triangle, with the job having equal position with the spouse. Others see things in terms of a tug-of-war, with the employee being pulled from opposite sides by spouse and job. Recruiter R.J. Wytmar has these suggestions to companies in trying to regulate the lives of their employees outside of work:

1. Don't play God. Any attempt to set up a standard of conduct for the employee's spouse will only complicate your evaluation or promotion of the employee. There is no ideal employee. Each has strengths and weaknesses so every selection is a compromise of a sort. So, there is no ideal spouse either from the employee's standpoint or the company's. Each has pluses and minuses, but if the employee is pleased . . . that's what counts.
2. Respect the privacy of marriage. It is imperative for the employee that their marriages not be the subject of company trial or scrutiny.
3. Avoid command performances. Companies enjoy knowing the spouses, but should not make the spouses feel on parade at company functions. If the spouse is made uncomfortable, the employee will be too.
4. Encourage involvement. It sounds contradictory but let the spouse know you want their support and knowledge of the employee's work. This is genuine involvement as opposed to using the spouse for company gain.
5. Permit natural growth. Give the spouse time to appreciate the company and hopefully develop the same loyalty as the employee. Company thoughtfulness toward spouses can create a desire to motivate the employees upward.

Some employees rise above their spouse's goals, and companionship is lost. Some employees succeed despite their spouses. The company must tread softly, for no matter which way it goes, marriage is a private affair—not company policy.

My generation was raised on the principle: "Children are to be seen and not heard." Today's youth are to be heard no matter what. The result is that everybody is talking now and no one is listening.

As adults we should set the example by being good listeners. This is an open invitation to our children to discuss problems with us instead of their peers or the neighbor next door. Sometimes we think we know our kids well enough to read their minds—we think we know what they're feeling and thinking even before they voice it. Maybe we'll find by listening we're not as smart as we think.

When we urge our children to confide in us, we're not talking about the "buddy-buddy" system. Age does present problems but we are there to guide them in the right direction.

There are some principles which encourage listening:

1. Don't put your children down automatically. They come to us not to be judged or criticized, but to be understood. If she breaks up with her boyfriend, you don't comfort her by saying "You're better off without him," or, "I never did think he was a good date for you." Much better to say, "Honey, I know it hurts that he hasn't called." This opens the door for a rewarding conversation for both of you.

2. Don't constantly define right and wrong. The children know this. That's why they're uptight. Knowing something is wrong doesn't relieve the desire to do it anyway. Letting them talk will usually lead them to accept the less exciting right instead of the temporary thrill of the wrong.

3. If you are secure as a parent, you find it no threat to say, "You may be right." A parent acting like he has all the answers reduces his image. "I don't know" is often a sign of wisdom.

4. Be cautious with sarcasm. The sensitive teenager is wounded by a sneer or by making fun of their choice of expressions. A sarcastic effort to put them down only diminishes us.

The golden rule works in listening too. Listen to your children as you desire your children to listen to you.

Having peace is more than just not having war. The United States is not at war, but would you say we are peaceful? Peace is an inner quality. Peace is a personal discovery and accomplishment.

I don't know Gertrude M. Puelicher but I appreciate her testimony. She writes:

> Are you searching for the peace that passeth understanding? The peace that the Nazarene carpenter told his disciples he was leaving with them? The peace that he designated as "my peace"? He differentiated between the peace the world gives and "my peace." You may remember that he comforted them with those loving words, "Let not your heart be troubled, neither let it be afraid."
>
> And that word "afraid" should remind you at once of God's promise as found in the book of Isaiah. "Fear thou not; for I am with thee: be not dismayed; for I am thy God: I will strengthen thee; yea, I will uphold thee with the right hand of my righteousness." If we would find peace, we must take that promise literally and rest in it. We can rest in it with assurance if we will but remember Paul's comforting words to Timothy whom he loved dearly: "For God hath not given us the spirit of fear; but of power, and of love, and of a sound mind."
>
> If you are earnestly searching for peace, then you must accept these promises, not alone with your mind but with your whole being. An intellectual acceptance is variable. It is too subject to change. An emotional acceptance has no endurance value. Like most emotional reactions it lacks permanency. The only practical acceptance is a spiritual one because when the Spirit within takes possession of our entire being, our personal world is awakened to the power of spiritual truth. Then as realization sets in, spiritual peace automatically results.
>
> Peace lies in our accepting the Omnipresence and Omnipotence of God as the only law governing our lives. However, and again I emphasize, mere intellectual acceptance is not sufficient. It is open to argument. We must live in obedience to that law by making it the dominating force of our existence. We must learn to live and move and have our being in God, in Spirit, in the Father within. He who will perfect that which concerneth us. Then will we be under the constant government of Omnipresence and Omnipotence. Then we will have attained the peace that passeth understanding.

War may be the easiest battle to stop. The struggles that polarize man can only be solved by people who can live with themselves for they have let God bring peace to their hearts.

Who is the boss of your business? The answer to this seemingly foolish question is of vital importance to both employers and employees.

We need to understand who the *real boss* of America's business is. Who is the boss? The founder of the business? No! The president? Not really! The general manager? The director of operations? The various department heads? No, none of these!

I am the boss of your business. I am the reason for this business and the reason for its prosperity. I am its guiding genius. I do more to promote and raise wages, to hire and fire than any executive. I must be served before I bestow my blessing. I am the alpha and omega. I am everything connected with the business. I am the foundation of its progress. I am its master because I am its patron—I am your customer!

Yes, when you get right down to it, the customer *is* the boss of any given business. What the customer buys and what the customer accepts makes your business succeed or fail. We need to constantly remind ourselves that a product is successful only when it is bought, not when it is manufactured. Goods are only good when they are sold.

If you produced a bad product, would you buy it? Neither would anyone else. If you purchased a flawed garment, would you return it to the store? So will another shopper who buys a piece of bad goods. If you brought home some fruit that was soft and squashed, wouldn't you return it to the supermarket? Of course!

You are no different from the people who buy your products or services; no different from the customers who shop in your store. They want the same things. They expect value for their dollar. They expect good service.

You see, we must keep in mind that a business is really run by the people who do the buying. The customer controls what we do, how successful we are, and even what we cannot do, as well.

We must guard against becoming so very busy that we forget the *customer*, who, after all, is the boss in a free market system.

There's more to healing than medicine . . . although I share your gratitude for every miracle drug that is introduced. Textile magnate John Hamrick has dedicated the resources of The Fullerton Foundation to seeking and training medical students who are committed to direct service to the patient. It has been rewarding serving as chairperson of the selection committee to interview these young people and witness their zealous compassion. They are dedicated to going head-to-head with their professors so, when trained, they can go heart-to-heart with patients.

It reminds me of the missionary doctor, seeing patients pass by a hospital enroute to his clinic. "Why didn't you save yourself the extra journey by stopping at the hospital?" the doctor inquired.

"You have different hands than they," came the reply.

Years ago in my own city I remember visiting the elderly mother of a friend. I asked her how she was feeling and she responded, "Here, here," and kept tapping her forehead.

I said, "Oh, Dear, I'm sorry you are experiencing a headache."

She replied, "Here, here."

Not understanding, I asked, "Are they going to have to do some surgery?"

Finally it came out when she said, "Here, right here," as she pointed again to her forehead, "is where Dr. Woody kissed me."

Yes, her doctor, Woodrow Tyson, knew that healing is more than textbooks and vials of medicine.

We're not doctors, but we may possess some healing qualities. In seeking the health of others the reward is the energy that throbs through us. Your medical kit may be just a phone call, a handwritten note, a few words of praise . . . or even a smile.

This excellent definition of freedom, entitled "Freedom Is Simple," was published some time ago by the *Louisville Courier-Journal*:

Freedom is a man lifting a gate latch at dusk and sitting for a while on the porch before he goes to bed. It is the violence of arguments outside election polls; it is the righteous anger of the pulpits. It is the warm laughter of a girl on a park bench. It is the rush of a train over the continent and the unafraid faces of people looking out the windows. It is all the "howdys" in the world and all the "hellos." It is YOU, trying to remember the words to "The Star-Spangled Banner." It is the sea breaking on wide sands somewhere and shoulders of a mountain supporting the sky.

It is the air you fill your lungs with, and the dirt that is your garden. It is the absence of apprehension at the sound of approaching footsteps outside your closed door. It is your hot resentment of intrigue, the tilt of your chin, and the tightening of your lips sometimes. It is all the things you do and want to keep on doing. It is all the things you feel and cannot help feeling. Freedom? It is YOU!

Describing freedom may be simple; preserving freedom may be more difficult. One researcher, looking across the span of mankind's history, concluded that there were nine evolutionary steps in the rise and inevitable collapse of a free society: (1) from chains of slavery, people rise to spiritual faith; (2) from spiritual faith, they generate courage; (3) from courage, they forge liberty; (4) from liberty comes abundance; (5) from abundance arises selfishness; (6) from selfishness, then to complacency; (7) from complacency to apathy; (8) from apathy, people degenerate to dependency; and (9) from dependency, back to bondage.

Preserving our basic freedoms in today's world takes a special kind of man and woman—individuals who are not for sale; people who are honest, sound from center to circumference, true to the heart's core; those with conscience as steady as the needle to the pole; men and women who will stand for the right if the heavens totter and the earth reels; individuals who can tell the truth and look the world right in the eye; people who neither brag nor run, flag nor flinch, who can have courage without shouting it, in whom the courage of everlasting life runs still, deep and strong; those who know their message and tell it; men and women unafraid to say "No" with emphasis and unashamed to admit, "I can't afford it."

If this modern era were nicknamed, it could well be called the "Age of Mental Stress." The pace and pressures of our lives seem to overburden our minds. And yet, life is not meant to be mean and miserable—it is meant to be lived well and happily. We are not meant to drink only of sorrow and pain, doubt and fear—we are meant to look forward to progress, to anticipate the new, to love greatly and laugh often, to share happily, to sing softly and cry with joy, to live life with meaning.

The true key to successful living is to control our minds and master our emotions, directing them to our benefit and not our destruction. Each of us has the power within ourselves to control our thoughts, our minds and our lives. We cannot live uncontrolled lives and still live constructively.

Such control is not as simple as it might appear. Many of us do not control our own minds. We all have witnessed strong, determined individuals with everything going for them fall under the weight of seemingly insignificant mental difficulties. We have seen fine people suffer mental torment because they have turned little despairs into mountains of defeat. And we have watched others give their minds to habits that will eventually destroy them—to alcohol, drugs and sensual pleasures that never bring real satisfaction!

What we dwell on in our minds comes out in our actions and behavior. As the Bible says, "As a man thinketh in his heart, so is he." Thoughts which pass through our minds and are gone cause no damage; those that remain trapped inside end up causing torment and despair. You *can* make a conscious decision to be happy. Abe Lincoln, with his rustic wisdom, stated, "Most people are about as happy as they make up their minds to be."

Napoleon Hill lists a dozen great riches of life that make worthy goals for all of us: "(1) A positive mental attitude; (2) sound physical health; (3) harmony in human relationships; (4) freedom from fear; (5) hope of achievement; (6) a capacity for fairness; (7) willingness to share one's blessings; (8) a labor of love; (9) an open mind on all subjects; (10) self discipline; (11) the capacity to understand people, and (12) financial security."

We must either use our will to master our minds and become servants of worthy goals, or our minds can be enslaved to destructive habits. Controlling your mind will bring you confidence.

Once a record is written, it remains forever written. This is one of the inexorable truths of our information-oriented society. Interested as I am in young people, I am particularly concerned about those who break the law—not only because the law was broken, but because of the penalty young people must carry with them the rest of their lives. Some time ago, the *Savannah* [Ga.] *News* carried this account of a judge counseling a young offender:

Because you have no previous conviction, I am permitted to give you parole; but if you never see the inside of a penitentiary, you will not have escaped the penalties of your crime. The record of your conviction will be here as long as the courthouse stands. Think of this, young people, the conviction record will be there as long as the courthouse stands. No amount of good conduct in the future can erase it. If you are ever called to witness in any court, some lawyer will point his finger at you and ask, "Have you ever been convicted of a felony?" The question will be asked with the purpose of casting doubt on your testimony; convicted felons are not believed as readily as other persons.

It may be that someday you will apply for a passport to go to some foreign country. You will not get it. No country will allow you to become a resident. Someday you may seek a position in the Civil Service. You may want to take a position of trust where a surety bond is required. On the application will appear this question, "Have you ever been convicted of a felony?"

In a few years, you will be 21 and others your age will have the right to vote. You will not. You will be a citizen of your state and country, but you will have no voice in public affairs. Your country is calling men to the colors, but the Army will never accept you, nor will the Navy. You may serve your country in the labor battalion, perhaps, but never behind guns. Yours may be the drudgery of war, but never the honor that comes to a soldier.

I am granting you a parole. A parole is in no sense a pardon. You will report to the men who have accepted your parole as often as they may ask. Should the slightest complaint of your conduct reach this court, your parole will be revoked immediately. You will not be brought back here for questioning or for explanations; you will be picked up and taken to prison without notice to you and without delay.

Advice on rearing children is not scarce. Usually such counsel tells us how to be good to our children. Every family has to develop its own lifestyle. We, for instance, are big on family conferences where we all sit together and level our complaints, criticisms or explanations of rulings.

Quite often I suggested to my children that since we would guide their destinies, at least until they were eighteen, that they could be smart and make the best of it.

Let me make some suggestions to young people who read *Today:*

1. Spoil your parents a bit. They aren't as young as they once were. Save them some steps by closing the door behind you—easy. Keep your own room—clean. Hang your clothes for neatness and long wear. Put dirty clothes in the hamper.
2. Don't pout. This undermines your parents' self confidence. Somebody has to be confident. Pouting puts forth your worst appearance and just cements the opposition to your desires.
3. Don't do idiotic things in public. One hand in the candy bowl is enough. Don't have a head-on collision with the grocery carts. Don't pull the can at the bottom of the stack. Must you keep saying, "When do we eat?" or "Let's go" when you just got there.
4. Listen to your parents. You're not quite as smart as you think. Sure, you have to learn something for yourself, but why not profit from your parents' experience? You can become "doubly smart" this way.
5. Try to answer by the third time your parents ask you a question. They may actually consider your answer valuable.
6. Tell your parents when something important happens to you. They might spill the coffee if they hear it secondhand from the neighbors. If what happens is good, let them burst with pride—after all, they have seen you at your worst.
7. Don't expect parents to reason with you all the time. The love your parents have given you should let you be assured they are acting in your best interest.

Most of all, parents have a right to their own lives. They are to love you but your desires are not to guide their every move. Your real importance is how you fit into the family puzzle to make it a complete, visible picture.

In every level of communication, there is a two-way street. We have been busy making parents feel guilty. Good parents generally produce good kids.

E ach time I visit London, I am disappointed and saddened to recall that only 1 percent of the population attends church or synagogue on any given weekend. In the early days of World War II, when London was being blitzed and living under a state of siege, an article appeared in the British press and was widely quoted on this side of the Atlantic. Though separated by time and geography, it may be worthwhile for us to take note of this compelling statement:

We have been a pleasure-loving people, dishonoring God's day, picnicking and bathing. Now the seashore is barred—no picnics, no bathing.

We have preferred motor travel to churchgoing; now there is a shortage of motor fuel.

We have ignored the ringing of church bells calling us to worship; now the bells cannot ring except to warn us of invasion.

We have left our churches half empty when they should have been filled with worshippers; now they are in ruins.

. . . The money we would not give to the Lord's work is now being taken away from us in higher taxes and cost of living.

. . . The service we refused to give God is now conscripted for our country.

. . . Lives we refused to live under God's control are now under the nation's control . . .

Europe's "continental Sunday" has now immigrated to the United States. Every Sunday is regarded as a holiday by many, many Americans, including distressing numbers of church members.

Do we really think we are smart enough to escape the folly of disregarding the Lord's day? We must not forget or ignore the Fourth Commandment. We must put God first in our lives now.

Achieving maturity means we have dedicated the biggest chunk of our lives to finding out how little we really know about life and ourselves. It's no wonder we feel youth is wasted on the young and wish we had the energy of years gone by. While we cannot recapture the past, we can contribute to the future.

Although aging robs us of youthful energy, some of us still stumble trying to step over our childishness. Here are some qualities of maturity that we didn't have in our youth:

1. Patience. In our youth, we said, "I want it now." As adults, we realize that instant gratification would keep us from enjoying our desires. The struggle or pursuit of goals nearly equals the reaching of them. As adults, we can look back as well as ahead, giving us a balanced perspective. With that mature perspective, we see the wisdom of denying ourselves some immediate pleasures in order to achieve lasting goals.

2. Calmness. In our youth, we fidgeted and couldn't keep still, burning up energy. Life was filled with highs and lows; we flared with temper; we overpromised in performance. As adults, we now see how restrained temper becomes added energy in the boiler of our beings. We accept life's highs and lows, realizing it keeps life from becoming monotonous.

3. Empathy. In our youth, we got emotionally distraught with our friends, crying and laughing together. As adults, we not only cry, but in a practical way try to relieve the burden so our friends may smile again.

4. Courage. In our youth, we had audacity, we bragged and, just as quickly, ducked away. As adults, we accept causes bigger than ourselves, feeling it is better to fail in a worthy cause than succeed in our emotional impulses.

5. Cooperation. In our youth, we went along to be one of the gang or we acted independently to prove ourselves. As adults, we cooperate because we are the family of men; such cooperation doesn't cause us a loss of identity, but indicates personal security.

6. Dependability. In our youth, we were starters, walking away from what we didn't like or what bored us. As adults, we are finishers—we make mistakes, but we work to make our mistakes good.

We're no longer young, but we may wonder if we have yet reached maturity according to these criteria. Hopefully, we don't think we have arrived, but are well on our way.

As I sit in airports waiting for planes, I enjoy watching people. At times it depresses me a little for I see so few people who are smiling. Of course, you can't smile all the time, but I see people who seem so tense and tired, I hurt for them. Still, how do you escape tension with all the problems of today?

My pastor friend, Dr. Harley Williams, wrote it well to his congregation:

Tension is the explanation of a multitude of ills. Only a few people live inwardly relaxed lives, but most of us exist in an attitude of "quiet desperation." The casualty list is long. William Muldoon, famous athletic trainer said: "Men do not die of disease but of internal combustion."

Some measure of tension is necessary. Loose violin strings will not play. But there is a difference in alertness and excessive strain. One is creative, another destructive. So many feel that they are all run down when the truth is they are all wound up. It is not the amount or kind of work we do, but the way we do it that really counts. What tires us is not work but strain. Some people, blessed with a physique and temperament to stand a lot, can take more than others.

You and I will never learn to have peace of mind or reach our fullest potential until we have learned, in Stevenson's words, "to set loosely in the saddle of life."

A good deal of strain is an unwillingness to accept situations that are beyond our control. We stubbornly resist things that we cannot change, and such resistance leads to inner stress. We must live flexible lives, letting God guide us. Our plans are often frustrated and delayed. I used to think people were just being pious when they would say, "The Lord willing." Not so anymore. One doesn't have to keep saying those words but he should keep thinking them.

The Psalmist (37th) testifies: "I have been young and now am old, yet I have not seen the righteous forsaken or his children begging bread." Jesus said in words that are radiant with trust, "Look at the birds of the air; your Heavenly Father feeds them. Consider the lilies of the field; if God so clothes the grass of the field, will He not much more clothe you?"

In a day when financial security is a goal after which we fret and strain, we need to relax and remind ourselves that our anxieties are only reflections of our lack of faith. In the end our very lives and all we possess are in the hands of God. How much wiser we are when we admit it, and let faith rule our hearts!

These are testing times, and I am disturbed that so many are flunking the test. Peace is internal, a gift offered by God.

Dealing with customers can be a challenge or a chore, depending on outlook and attitude. There are customers who take advantage of you and it must gall you to have to placate them. But remember, when you are bending in every direction to satisfy the customer, you are getting what you want—a sale. Secure individuals can humble themselves, while the insecure are sensitive and defensive.

If you serve customers and wait on people in your work, take comfort. At other times, when you are shopping, you are on the other side of the counter. Perhaps the Golden Rule applies here—treat the customer exactly as you want to be treated when you are buying.

Here are some reminders that might serve as a good attitude refresher:

- A customer is the most important person in any business.
- A customer is not dependent on us; we are dependent on him.
- A customer is not an interruption of our work; he is the purpose of it.
- A customer does us a favor when he comes in; we are not doing him a favor by serving him.
- A customer is part of the business, not an outsider.
- A customer is not a statistic; he is a flesh-and-blood human being with feelings and emotions, like ourselves.
- A customer is a person who comes to us with his needs or his wants; it is our job to fill them.
- A customer is deserving of the most courteous and attentive treatment we can give.
- A customer is the lifeblood of this and every other business; without him we would have to close our doors.

If you have children in college, here is a witty, as well as thought-provoking, essay on the traits of a good roommate, paraphrasing First Corinthians:

Though I speak in language of Browning and Shakespeare, and have not love toward my roommate, I am becoming as a sounding drum or tinkling test tube.

And though I have the gift of a Phi Beta Kappa brain and understand the mysteries of Einstein, Eliot, Plato, and Niebuhr, and have an objective knowledge of chemical formulas, scientific hypotheses and historical phenomena; and though I have all the self-confidence and self-reliance to believe I can achieve anything, and have not love and understanding toward my roommate, I am nothing.

And though I have the innate gifts of a campus leader and understand the corporate needs of the student body, but fail to see the personal requisites of one who shares my room, it profits me nothing.

And though I bestow all my natural abilities on a dozen campus organizations, and though I give my time and energy indiscriminately to extra-curricular activities and do not love and consider my roommate, it profits me nothing.

And though I can preach in glowing terms of God's transcending love, and though I never reject an opportunity to make a speech at noonday devotions on Christian living, and though I give my strength eagerly to any and all activities of the Student Christian Association, and do not let love guide my relationship with my roomate, it profits me nothing.

We will conclude tomorrow . . .

Here is the continuation and conclusion of the guidelines for a good roommate, modeled after First Corinthians:

Love is patient and kind from morning until midnight. Love is not envious of a roommate's clothes, car or dates. Love does not "put on airs" regarding family, fortune, scholastic achievement or campus popularity.

Love is not rude, no matter how small the dorm room, nor how long the hours of study the night before, nor how frustrating the events of the day.

Love values the rights of others, when friends come by for a midnight snack and my sleepy roommate has retired, or when I have to study late and my roommate finishes early. It turns down the volume of a favorite radio program when my studious partner is grappling with advanced calculus.

Love is not easily provoked, but cultivates understanding and restraint when disagreements occur, and love has the maturity to discuss these calmly at a discreet time.

Love is not resentful over collegiate honors, club awards, and campus responsibilities that bypass me and select my roommate, but it genuinely rejoices in every good thing. Love is sympathetic when things go wrong, exams are failed, funds are low or engagements are broken.

When you were a child, you thought, spoke and acted like a child; but now that you are a college student, you must put away immature actions.

Love never fails. It never fails to accept the other as a distinct personality, made in the image of God. It never fails to recognize the spiritual potential in another person for the fulfillment of God's purposes.

Love never fails to give its best in a friendship that grows, enriches, strengthens, and blesses your roommate and you!

We all probably tend to take our clergymen for granted, calling upon them in times of trouble and need, while otherwise excluding them from our thoughts. *The Messenger*, in an essay entitled "What I Owe My Pastor, Priest, Rabbi," offers some thought-provoking insights:

I owe him respect as the ambassador of God, sent to teach me a better way of living than the selfish, sordid existence I might be guilty of but for his guidance.

I owe him trust, that he may be free to serve the church unhampered by criticism and faultfinding.

I owe my pastor, priest or rabbi the protection of kindly silence by refraining from repeating, in his presence, the slander of unkind gossip that would worry him and keep him from doing his best.

I owe him prayer, that God may make his service a blessing to everyone with whom he comes in contact.

I owe him enough of my time to help in his work, wherever he may need me.

I owe him encouragement when vexation and annoyances make his work difficult.

I owe my pastor, priest or rabbi attention when I go to church or synagogue, that he may not be annoyed by seeing in my careless, inattentive actions that I am not interested in what he is saying.

"S omeday after we have mastered the wind, the waves, the tides and gravity, we will harness the energy of love: then for the second time in the history of the world, man will have discovered fire," wrote Teilhard de Chardin. Are we having a reevaluation of relationships to each other?

The family is being re-discovered, and so are neighbors and neighborhoods.

Whenever we say "friends" we distinguish from "family." This I consider a mistake. One of our troubles is that we take family for granted and assume they are friends, but we know better, don't we? Families must work at building friendships between the members.

Friendship is dependent upon believing in each other. This believing overlooks at times a bit of the shabby, the shoddy, and the shameful. We find it easy to be calculating, conniving, and cunning in our use of people. Friendship depends upon openness, compassion, and sympathy.

Real friendships span space and time. Friends don't come and go in our lives. We may have periods of time together and then be separated, but a person never comes into our lives and then leaves. The person leaving always leaves a bit of self behind.

The ground rules for friendship include: Don't take friends for granted. It is not enough to feel grateful for friendship inwardly. There must be moments when we express gratitude; there must be expressions of appreciation, courtesy, happiness, and just plain love. These acts of friendship are not only for friends we face eyeball to eyeball. Today might be the day to write a note to a distant state or make a long distance call. Even a friendship gift might be appropriate.

You might protest—real friends remain whether seen or unseen, contacted or uncontacted. True. You don't have to do deeds to preserve friendship but just because you value the person as a friend. However, your act of generosity may come at a time when your friend needs the lift your thoughtfulness can provide.

How fortunate I've been. My best friends have included my Grandfather Steere—my mother—my father—my children—and most of all, my wife Buren.

Boredom and regimentation are a state of mind—only you know if and why you are bored. Your job may look exciting to others, but to you it could be sheer boredom. And with boredom, come fatigue, depression and a loss of purpose.

The only prevention for boredom I know of is enthusiasm. That's "Catch-22" thinking, you say—if you were enthused you wouldn't be bored. The great American poet Walt Whitman claimed that he found himself and set himself free through enthusiasm.

Here are some tips to help rediscover the enthusiasm you once had in your work:

Stop feeling sorry for yourself. Don't deceive yourself into thinking everybody else has a fun job while yours is boring. That sort of jealousy and chafing may be what is keeping you from advancing in your job. Feeling sorry for yourself, you have placed yourself at the pinnacle of selfishness and your world has shrunk to the narrow dimensions of your own life. There are many who have it tougher, many with no jobs at all, many who cannot stand their jobs.

Define your goal and set a timetable for accomplishing it. Rather than being depressed over what you don't get, identify what you want and plan to reach. View your current job as a stepping stone to future opportunity. Goals put you on the spot and demand patience.

Don't waste time and energy regretting what didn't happen in the past. Don't run yourself down, learn from yesterday's failures and then forget about failure.

Gather together with enthusiastic people. Like wind-drafting in auto racing, using the speed of the car in front to pull you along, enthusiastic people can bolster your enthusiasm. Enthusiastic people are contagious; bored people only add to your problem.

Most of all, remember that enthusiasm means God is in you. When things are at their worst, keep in mind the psalm that says, "This is the day the Lord has made, I will rejoice and be glad in it."

E very morning lean thine arms a while upon the window sill of heaven, and gaze upon thy Lord, then, with the vision in thy heart, turn strong to meet the day," wrote Thomas Blake. Such is the essence of optimism.

The cynic may claim that optimism means hiding your head in the sand, avoiding the reality of the world around you. Actually, optimism is facing life and looking for the good side of things. Usually we find what we seek.

Ralph Waldo Emerson believed there was something stronger than any circumstances confronting us; that thoughts rule the world and that optimism results from positive thinking. The apostle Paul, writing to the Philippians, gave this basis for optimism—"Whatsoever things are true, whatsoever things are honest, whatsoever things are just, whatsoever things are pure, whatsoever things are lovely, whatsoever things are of good report: if there be any virtue, and if there be any praise ... think on these things."

We are the object of peer pressure in our social life. The same holds true of our thinking patterns—criticizing and condemning becomes the "in" thing to do. But, a good day is when you break through the walls of pessimism and see the good in each situation. You soon see colors hidden from most eyes, you hear music from the treetops, your menial tasks become fun. When you spend your mind and vision looking for good, your disposition changes and your optimism rubs off on those around you. The price of optimism is a willingness to volunteer your strength to correct what others see as bad.

The "puritan work ethic" is alive and well. This view may be a minority opinion since we hear many business leaders proclaim that "nobody wants to work anymore" and others conclude that "today's young people are just plain lazy."

There is no denying that today's generation works for different reasons than the previous generation. Generally, we are not as "hungry"; life is easier economically. Plus, political vote-getters, in league with pseudo-sociologists, have bribed the public by making it possible for able-bodied people to receive income without working for it. And superficial job security obtained by organized labor has made fringe benefits, vacations and retirement pay more important than job excellence.

Adding fuel to the problem, business has been unable to get its message across. As a result, big business is bombarded by the news media, in turn, causing employees to mistrust their employers and conclude that the company thinks only of making a profit—and too much profit, at that.

The company does not force boredom upon its employees—boredom arrived along with the Industrial Revolution. Mechanized work and assembly-line production are boring, but efficient and lucrative. Mechanized assembly work made America the leading industrial nation and raised pay to the point where 80 percent of us now think of ourselves as middle class. In return, we have come to view this labor-saving technological work with disdain and something done only for money. As a result, enthusiasm and loyalty are missing from the workplace.

Loyalty is something I need to practice for my own sake, whether or not my employer demands it. I must work where I have confidence in the company, in its management, in its products and services. Then I think of work as the revelation of myself, as the way I use my talents and skills. What I don't use, I lose, so I must work even if I could get by without working.

We all have trouble sleeping occasionally. At times, there may be a good reason for our restlessness; at other times, for no apparent reason, we cannot fall asleep. More and more research is being conducted on the process of sleep and, if a single phrase sums it up, it is, "If you have trouble getting to sleep and you're over 30, relax—you're normal." It might be reassuring to learn that sleeplessness is a normal aging process. Here are some other interesting findings:

- By the age of 45, most people awaken about three times during the night.
- As people grow older, they dream less and awaken without finishing the dream.
- In older age, the deepest sleep, or Delta sleep, tends to disappear.
- Studies show that good sleepers fall asleep within 7 minutes, while poor sleepers take at least 15 minutes to fall off.
- Poor sleepers tend to be more anxious, introverted and neurotic than good sleepers.
- Sixty-year-olds sleep longer than persons of any age between 20 and 60.
- Thin people sleep longer than fat ones.

Sleep is a complex process, a process of aging. No wonder the family doctor always asks how we are sleeping—it's more than idle conversation, sleep is essential to good health.

One of the most tragic mistakes our generation has made is the attitude we have instilled in our children toward education. We have made compulsory education sound as though our kids are doing something for their parents, rather than the other way around. We have made college students feel they are doing their parents a favor by attending.

More than a century ago, while Mark Hopkins served as president of Williams College in Massachusetts, a wealthy young student was caught defacing college property. Brought in to face the college president about criminal deeds, the cocky young man pulled out his checkbook to pay for the damages.

President Mark Hopkins stared into the youth's defiant eyes and said, "Young man, no student can pay for what he receives here. Can you pay for the sacrifice of Colonel Williams who founded the college? Can you pay for the devotion of half-paid professors who taught here in order that youths like you might have an education? Every man here is a charity case."

What a valuable lesson for every student to learn. Students who resent going to school should be aware how their parents struggle to make ends meet, paying higher taxes that make public education possible. College students should be aware that even after their parents have paid for tuition and board, that only amounts to one-third of the costs of educating them. The rest comes from taxes and gifts to state schools and totally from gifts and donations to private colleges.

Education is the finest illustration that our generation cares about its young people. No matter your wealth, race or creed, each of us is a charity case. You and I are debtors to all who believe in us and provide for us. Education is not a punishment—it is an open-ended invitation to a great adventure given to each of us at great sacrifice.

Today I honor you who are willing to accept the loneliness of leadership. Harry Truman talked about the loneliness when you accept the premise that "The buck stops here."

Back in pastoral days I recall a member saying, "Pastor, I'll try to do better each Sunday. I'll make my pledge and pay it, but I don't want any office or leadership responsibility in the church. I just want to be a member." Many of you who are leaders feel that way at times, don't you? You wish you could be just a regular employee and not shoulder leadership decisions and responsibilities.

You who are very conscientious worry lest a part of your problems result from not leading as forcefully as you wish. Let me make three suggestions about leadership:

1. Use your personality. A key to success is communication. Your communication strength is when you do it naturally at work. One executive lamented, "Industry teaches foremen how to fill out forms, not how to lead." If you lack confidence, you become uptight and that stilts your personality. Let your communication be the essence of yourself, the total of your qualities. The basis for such naturalness is when you don't "cop out" by saying, "They want it," but state firmly and kindly, "We've decided."

2. Keep your humor. The value of humor in interpersonal relationships has been proven again and again. Humor can create goodwill. Humor can bring people together. Humor can calm unruly tempers and take the sting out of rebuke. Of course, I mean humor that is not offensive and is kind.

3. Be friendly. The leader who stays aloof doesn't identify himself as a leader, but as an insecure person afraid of mixing, lest someone see through him. Develop the image and attitude that reveals you as a friend who is genuinely interested in employees and their problems.

As a leader, you may have been hired for your technical skills but more because of your ability to lead people. The loneliness of leadership is because you step out ahead . . . but people soon follow.

W hy do some people attract while others repel? Why are some people like a magnet while others are like a blowing fan? Is it because of physical attractiveness? I've met some handsome but repulsive snobs. I've met some well-mannered "blokes" as well as practical bores. There is no simple way to explain personal charm but there is a basic attitude.

When someone wants to be more attractive or desirable, we try to reform them or make actors out of them. We try to make them become someone completely different or we try to moderate them. Our advice would go something like this: "Refine your tastes, subdue your feelings, control your speech, dress more fashionably." The result—a non-entity. You meet that made-over person on a dozen corners. You've asked them to lose their peaks and valleys and become a flat plateau.

The basic to becoming alive and attractive is showing genuine interest in other people. You consider them as smart as you; you consider them as important as you; you let them know you know they are alive. You become a people-watcher, not to be nosy but to be more understanding. The resulting warmth makes you appealing.

What do you look at in your neighbor to better help him? You see what they value. What a man or woman buys can be an index to their character and needs. If they drive an expensive car and wear quality clothes, they enjoy the finer things and don't mind paying for them. If they are fine and gaudy, you know they are paying for attention. Those with the small car and less flair tell you they are practical and not as interested in impressions.

What do you know about the other person's hobbies—the books they read—the sports they enjoy? What about their faith—their religious life—their personal or family problems—their goals in life?

When you become interested in the other person, you are reaching out, and in most instances, they reach back. The most basic way to let people know you care is by showing a genuine interest in them.

Have your found yourself suddenly overeating or oversleeping, dropping hobbies or forgetting about exercise, having only perfunctory sex or meeting criticism with open hostility? Any of these signals could mean that you have gone sour on your job—you overeat, but the food tastes lousy; you oversleep as an escape, but aren't rested.

Job satisfaction is not an impossible dream. But first, we have to understand that job satisfaction does not mean that we like everything about our jobs. Part of being satisfied with your job actually comes from knowing that you have done well what you don't particularly enjoy. Like other emotions, irritation can be helpful if controlled and focused—it can charge you up.

To gauge whether or not your own job is good, you have to employ the "on-balance" method of measurement, comparing your job to other options. You know you cannot find the perfect job, but you want one that makes maximum use of your abilities and provides adequate financial rewards. Work can be a burden *or* it can be the way you provide for the family you love. Work can be tiresome *or* it can be the way you achieve respect in your community. Work can be depressing *or* it can be the means for achieving self-respect.

Here are some questions to ask yourself to help judge your job:

- Do you feel and act as though you're doing the company a favor by showing up?
- Do you feel that obvious company problems are management's fault and responsibility or do you try to help solve them?
- Do you withhold advice or suggestions because you feel it is none of your affair?
- Do you take advantage of every coffee break, adding a few minutes to each end?
- If a rush order was necessary, would you consider working through your break so you could feel you had really helped the company?
- Do you do exactly what you're told and no more, or do you go the extra mile, looking for more to do after you have completed the basic tasks?
- Are you careless and sloppy when you can get by with it?

When we begin to take our work for granted and forget to count our blessings, our job becomes boring. When that happens, instead of overeating or oversleeping, instead of ruining a marriage or becoming intolerable, we must look inside ourselves. The difference between a good job and a bad job is not the particular company or the work, but our attitude. Remember, one person just pounds nails while the other crafts furniture—the difference is attitude.

A determined man can do more with a rusty wrench than a loafer can do with all the tools in a machine shop," an author once wrote. Determination and ambition are the fuel of accomplishment.

Some 2,000 years ago, the Roman philosopher Cicero described six mistakes to avoid in the pursuit of personal accomplishment:

1. The delusion that personal gain is made by crushing others.
2. The tendency to worry about things that cannot be changed or corrected.
3. Insisting that a thing is impossible because we cannot accomplish it.
4. Refusing to set aside trivial preferences.
5. Neglecting development and refinement of the mind, and not acquiring the habit of reading and study.
6. Attempting to compel others to believe as we do.

Accomplishment in our lives is closely tied to human relations. As Don Laird said, "You will get much done if you crack the whip at yourself." Here are some important words to master in our pursuit of accomplishment:

- The six most important words—"I admit I made a mistake."
- The five most important words—"You did a good job."
- The four most important words—"What is your opinion?"
- The three most important words—"If you please."
- The two most important words—"Thank you."
- The one most important word—"We" and, by contrast, the least important word—"I."

Perhaps the finest blueprint for accomplishment are the words to a hymn by Howard Arnold Walter:

I would be true, for there are those who trust me,
I would be pure, for there are those who care;
I would be strong, for there is much to suffer;
I would be brave, for there is much to dare.
I would be friend of all—the foe, the friendless;
I would be giving and forget the gift.
I would be humble, for I know my weakness;
I would look up—and laugh—and love—and lift.

Former Maine Governor Kenneth M. Curtis gives this advice to young people entering business. He suggests hard work and sincerity and then adds, "There is really no magic formula for success. Perhaps the most important thing is not to worry about success, but to try to do things that are right. Always be honest and deal fairly with others."

In the years since World War II, we have probably placed too much emphasis on college credits and graduate business school training as the road to success. This overemphasis on formal education may delude the college graduate into thinking education is a key to entitlements or may brainwash those lacking a higher education into thinking they can never reach the top because of educational limitations.

What really is an education and what is an educated person? Educated men and women:

- Can rise above their prejudices and previous conclusions and maintain an open mind.
- Are willing to learn something new and don't view progress as a threat to their basic beliefs.
- Listen to all information given and seek additional facts to make decisions coolly and carefully.
- Don't laugh at another's ideas, seeing no threat in a new idea and feeling there can be a kernel of good in the wildest idea.
- Keep a card or notebook handy to record their daydreams and creative ideas when their minds are free-wheeling.
- Maximize their strong points and don't hide their weak points, knowing their strengths outbalance their frailties.
- Know what they can do and do it with pride.
- Know what they cannot do and are humble enough to ask others who can, rather than blunder through and hurt their company or cause.

In essence, the educated person believes in preparation, not luck; believes in discipline of good habits, not conniving; believes all things can be beautiful, not tarnished.

Have you ever considered the effect of a sincerely deserved compliment? Just saying the nice thing can turn another's day from gloom to sunshine.

Not long ago, I discovered one of the secrets of an old friend's graciousness. For more than two decades, I have shared a warm friendship with Mississippi banker Stanley Levingston. I have always been impressed with his capacity to lift my spirits with a kind word or deed. His mother died several years ago, and I later discovered her favorite poem, which helps explain Stanley's attitude when raised by a mother with this philosophy.

The living need the flowers that we strew upon the dead;
The flowers of human contact, the kind words to be said,
The handclasp given in silence, the touch upon the brow;
These priceless human blossoms—the living need them now!
How often those we cherished lie in the graveyard shade
Decked with those floral emblems which, oh, so quickly fade!
Who, while we had them with us, longed, had we only known
For more of the fadeless blossoms, in God's own garden grown.
The living need these daily, all through their years of life,
To ease the bitter heartache, to soothe amid the strife,
We may honor the lifeless body as we lay it under the sod,
But—it's what we owe the living that we answer for to God!

Today is your opportunity to give the compliment that could change someone's dreary day into one filled with sunshine. Try it—the giver is always more blessed than the receiver.

Gee, but all the other kids are getting to do it!" When was the last time your children used this high-pressure argument on you? Probably the very last time your kids wanted to do something they knew you felt was not best for them—and you knew that all the other kids were using the same argument on their parents. We think of this age-old ploy as childlike, but do we ever grow up? Or do we perhaps merely couch the argument in different terms?

In his book titled *Beggars in Velvet*, the late Dr. Carlyle Marney related the story of a group of boys from the so-called "best families"in his neighborhood. The boys broke more than 300 windowpanes in a new school building, were apprehended and held in custody. The judge asked a respected psychologist to interview each boy separately. To the surprise of all concerned, not a single boy approved of the vandalism they had committed as a group. Each boy stated with firm conviction that he knew breaking the windows was wrong, but he went along with the group because all the others approved of it.

We all, perhaps, know personally of a similar story. A new family moves into town, the youngsters fall in with a new gang of kids and, in order to be accepted, go against their sense of right and wrong. It can produce tragic consequences when our hopes of being popular hinge not on what we think of others, but on what others think of us.

We can at least understand, if not altogether excuse, young people going along with the crowd for the sake of acceptance. But what about you as an adult? Are you living a masquerade? Are you living beyond your means and falling deeper into debt to impress your neighbors? Do you complain about your job because everyone seems to gripe and you would feel awkward praising your employer? Do you drink too much just to be one of the gang? Do you criticize your spouse simply because someone else did, and it seems corny to say you love your mate? Do you wink at unfaithfulness because you fear that your own faithfulness will make you appear somehow less appealing? Do you laugh at filth and profane God because everybody else does?

The best way to make a lasting impression on others is to first please yourself—and your God. Respect and long-term relationships are built on integrity.

Charron wrote years ago:

> He who receives a benefit should never forget it;
> He who bestows should never remember it.

A couple of years ago the Horatio Alger Association honored Harry Gray as one of its recipients. Mr. Gray is retired chairman and chief executive officer of United Technologies. In being presented the award, he was correctly identified as "a legend in his own time," who's been on the cutting edge in giving our nation leadership in technology, especially as it relates to aircraft engines. In responding to the introduction, Mr. Gray made several points—or several approaches to the same theme—anything he had accomplished to make him deserve the award was because of the help he had received from others.

All of us have received help, so the real question is, have we taken time to say "thanks"? Who are the people that, at a crucial moment, put a hand on your shoulder, did you a favor, said a word of encouragement, stood by you when all others turned and fled? When is the last time that you thanked them? Chapter ten of my book, *How the Best Is Won*, begins with a story about Jack Twyman, chairman of Super Foods, Inc. He is recognized as taking a company that was literally bankrupt and making it as fine a performer as we have in the industry today. Maybe, however, I wasn't writing as much about Jack as I was about Brother Matthew. My publisher asked, "Who is Brother Matthew?" I replied that it wasn't important; he was just a teacher at Pittsburgh Central Catholic School, but he was more than that.

When Jack Twyman was cut three consecutive years from his basketball team, Brother Matthew took Jack and others who were cut and made a scrub team that played all the industrial teams in the Pittsburgh area, and prepared Jack to make the varsity in his senior year. More than making the team, he let Jack know there was not any reason to ever be intimidated again; he could, with extra effort, achieve his goals. It was Brother Matthew in the shadows who saw Jack Twyman become All-State with one year of experience; All-American at the University of Cincinnati; All-Pro for a decade, and a member of the Basketball Hall of Fame. Could Jack have made it without Brother Matthew? Who knows—but his teacher introduced him to that strange law—"strong resolution always attracts unknown resources." That's the same thing the person did who helped you and me. They simply turned the key that transformed the wall into a door.

So this is a good day to just say "Thank You" to persons who opened doors for us—if they're still living; or pause to memorialize them in our thoughts if they've gone on to be with God.

W hat is human life? What is your life? Being human isn't an excuse for indifference, but a challenge to strive for perfection. What is human life?

HUMAN LIFE is a grant, privilege and blessing created by a higher power that permits man to talk, think, act, lead, work, and engineer things for the good of mankind and the Heavenly Father. HUMAN LIFE is something a person cannot start or finish all by himself. Neither can we live without dealing with each other in giving and getting services and goods for a price as well as for those beyond price from a good neighbor or friend.

LIFE may find itself in four degrees of CITIZENSHIP. First, those who can and will do his share, carry his part of the load of his community, belong to all that he can and should, pay his bills, support his family, his church and ever extending a helping hand within the scope of ability and reason. This is a pretty good degree of CITIZENSHIP.

Secondly, there are those who would, if they could, do all that group one is doing if their means and abilities would permit. Their good attitude will some day cause them to move up the ladder into group one, and some of group one may slip down because of complacency.

In the third group, there are those who could and should be in the number one group but instead, because of selfishness, somehow want all the fun and all the wealth and forget the responsibility of CITIZENSHIP to those who have helped him first and possibly last—the ungrateful soul who has been successful at least to a point.

In the fourth group are those who truly never find themselves and who never seem to care about paying any rent for living and place no value on a soul at rest.

LIFE is a ladder that we are constantly climbing up or sliding down; and a good question for all of us today is, "Where am I and where am I headed on the ladder?"

Are we standing on the ladder where we could stand, or should stand, and does this have any relationship to the promise, "The first shall be last and the last shall be first"? Everyone is good enough to be FIRST in something worthwhile and not be FIRST in something below the base of the ladder that has no value in services or goods.

These excellent paragraphs are from an unknown author.
The gift is being God's highest creation. It is a privilege to be born and live. Our acceptance of responsibility indicates our gratitude and maturity.

Is your job paying off? You are making a living, but are you satisfied, do you feel your job is paying off? There are dividends, other than salary, that should result from your work.

If your job is paying off, the first and foremost dividend should be a *sense of accomplishment*. You need to feel that you are part of something worthwhile and that you are making a meaningful contribution. The Russian author Dostoevski wrote it well, "If you want to punish a man and punish him so severely that even the hardened criminal would quail, all you have to do is make his work meaningless."

A second dividend you should be receiving from your work is *pride*— pride in the place where you work, pride in your company's products or services, pride in your fellow employees.

Another dividend that some may question is *fun*. Your work should contain excitement and zest. Certainly, all of our jobs at times have portions that are boring, grinding and sheer drudgery. But if that's all you have, then your job is not paying off; if your work has no fun, you have to decide whether to change your job or your attitude.

An additional dividend is a *sense of belonging* or the feeling of teamwork. You feel important when you share common goals and achievements with others; your contribution multiplies through your fellow workers doing the same task.

A final dividend is the feeling of *growth*—growth as an individual, growth in skills and influence, growth in opportunities, growth in challenges.

If your work is not paying off, you face two possibilities—either upgrade your job through better performance or look for another job. The grass may appear greener elsewhere, but it might be more rewarding to change yourself rather than change jobs.

Be sure your sin will find you out" is one of the most misunderstood sentences in the Bible. It is not the threat that it first appears to be; it is not a warning that our wrongdoing will be discovered by others.

The cynic may claim that there are only two types of people—those who get caught and those who get away with it. The Biblical reference means not so much that others will find out about our sins, but that we will be found out by our errors. Being haunted by our own mistakes is among life's most painful experiences. When we are caught, we tend to defend ourselves or launch into self-justifying excuses. All that will do is make us miserable.

We need to ask ourselves basic questions about our own actions and behavior. Rotary International calls it a four-way test:

1. Is it the truth?
2. Is it fair to all concerned?
3. Will it build goodwill and better friendship?
4. Will it be beneficial to all concerned?

We might embellish these questions as we seek to analyze our own actions:

1. Does what I am about to do involve my best self? I am many people—I can be greedy and grasping, putting my own interest above all else; I can be angry and lustful; I can be casual and negligent. Or I can give my best moral self.
2. Will I have to keep what I do a secret? Secrets mean operating in the dark, and too much time moving about in the dark will eventually lead to a fall.
3. Where will this act lead me? Real problems usually begin with a seemingly insignificant decision—but a wrong minor decision can have the same effect as one drink to the alcoholic.

No weight we have to carry in this life will bend our backs and break our spirits like carrying guilt, burdened by the knowledge that our best self has been lost amidst our ambition. Strength comes from purity of thought and action.

Money is a curious thing. We all need it; we all think we never have enough of it. A modern novel set in the days after the stock-market crash of 1929 contains an exchange between a bartender and a hard-drinking customer—"Did you lose a lot in the crash?" asks the bartender. "I lost everything I really wanted in the boom," comes the reply. Like the character in the story, the trick is to make sure we use money instead of letting money use us.

Benjamin Franklin wrote, "Money has never made a happy man yet, nor will it. There is nothing in its nature to produce happiness. The more a man has the more he wants. Instead of its filling a vacuum, it makes one. If it satisfies one want, it doubles or triples that want another way. That was a true proverb of the wise man, rely upon it; 'Better is little with the fear of the Lord, than great treasure, and trouble therewith'." As we chip away at a mountain of bills, it's hard to imagine that money could pose a danger. Consider the following:

1. Too much money can erase your noble goals, diluting your dedication to helping others and bettering your community. With too much money, without great care, you have only one passion—how to make more money.

2. Climbing the money tree can destroy character and morals. The climb can mean stepping on others' shoulders, manipulating people; if you start to slip, you pull others down in your desperation to make the climb.

3. Too much money leads to ego-inflation. Where once you gave credit to God or your parents or your spouse or your co-workers, now you talk as if you did it all.

4. Money can become your god, blinding you to the needs of others. You may dream of a vacation hide-away—a worthy goal unless it's nothing more than a subconscious avoidance of human needs, an escape from helping others.

5. Money can ruin a family. To ensure your children have it better than you did, you overgive and overprovide. In the end, they see the possibility of money without work.

In our pursuit of money and attempts to use it wisely, we can learn from the wisdom of John Wesley, who wrote, "Make all you can. Save all you can. Give all you can."

We often hear about employees' rights and teachers' rights and players' rights, but seldom, if ever, about the rights of bosses or the rights of principals or the rights of coaches. Somewhere along the way, in our zeal to gain equal rights, we overlooked our concern for management.

In the hue and cry over protecting the workers, we forgot that management is also composed of employees. More than likely your supervisor doesn't own the company, but is hired just as you are. Likewise, the principal of the school is under contract to the school board, just like a teacher. And the coach of the professional team is pressured by the owner and general manager.

We want fair and honest treatment *from* those in authority over us, but are we equally willing to *give* such consideration? Many good managers lose their jobs because they were too willing to pacify employees who took advantage of them—as a result, the work suffered. A part of a manager's or supervisor's job is to be constructively critical. But often we reject such advice and carry a grudge to the point of creating a minor undercover rebellion.

Keep in mind the following in your relationship with your own boss:

1. Your boss is usually looking at the overall picture, while your vision is limited to your particular job or section.
2. You don't have to accept at face value every single direction from your boss—but don't blast back. Instead, ask for the reasoning behind the suggestion or change.
3. When you have a problem, bear in mind that the other employees have their problems. Your boss has to be concerned with them all and cannot be overly concerned with only one.
4. If you offer a suggestion and your boss turns it down, don't necessarily stop there. If you truly believe you have a worthwhile idea, come back and try to sell it again—the initial turndown might be due to the wrong timing or approach.

The Golden Rule works horizontally between you and your fellow employees. Remember that the Golden Rule is just as essential working vertically between you and your boss. You have rights and feelings—but so does the supervisor, the principal, the coach.

I do a lot of traveling overseas, having spoken in 24 countries of the world. I never fail to be impressed by the wonders of our globe—and I never fail to get a lump in my throat when I return to our shores. Nothing expresses the feeling I get each time I wing over the Statue of Liberty quite like Henry Van Dyke's poem "America For Me":

'Tis fine to see the old world, to travel up and down
The famous cities and places of renown,
To admire the crumbling castles and the statues of the kings.
But now I think I've had enough of antiquated things.
So it's home again, home again, America for me.
My heart is turning home again and there I long to be
In the land of youth and freedom beyond the ocean bars
Where the air is full of sunlight and the flag is full of stars.
O, London is a man's town, there's power in the air
And Paris is a woman's town with flowers in her hair.
It's sweet to dream in Venice. It's great to study Rome.
But when it comes to living, there's no place like home.
I liked the German firwoods in green battalions drilled.
I liked the gardens of Versailles and flashing fountains filled.
But, oh to take your hand, my dear, and ramble for a day
In the friendly western woodland where nature has her way.
Now I know Europe is wonderful; yet somehow seems to lack.
The past is too much with her and the people looking back.
The glory of the present is to make the future free.
We love our land for what she is and what she is to be.
O, it's home again, home again, America for me.
I want a ship that's westward bound to plow the rolling sea.
To the blest land of room enough beyond the ocean bars,
Where the air is full of sunlight and the flag is full of stars.

Did you ever visit the House of Mirrors at the carnival or county fair? It was fun, wasn't it, as one mirror made you thin and another made you a contender for the circus fat man? In a way, children do the same for us. Each child is a mirror of sorts in whom we see ourselves exaggerated in one form or another.

Most of us find ourselves a bit scared at times and disappointed as our children grow. We're not so much disappointed in our children as we are in ourselves as we see some aspect of ourselves exaggerated in our children.

If we are having trouble relating to our children and feel they are impossible to understand, we might become haunted. Haunted because a psychiatric study of parent-child relationships has shown that individuals who experience difficult relationships with their children usually had a difficult time when they were children handling hostility toward parents or brothers and sisters. If the desire is that a happy family replace your own unpleasant childhood, then extra effort must be put forth, for usually the cycle repeats itself.

Of course, there are exceptions or additional problems. If you have a gifted child, you will find it more difficult to keep that child happy. Gifted children are often one step ahead of the baby talk or the level the parents feel to be normal. They fight to find themselves and not lose their confidence, which is being undermined by parents who suppress new ideas and make them feel obstinate.

When starting to school gifted children have the problem of jealousy from classmates so they either hide their "light under a bushel" or become loners.

Also, parents have trouble identifying the maturing differences between boys and girls. All children have fears but even these vary by sex. Florida State University studies show that girls' fears tend to focus on the immediate present—the here and now. Boys have more intense fears of the future. In our effort to treat our children equally, we must know that equal doesn't mean alike.

Our children make our homes a house of mirrors. We have to accept what we see and not hope to dream away the unattractive but put emphasis on the good we see.

In the last decade I've probably lost over one hundred pounds—gained ten—lost five—gained two—lost four. You know how it goes. We're so blessed in America that many of us constantly fight the battle of the bulge. As a result, if you want an instant best seller, design a new crash diet—one that promises much with little effort.

Overeating and lack of exercise may well bury our nation. We do have people who play down exercise, claiming exercise stimulates the appetite and may cause weight increase. Dr. Laurence Oscat, while at the University of Illinois, reported that it is false for us to think an hour of exercise is like a day of physical labor, which would certainly increase one's appetite.

What I've had to learn is that there is no easy way to weight loss or weight control. Also, we respond differently to the same diet. The keys to diet are patience and dedication.

The so-called "crash" diets seem to give quick weight loss but usually when the pounds drop quickly, they seem to return equally fast when the diet is stopped.

Sound advice on a diet seems to include:

A proper balance providing all the nutrients the body needs to maintain itself. This can be done with calories reduced.

Usually it is best to eat three meals a day. Cutting out a meal may lead to overeating when next you do eat. Some experts suggest you not eliminate what you crave but counterbalance by eating less of something else. No diet will work with snacks between meals or food doused in butter or covered with rich sauces.

It is good to keep records forcing inventory of what you eat. Also, it's good to choose a diet that contains enough variety to avoid table boredom.

Along with many of you, I've tried most of the diets. I've wanted the easy way out. I've asked my wife, Buren, to help me. However, like any self-improvement, it must be my desire and willingness to sacrifice to reach the goal. Wishful thinking must be translated into reality.

I've met a few people who have suffered from lack of appetite. Often I've wished I could compromise with them, giving some of my appetite for their lack of it. Again, this would be the easy way—and, again, just wishful thinking.

An excellent article featured years ago in *Sunshine* magazine under the title "The Joy of Work," provides food for thought and fuel for action to all of us who work at anything:

> The joy of doing one's work is the purest, least diluted, most permanent, divine and abiding joy of which a man is capable. Behind work is rest; behind all good craftsmanship is unstained satisfaction; behind effort, heaven. Work is no punishment; it is the most redemptive of things.
>
> He who loves to work gains all the favors of the gods. He gets health, for there is no tonic so efficient to the body as work. He gets joy, for the most perfect joy of which we are capable is the putting forth of all one's powers. He gets fellowship, for there is no companionship so pure and wholesome as that of those who work together at some worthy business or cause. He gets self-respect, for there is no satisfaction so great as the consciousness of having done well that which we have undertaken to do. He gets faith, for all belief in the laws of goodness comes from the doers. Human blessedness is not found in success, but in effort; not in arriving, but in traveling; not in the wages of work, but in the very work itself.

Achieve joy in your labors and, in return, receive the blessings of health and fellowship, self-respect and faith. Jobs are what we seek; careers are what we make ourselves.

There is a stubborn, unbending reality about life that we all must face. Life can be hard and painful, as well as easy and beautiful. Jesus said, "In this world, you shall have tribulation." Grief and pain are a portion of every person's life in due time.

And yet, grief is not the whole of life. We must remember that the only cure for grief is action. "The show must go on," so the saying goes, and in so doing we rediscover the freshness of hope by not allowing grief to paralyze our freedom and leave us with stagnant spirits and lingering gloom.

The show does not go on, however, without confronting our feelings of pain and loss. Sometimes, the loss of a loved one seems to remove our very reason for existence. Edna St. Vincent Millay described this empty feeling so well, "Life must go on; I forget just why." Life, indeed, must go on and we dare not forget why!

We were born to fulfill the promise of our lives—not only when the days are bright with joy and happiness, but also when they are heavy with sorrow and dark with despair. We were given life so that we could witness to our faith in God and in life itself—not only when the sun is shining, but also when the clouds hang low and the fog of doubt and gloom envelopes us.

Contrasting with the mood of Edna St. Vincent Millay are the words of Tillie Olsen, who, in spite of loneliness, fear and pain, said, "There is still enough to live by." Often, the recollection of happy moments in treasured yesterdays will make a smile break through our tears. Instead of despairing over present loss, we can feel grateful for past joys.

Dr. Harold Blake Walker tells of writing a letter of sympathy to a woman whose husband had died. She wrote back: "Everyone loved my husband. He always went out of his way to lend a helping hand, whether it was to a window washer or a lonely boy. I am deeply grateful for my memories." She still had enough left to live by.

The hardness and pain of life are tempered by times of refreshing peace and joy. We cannot dull life's hard edges by refusing to face up to life's hardships. Instead, we must realize and understand that our courage in such times is witness to our faith in God; and with that courage, we can sustain the lives of others who mourn.

Using the term "square" to refer to someone slightly out of step with the social norm might be a bit outdated and outmoded. The message contained in "All Squares Please Stand," however, is timeless, and has appeared over the years in publications as varied as those of Rotary International and the Boy Scouts:

Square, another of the good old words, has gone the way of *love* and *modesty* and *patriotism*—something to be snickered over or outright laughed at. Once there was no higher compliment you could pay a man than to call him a "square shooter." The ad man's promise of a "square deal" was as binding as an oath on a Bible. One of those ad men, Charles Brower, says he is fed up with the way this beat generation is distorting and corrupting our time-honored vocabulary. He said most of this first, but we second his motion.

Today's "square" is one who volunteers when he doesn't have to. He's a guy who gets his kicks from trying to do a job better than anyone else. He's a boob who gets so lost in his work that he has to be reminded to go home. A square doesn't want to stop at a bar and get "all juiced up" because he prefers to go to his own home, his dinner table, his own bed. He hasn't learned to "cut corners" or "goof off."

This "creep" we call a square gets all choked up when he hears children singing "My Country 'Tis of Thee." He even believes in God and says so—in public! A square lives within his means whether the Joneses do or not, and he thinks his Uncle Sam should, too. A square is likely to save some of his own money for a rainy day rather than count on using yours. He gets his books from the library instead of the drugstore. He tells his son it's more important to play fair than to win.

Imagine! A square reads Scripture when nobody's watching, prays when nobody's listening! He believes in honoring father and mother, "doing unto others," and that kind of "stuff." He thinks he knows more than his teenager about cars, freedom and curfew.

You misfits in this brave new age, you dismally disorganized, improperly apologetic ghosts of the past, stand up! Stand up and be counted! You squares who turn the wheels and dig the fields and move mountains and put rivets in our dreams. You squares who dignify the human race, you squares who hold the thankless world in its place. We thank God for every one of you.

Charles Schulz and his "Peanuts" comic strip characters have offered many humorous definitions of what happiness is. Happiness is a warm puppy or a date with your best girl, according to Charlie Brown, Snoopy and the rest of the gang. But these things are only fleeting and temporary; they offer no real, lasting happiness. Mankind has been searching for the meaning of that evasive quality—real, lasting happiness—since the dawn of civilization.

No two people completely agree on just what happiness is, though we all have our own ideas and misconceptions about it. Dr. E. D. Anderson, a noted authority on emotional problems, has compiled a dozen traits an individual must possess to be genuinely happy—oddly enough money is not included: "(1) A joy of living; (2) a joy of learning; (3) a sense of humor; (4) love of beauty in music, nature, art, and literature; (5) interest in and love of people; (6) respect for ability and wisdom, and recognition of the importance of a job well done; (7) courtesy, kindness and sympathy toward others; (8) deep religious convictions and beliefs; (9) independence of thought and spirit; (10) confidence and respect for your own abilities and talents; (11) a feeling of belonging to the family, community, nation, and world with a willingness to take the responsibilities that go with that feeling; (12) the ability to give and receive love."

This last trait, according to Dr. Anderson, is the most important of all and the most difficult to achieve. Our personal ability to love produces love in others, in much the same way that being interested in others makes us interesting to them.

The search for real, lasting happiness can have an impact far beyond our own personal gratification. "If we can produce a generation of happy people," theorizes Dr. Anderson, "that generation will solve its own problems and the world's problems with a minimum of strife. The world's problems start with the unhappy individual."

In our quest for happiness, let us remember that happiness is not found, but deserved; not learned, but earned.

To paraphrase an old saying, "Laugh and the world laughs with you, grumble and you grumble alone." The plain truth is, no one likes a grumbler. The whining, discontented person is difficult to enjoy; the constant complainer is a nuisance and a burden to all those around them. These eternal pessimists, with their small and petty outlooks, live lives robbed of dignity and worth and joy.

Worst of all, the constant grumbler lacks a sense of humor. The ability to laugh with others and at ourselves is a sure cure for depression and moodiness.

You just might see someone you know in "The Grumble Family," a thought-provoking poem by an anonymous author:

There's a family nobody likes to meet,
They live, it is said, on Complaining Street,
In the city of Never-Are-Satisfied, the River of Discontent beside.
They growl at that and they growl at this,
Whatever comes, there is something amiss;
And whether their station be high or humble,
They are known by the name of Grumble.
The weather is always too hot or too cold,
Summer and winter alike they scold;
Nothing goes right with the folks you meet,
. Down on that gloomy Complaining Street.
They growl at the rain and they growl at the sun;
In fact, their growling is never done.
And if everything pleased them, there isn't a doubt,
They'd growl that they'd nothing to grumble about!
And the worst thing is that if anyone stays
Among them too long, he will learn their ways,
And before he dreams of the terrible jumble,
He's adopted into the family of Grumble.
So it were wisest to keep our feet,
From wandering into Complaining Street;
And never to growl, whatever we do;
Lest we be mistaken for Grumblers, too.

Most of us are blessed with mediocre capacities, average abilities and rather ordinary personalities. But we learn to make the most of what we have.

J. Willard Marriott, founder of Marriott Hotels, penned a few guidelines to pass on to his son. They are too important not to pass on to you:

1. Keep physically fit, mentally and spiritually strong.
2. Guard your habits—bad ones will destroy you.
3. Pray about difficult problems.
4. Study and follow professional management principles. Apply them logically and practically to your organization.
5. People are Number One—their development, loyalty, interest, team spirit. Develop managers in every area. This is your prime responsibility.
6. Decisions: People grow by making decisions and assuming responsibilities for them.
    a. Make crystal clear what decision each manager is responsible for and what decisions you reserve for yourself.
    b. Have all the facts and counsel necessary—then decide and stick to it.
7. Criticism: Don't criticize people but make a fair appraisal of their qualifications with their supervisor only (or someone assigned to do this). Remember, anything you say about someone may (and usually does) get back to them. There are few secrets.
8. See the good in people and try to develop those qualities.
9. Inefficiency: If it cannot be overcome and an employee is obviously incapable of the job, find a job he can do or terminate now. Don't wait.
10. Manage your time.
    a. Short conversations—to the point.
    b. Make every minute on the job count.
    c. Work fewer hours—some of us waste half of our time.
11. Delegate and hold accountable for results.
12. Details:
    a. Let your staff take care of them.
    b. Save your energy for planning, thinking, working with department heads, promoting new ideas.
    c. Don't do anything someone else can do for you.
13. Ideas and competition:
    a. Ideas keep the business alive.
    b. Know what your competitors are doing and planning.
    c. Encourage all management to think about better ways and give suggestions on anything that will improve business.
    d. Spend time and money on research and development.
14. Don't try to do an employee's job for him—counsel and suggest.
15. Think objectively and keep a sense of humor. Make the business fun for you and others.

When you were daydreaming as a youngster, which hero were you—Buck Rogers, Flash Gordon, Little Orphan Annie, Jack Armstrong, the All-American, Tom Mix, Captain Midnight, the Green Hornet? All of us dream of being heroes, though we may not admit it.

When you have dreams of being a hero, you're not alone. It seems all of us have such fantasies at one time or another. The knight in shining armor on the white horse is a life-long hero.

When we were children we listened to the radio that used our imaginations far beyond TV. Then out to the yard we'd run to reenact what we'd heard, placing ourselves in the hero role.

There is inbuilt in us a desire to excel, to go beyond our present limitations, to win the applause of the public.

Fantasies are a healthy escape. I'm only bothered when people dream of dying while doing some noble act that will leave a pleasant picture in the mourners' minds. The death wish I never find healthy.

I feel sorry for the adults who feel they've outlived their possibility of dreaming. Parents need to daydream to escape family pressures. Daydreams can help in the dentist's chair or some task you find unpleasant.

Daydreams aren't all wasted. Some of our finest firemen or policemen are fulfilling childhood dreams. Many of our best pilots flew imaginary planes in imaginary wars long before they saw the inside of their first plane.

Some people allow their imagination to "free-wheel" through daydreams and discover solutions to real life problems.

Some people, remembering their young dreams, later join volunteer associations like rescue squads to fulfill lingering fantasy.

America historically has been a nation reaching beyond normal limitations because man has dreamed of himself as a hero. This isn't egotism but a willingness to put one's self on the spot.

Let your dreams roll on and, who knows, you may still be the knight with the shining armor on the white horse.

Time is our only possession that cannot be recovered and restored. Time is spent only once, for better or for worse. Our allotment of time can be wasted by outside influences and other people; but more often than not, we rob ourselves of time in seemingly innocent, yet destructive, ways:

Self-indulgence. We tell ourselves how hard we have worked to get where we are—regardless of where it is—and prescribe extra doses of golf and tennis as necessary for survival. In more subtle ways, we linger longer in the showers each morning and take longer to shave and dress.

Socializing. We tell ourselves how necessary it is to care about people. In selling, we believe that contacts lead to sales. We must each ask ourselves if we are making constructive use of social time or merely wasting time feeding our own egos with idle conversation.

Overdoing it. We tell ourselves that it is important to do a job thoroughly and well. Yet we can actually waste time by staying in one place too long. Managers who cannot delegate, who cannot trust their employees, waste time doing what others should be doing. Insecurity can cause us to overdo a project rather than moving on to the next task. If we keep touching up a photograph, for instance, eventually it becomes distorted.

Daydreaming. We tell ourselves that imagination is a personal asset. When our imaginations take the form of idle daydreaming, however, we can become ineffective. Daydreaming about what we want to happen, while neglecting what is happening, actually determines what will be. Daydreaming about the upcoming weekend can lessen our productivity and make us resent our job. Daydreaming about the promotion that went to another can jeopardize the job we have. Daydreaming about yesterday's mistake can make us insecure and ineffective today.

Remember, time is a valuable asset that cannot be saved or stockpiled, reclaimed or recovered. Use it wisely.

"Every great and commanding movement in the annals of the world is the triumph of enthusiasm... Nothing great was ever achieved without it," wrote Ralph Waldo Emerson.

Enthusiasm does not necessarily entail great noise and motion, such as the hoopla generated at a sales convention or political rally. We may reveal our enthusiasm with jubilation or we may be reserved and quiet. Enthusiasm means God is working within us; enthusiasm is the inner energy to seek our goals.

An unknown author depicted enthusiasm in the following way:

Enthusiasm is reason gone mad to achieve a definite, rational objective.

Enthusiasm is inflamed by opposition, but never converted; it is the leaping lightning that blasts obstacles from its path.

Enthusiasm is the X-ray of the soul, that penetrates and reveals the invisible.

Enthusiasm is a contagion that laughs at quarantine and inoculates all who come in contact with it.

Enthusiasm is the vibrant thrill in your voice that sways the wills of others in harmony with your own.

Enthusiasm is the "philosophers' stone" that transmutes dull tasks into delightful deeds.

Enthusiasm is a magnet that draws kindred souls and irresistible force and electrifies them with the magnetism of its own resolves.

Capitalism or private enterprise or free enterprise is not a system in the sense of having been invented by someone in history. Our economic system is the natural result of allowing free people to freely exchange their abilities, their skills, their dreams, their wisdom. With that mutual exchange, we become collaborators in the pursuit of common goals.

Private enterprise is much more than a system of dollars and cents, it is a way of life. It is the freedom to control where we work, to decide what we want, to determine what we give. The foundation of our nation, as Thomas Jefferson wrote, "is the equal right of every citizen, in his person and property, and in their management."

This freedom does not mean living an isolated existence, totally unto ourselves, without concern for others. With the right to earn comes the privilege of providing for those we love. With the right to prosper comes the opportunity to enhance our self-worth by sharing what we have with others.

Too quickly and too easily, we want to dismiss the unfortunate from our view, blaming them for their own problems. But would we blame the child for a birth defect? Would we blame the blind for being sightless or the deaf for not hearing? Would we blame the farmer for flooded fields in the springtime? Of course not! Misfortune, in large or small doses, befalls each of us through no fault of our own.

The true marvel of our economy is that it is the only system that pumps forth with a heart. Free enterprise provides the opportunity to freely give, to freely share, to freely help others.

What can we do when we feel anxious or apprehensive, when we feel down or uptight? The extension family relations specialists at the University of North Carolina offer several practical suggestions for combating the distress and tension that come with such emotions:

1. Talk out the concern. Discussing a problem can be a great release. We tend to hold everything in, to shield our families from problems of the workplace. Yet talking over our troubles can help, and involving the entire household and sharing the problem can unite the family.
2. Express feelings. Let someone know your warmth and love. Even hostility should be expressed in some constructive manner. Let it out.
3. Do something for someone else. Quit feeling sorry for yourself. Even when you feel like hibernating, reach out to help another person.
4. Plan a break or diversion from normal routine. Take part in after-work recreation; take up a hobby you've always wanted to try. Be sure to take a vacation, preferably without too many plans and constraints. Make it a time of relaxation. Loaf a little every day; make yourself comfortable doing nothing.
5. Review your work and purposes. Reevaluating goals, whether a businessman or housewife, is a necessary process in order to obtain a degree of satisfaction.
6. Be less critical. Criticizing yourself, just as when criticizing others, can leave you feeling depressed. We can demand too much of ourselves, just as we demand too much of others. Instead, be realistic about your strengths and weaknesses, and learn to live with them.

Weather and personal problems are two topics everyone talks about, but no one changes. These six suggestions might be a starting point for bringing stability and calm to your life.

During election month, it is especially essential that we retain our national sense of humor. The following analysis of the differences between Republicans and Democrats comes from no less a repository of humor than *The Congressional Record*:

The people you see coming out of wooden churches are Republicans.
Democrats buy most of the books that have been banned somewhere.
Republicans form censorship committees and read them as a group.
Republicans are likely to have fewer but larger debts that cause them no concern. Democrats owe a lot of small bills. They don't worry either.
Democrats give their worn-out clothes to those less fortunate. Republicans wear theirs.
Republicans employ exterminators. Democrats step on bugs.
Republicans have governesses for their children. Democrats have grandmothers.
Democrats name their children after currently popular sports figures, politicians and entertainers. Republican children are named after their parents or grandparents, according to where the most money is.
Republicans tend to keep their shades drawn, although there is seldom any reason they should. Democrats ought to, but don't.
Republicans study the financial pages of the newspaper. Democrats put them in the bottom of the bird cage.
On Saturday, Republicans head for the hunting lodge or the yacht club, while Democrats wash the car and get a haircut.
Republicans raise dahlias, Dalmations and eyebrows. Democrats raise Airedales, kids and taxes.
Democrats eat the fish they catch. Republicans hang them on the wall.
Republicans have guest rooms. Democrats have spare rooms filled with old baby furniture.
Democrats suffer from chapped hands and headaches.

In light of these probing observations, perhaps that is why the Independents are growing faster than either party!

Life is more complex today, whether we live in the open country or in the heart of a major city. Also, large numbers of children are being raised in one-parent homes, because of divorce or the death of a parent. The most important factor, however, is that we do not allow social changes to alter or corrupt our moral values of our homes.

The home may be in a trailer park, a one-room apartment, a farmhouse or a beautiful abode professionally landscaped. Still, in such places, no matter the size, shape, or location, children can have good homes if we hold fast to some basic attitudes:

1. The children must be loved, wanted; and they must know they are.
2. We must accept the responsibility as parents that we are to be the child's guide; that our best teaching is not by what we say as much as where we put our steps that they can walk in.
3. In our times of relative affluency, we must try to retain that fine line between giving too much or too little to each of our children.
4. We must not let our fear of impending danger make us paranoid, for the child must have some time and space of his or her own.
5. Discipline is part of parental responsibility, but the poise, patience, self-restraint and personal mastery we want the child to have must be first demonstrated in us.
6. Mistakes must be corrected, but not with a sense of vengeance and raw punishment, nor with the feeling that the mistakes will be remembered and brought up again and again.
7. If we expect our young people to do big things later on, it must be that they're to build on the encouragement we give now to such little things as taking the first step, saying the first words, reading the first sentence, and making the first clumsy gift.
8. We must let the child feel that the one place he or she can say what's on their mind is in the home, even if we have to bite our tongue.
9. That houses or apartments do not become homes by furniture or design, but by atmosphere; and that there is merit to the old line that the family that prays together, stays together.

Sunday, Week Forty-Four

We speak of love being spontaneous but there are also aspects of it that are routine. For instance, I can't imagine a daughter who loves her father more than my wife, Buren, loves her "Papaw." She calls him at least three times a day. That's very routine. Many times I overhear her saying the same words she's used the day before. It is very routine. She calls at almost exactly the same time each day. That's very routine. Yet, if you could hear the tone of her voice as well as see them when they are together, you would understand that their love is fresh and spontaneous for each other. Spontaneous love most often comes to those who have a routine plan in sharing their affection.

In my business, traveling an average of one thousand miles each business day for over a quarter of a century, I'm grateful that Buren has been able to travel with me on a number of the trips, but the fast pace of going from one city to another would be unfair to impose upon anyone you love. So there are many, many days that we are away from each other, which we have used only to strengthen our marriage. Again, we have a routine—with few exceptions, no matter where I am in our country or the world, in fact, I call her at 11:00 P.M. her time. You might consider that thoughtful to have such a routine. I don't know about it being thoughtful, but I know it's necessary. Actually, I can't measure how much it means to her, but it puts the proper closing to many a day, lets me relax with warm thoughts as I go to sleep. That's very routine. We don't spend a great deal of time trying to think of creative things to say to each other but it does allow an opportunity to catch up with the news at home and hear details about the children when they were growing up. But most importantly, it is just to hear her voice and to know that no matter what has happened that day, she shares in it—whether it's been a day of achievement or failure to meet objectives. I know that none of this infringes on her love for me. Though all may doubt me, she believes in me. So if we have a spontaneous love, it is because we protect it through the routine.

Don't minimize saying the words "I love you," nor play down a gift that you choose to give on the spur of the moment, but the routine becomes a launching pad for spontaneous bursts of affection.

Can you be a positive thinker? There's no reason why not. Can you always be positive? There's no way you can. Being a positive person doesn't mean not having any negative thoughts.

We cannot be positive all the time. In fact, if we are never negative, how can we tell if we're positive? Moliere understood this, saying, "Unbroken happiness is a bore; it should have ups and downs." And George Bernard Shaw even went so far as to shout cynically, "A lifetime of happiness! No man alive could bear it. It would be hell on earth."

Life has negatives; life has downs. The issue is whether you can retain a positive attitude, and not give up even when your heart is breaking. What we have mistakenly done is to take a superficial approach, in effect saying that we ought to smile all the time because, after all, "every day, in every way the world is getting better and better." But perhaps, not so in your world today—your heart is breaking, and for you to smile would be totally dishonest.

So, being positive doesn't mean making believe all is always okay. Being positive does mean hurting and licking your wounds, but also building on the bad and the setbacks you have confronted.

Arnold Glasow believed, "The best way to achieve happiness is to learn to live without it." The ability to go forward when others would consider the road blocked says something about the quality of character.

Being overly critical is a trait we thoroughly dislike in others—and need to guard against claiming for ourselves. This advice offered by the *Southern California Baptist* may provide some insights:

> Anybody can be a critic. It takes no special talent or training. In fact, a noticeable lack of both is a decided asset to those who want to establish a reputation for being a critic.
>
> For those who have never filled the role of critic, finding fault with everything and everybody at one time or another, consider a few simple guidelines to help you get started. With enough practice, it will come naturally.

1. Be dogmatic; act as though everyone else is not quite as smart as you.
2. Have something to say on every issue, whether you know anything about it or not.
3. Be quick to say, "I told you so," whether you did or not, because no one will remember whether you did or not.
4. Let several other people speak first when something is being discussed. Then you can point out why they're all totally wrong.
5. If you are cornered in an argument, ask an irrelevant question.
6. Don't often expose yourself to the facts or consider both sides of the question. Nothing can so dampen the ardor of the critic as a little enlightenment.

The quality of leadership has been defined and dissected, summarized and theorized. It is more than charisma, more than mere charm, and not always unusual talent—but the ability to supply something people need or to take them where they want to go.

Certainly no two leaders are alike, but there are several common characteristics found in those we respect and follow:

1. *Leaders are sponges.* Just as the teacher is usually the best student, leaders have a curiosity that keeps them searching for new ideas. And finding those ideas, seeing their uses and applications. It is not unusual to see leaders taking copious notes; they have no false pride to keep them from learning.

2. *Leaders are listeners.* Listening is not clearing your desk and appointment calendar to give someone your time. Listening is anxiously waiting to hear. For some, a personal conference is a chore; for others, listening is the hotline for knowing how to lead better.

3. *Leaders are solicitors.* Leaders solicit ideas from those around them. When they say they have the best employees, it reflects a strong belief that they can and do learn from their employees. Leaders are sensitive, thoughtful, aware and responsive. Leaders know how to ask clear and concise questions that pick employees' brains and lead to a creative solution.

4. *Leaders are planners.* Planning begins with an evaluation and discipline of the leader's personal time. They set goals and work on problems that stand in the way of the goals. Leaders know how to focus their total mental and physical power on the relevant problem. Leaders logically and orderly arrange their priorities.

5. *Leaders are patient.* Although anxious to achieve progress, leaders know that progress is one solid brick at a time. Leaders make certain they understand first before judging harshly what appears to be an unreasonable delay.

6. *Leaders are servers.* The higher they rise, the more conscious leaders are of serving the needs of their employees. Leaders realize that those employees have brought them to their heights and that those employees are the indispensable key to further progress.

*T*he *Messenger* carried this advice to "Be Careful What You Say":

In speaking of a person's faults,
Pray don't forget your own;
Remember those with homes of glass
Should seldom throw a stone.

If we have nothing else to do
But talk of those who sin
'Tis better we commence at home
And from that point begin.

Some may have faults, and who has not?
The old as well as young.
Perhaps we may, for aught we know
Have fifty to their one.

I'll tell you of a better plan.
You'll find it works full well.
To try my own defects to cure
Before of others' tell.

And though I sometimes hope to be
No worse than some I know,
My own shortcomings bid me let
The faults of others go.

Then let us all, when we commence
To slander friend or foe,
Think of the harm one word would do
To those we little know.

When young people are asked to develop their own codes of conduct, they are usually tougher on themselves than we parents would be on them. Not long ago, a regional PTA asked teachers at several senior and junior high schools to have their students prepare a paper on the subject: "What are the things that you wish your parents would do or not do?" To keep the answers objective, the students were told they needn't sign their names. No other guidelines were given, other than a suggestion that they write off the top of their heads whatever came to mind first.

We could anticipate some of the answers; others may surprise you. Following are the most common requests of what youth wanted their parents to do or not to do:

Be stricter.
Be more dedicated to church work and go to church as a family.
Be fun-loving.
Treat my friends like they were welcome.
Try to understand me and my friends.
Don't treat me like a child but depend on me more.
Tell me right from wrong, but don't be too harsh about it.
Not to fuss at me before other people.
Not to curse . . . not drink . . . not smoke.
Answer simple questions without giving a lecture.
Ask my opinion instead of demanding.
Be trustworthy.
Sometimes it takes me a long time to explain why I did something and I'm convicted before the trial begins.
I would like my parents to be more thoughtful of one another . . . love one another . . . love me.

The survey seems to indicate that our young people reject the permissive, open, no-commitment society in favor of a stricter, disciplined society embracing what we parents call traditional values.

Let's use these findings as a challenge and an incentive for us as parents to set the example, to be the kind of parents our children want.

If the United States is being out-traded in the world, it may be because we have forgotten some basic definitions. Trading indicates an exchange, and exchanges take time. Could it be that coming out of World War II and for a decade controlling one-half of the world's GNP, it was natural that we would become somewhat arrogant? This arrogance became translated into our thinking we could just jump in, "cut a deal," and move on to our next item of business. We want quick, fast business transactions while the rest of the world barters—or negotiates. Bartering is an ageless art form of business. The earliest story I read was about the negotiations between Esau and Jacob in the Old Testament.

As IGA has moved dramatically on the world scene and globalization has become an important part of our business, I've enjoyed the opportunities to "barter" or "negotiate." Our State Department is somewhat fascinated with the relationships we've built with Japan, even to the point that, in the stores in that country, the employees wear uniforms that are "Made in America." All of our negotiations have been pleasant—strenuous, lengthy, but it is not easy to build a bridge across cultures as contrasted as the United States's and Japan's. Also, in our Australian growth we had to remember that sometimes we can be "divided by a common language." We must not assume that because we seem to use the same words that there is not national identity and integrity behind them. Sometimes the same words carry different emotional baggage depending on which country they're coming from. We have done all of our world expansion built on a premise that we will never be guilty of saying, "When in Rome, do as Americans do."

When asked where I received advice, it has come from two sources: from the Syrian/Lebanese heritage on my father's side, where negotiating is just a way of life, and the other source took me back to the early days of America. One of the books my parents insisted I read when growing up was the autobiography of Benjamin Franklin.

Mr. Franklin wrote that when you negotiate with someone, first be clear in your own mind about exactly what you want. Second, do your homework. As much as possible, be able to anticipate the questions and negotiating points. Third, don't expect to win or make a sale or sign an agreement on the first time, or the first half dozen times. The first visit may just help both clear the air or begin the thinking on the part of the other person that they may want to do business with you. Fourth, if at all possible, you want to make the other person feel a sense of friendship so that you're negotiating in terms of his needs, his wants, his advantages which, in turn, will assure mutual benefit.

Think what could happen if we truly understood the logic of the Golden Rule—treat others well for you want to be treated well by them. You know how an unkind remark cuts you, so don't make one about another. Think how you are crushed by someone shouting at you, so don't shout at others. We all wilt under constant criticism so be careful that any criticism of others is justified and constructive. Dishonesty and deception make you feel like a fool—be honest with others, even if it hurts. When someone slights you it makes you feel lonely and insecure, so always make others feel wanted.

Relationships are very fragile; an unkind word in a moment of haste can destroy what it took years to build. We're fortunate if we can honestly say we have a dozen real friends . . . those who stick with us through thick and thin.

Well over a century ago a visitor at the White House asked President Abraham Lincoln his definition of a friend. He slowly replied, "My definition of a friend is one who has the same enemies you have." Let me share some additional definitions of a friend:

True friendship is like sound health; the value of it is seldom known until it is lost.

You can make more friends in two months by becoming interested in other people than you can in two years by trying to get other people interested in you.

A true friend is somebody who can make us do what we can.

Friendship consists of forgetting what one gives and remembering what one receives.

A friend is one who knows all about you but loves you just the same.

Silence makes the real conversations between friends. Not the saying, but the never needing to say is what counts.

Most fortunate of all are those who consider their wife or husband to be their best friend.

The harder I work and the less I scheme, the better my luck seems to be. You might guess correctly from that personal philosophy that I am not a gambler by nature. In fact, I feel a bit sympathetic toward people who go through life looking for that one big payoff.

Even though I am not a gambler, I am fascinated by watching the casino crowds when I have occasion to be in Las Vegas. I remember once standing off to the side and intently watching a group of older women playing the slot machines. As I watched, I began to transfer human characteristics to the "one-armed bandits" of chance.

I noticed that the slot machines kept their arms at their sides and only worked when they were forced to work. And when they were forced into action, they responded with style, noise and excitement. This made me think of some people who must be coerced into action and work like eager beavers until you turn your back. Then, like the slot machines, they become idle again.

I noticed that the slot machines took everything that was offered and seemed to want more. I thought of people who get healthy raises, better hospitalization, longer vacations, more benefits and never breathe a word of appreciation, but act as if they expect even more.

I noticed that the slot machines always spin their wheels while they work. I thought of people who proclaim how hard they are working, but much of it is spinning wheels. Effective work is not necessarily giving your energy, it is priority and knowing what to do first and what is most important. We can become tired from frustration faster than from labor.

My intent in comparing human beings to slot machines was not to belittle us, but to help us overcome our negative tendencies. By giving your best, not like a machine but like the warm and creative person you are, it will be no gamble for your company to have you in a position of responsibility.

If each of us could have one grace, I would wish for us the grace of giving. The great people of this earth share a common characteristic—generosity. They share their lives and their means.

There is an amazing secret about giving—you cannot outgive God. Share what you have in helping others, and you will find a joy and richness of life you've never known.

I learned this secret at the age of eighteen, working my way through college. I was playing baseball, but in those days a scholarship was just that—help on tuition and no more. Also, I was participating on the debate team and serving as an apprentice at a local church. It was summertime, and funds were short when I went to hear a missionary tell about his work in a foreign land: the suffering of the children, the starvation of the people, the need for medicines. Something stirred in my heart. I wanted to give, but all I had to my name was five dollars, and all I had to look forward to were the two dollars that my folks could afford to send me each week. That five dollars seemed to burn a hole in my pocket, and I knew I had no choice but to place it in the offering plate, for no matter how dire my circumstances, they didn't compare with what the missionary had just described.

The next morning (Saturday) I felt somewhat noble skipping breakfast because I was broke. When the mail arrived that Saturday morning I knew it always had the letter from home, but this time it didn't arrive. There was not the two dollars I expected. My noble feeling turned into hunger pangs as lunchtime came and went, followed by the passing of dinnertime without food. However, I knew if I could just hold out until the next day, someone at the church always invited me to lunch.

In the congregation were the Irvins, who had been very thoughtful toward me. So much so that I called them Uncle Howard and Aunt Kathleen. With less pride, I could have gone to them already, but I didn't. Unbeknowing to me, Uncle Howard said to his pastor, "You know, our young assistant hasn't been home to see his parents and school will start soon. I want to offer him a car to make the trip and money for gas." At the close of the worship service the pastor mentioned the conversation he'd had with his deacon, Howard Irvin, and he said, "Why don't all of us give this young man, who's meant a great deal to this congregation, a trip home to see his parents." So now I had a low-mileage 1948 Ford, full of gas, with one hundred fifty dollars in my pocket, enough to comfortably drive home to Binghamton, New York, and also to invite my brother Ted to make the trip with me! I was stunned.

And I learned the secret of giving . . . you cannot outgive God.

Our country is undergoing a resurgence of the American spirit! This spiritual rebirth is reflected in our value systems today:

There is an encouraging *wave of optimism* in many quarters. Or defining optimism another way, we are again dreaming. For a period, we seemed to be afraid lest our dreams be nightmares. In business, we see people breaking out of the security of the corporate structure to join the high risk venture of the entrepreneurs.

Not only are we dreaming, but there is a *willingness to accept responsibility*. We still have the many whose basic effort is to shout for their entitlements, those who are determined to remain poor enough to milk every benefit of welfare. On the other side, we see those willing to dream and, in turn, willing to risk. This natural progression means an acceptance of responsibility for chasing a dream.

There is an encouraging *willingness to prepare for living*. There are many indicators that people want to do more than merely exist—the army of adults going back to school at community colleges; the increase in correspondence courses; the influx of audio and video educational tapes; the increased use of our public libraries; the organization of study groups; the increasing number of serious, educational paperbacks in bookstores; a growing do-it-yourself spirit, not only as a money-saver, but as a challenge. This surge of preparation represents a new vitality. The mind and the spirit are coming alive with force.

The last building block is a *spiritual thrust*. As the "electronic church" levels off and many famous radio and television personalities plead for funds to stay on the air, local churches are experiencing new energy. Such churches ask for pledges of commitment, strengthening themselves by asking their people to affirm themselves.

S ome years ago, a sportscaster asked Coach "Red" Blaik of Army to explain the phenomenal success of his former assistant Coach Vince Lombardi. Coach Blaik replied, "Vince is motivated to success, to win if you will, not for personal glory, but for the personal satisfaction that comes with great accomplishment."

If I had a single wish for each of you—no matter how insignificant you consider your job, no matter how humble you consider your role in life— my wish would be that you might see your job as extending beyond yourself. We have no difficulty feeling that the artist, the politician, the athlete, the teacher all extend beyond themselves. But so do you!

Our entire system of enterprise in this country is based on the initiative of the individual worker; the pledge of the individual worker to make a good product; the service of the individual employee to the customer. When we see our work as a means of personal achievement and satisfaction, we then see our work as more than just a paycheck. Supporting your family is a basic necessity and your fundamental concern, but it is also necessary to find fulfillment in what you do to care for your family.

You work so that you might live hopefully, your work is a vital part of your living.

People who are always looking for trouble usually end up finding it. It is possible to wish trouble on yourself through negative thinking. Rather than overlooking or minimizing potential trouble, such people give a possible problem center stage. Enough trouble comes to each of us without going out in search of it.

There once was a woman who was always hearing burglars in the house. One night, she whispered softly to her husband, "I tell you, there is someone in this house." The husband knew from experience there was no use arguing. The quickest answer was to turn on the lights and take a look. He sleepily crawled out of bed, felt his way into the living room and switched on the lights. To his surprise, there stood a burglar with his arms full. The burglar dropped the loot, pulled out a gun and muttered to the man of the house, "Say a word and I'll kill you." Now very much awake, the husband said, "Mister, you can keep everything you've picked up, but I'd like to make one request of you." "What's that?" replied the burglar. The husband explained, "Before you leave, I'd like you to come upstairs and meet my wife. You see, she has been looking for you for 20 years."

People who start off each day looking for trouble are the first to complain when it is found. We all know people who cannot enjoy good health today because they are worried about getting sick tomorrow. We may know people in business who cannot accept today's profits for worrying about tomorrow's losses. At the other end of the spectrum, we cannot go blithely on our way ignoring danger signals. Whistling in the dark never eliminates the danger.

The key is to face the problem with the attitude that you can solve it. Without minimizing the problem, believe that you can overcome it. Keep in mind that the trouble-seeker moans, "Why?" The problem-solver asks, "Why not?"

It always pleases me when I find that corporations want to help their employees, whether it be with a drinking problem, depression, drugs, or divorce. Employers don't want to be nosey, but they want to help. There is a fine line between getting too personal and not caring. So, when a person is in trouble and you arrange a meeting, you have to be sure you're tactful and, most of all, plan the meeting in a comfortable, private setting. Don't waste a lot of time with small talk but describe the specific behavior as you see it from your standpoint. You're not asking the cause but you're there to help if they want to share their problem with you. You're simply saying, "Please tell me what's going on in your life. Why are there problems on your job? We don't want to lose you but your present behavior is less than acceptable."

If you see is as a serious matter, then ask if they will accept counseling or outside help; or put them in touch with your own group, if you have one that is collectively fighting the alcohol problem, depression, or drugs. Most of all, don't threaten firing. The employee knows that's a possibility already, but encourage the employee to accept your offered help.

Coupled with that, let's make a check list of what I feel most employees would call their "wish list."

1. I want a regular evaluation of my performance and my pay, compared to what someone in my job in another company would be receiving.
2. I want to feel that management respects me and appreciates my contribution as much as I appreciate having my job with the company.
3. I like recognition when I do a job well. A small pat on the back goes a long way and makes me more willing to accept criticism.
4. I want a chance for advancement, to have my ambitions realized.
5. I want my work to be interesting—knowing, though, it is my obligation to take even the routine and make it interesting.
6. I want a sense of security, assured that if I do my job well, I have hope for the future.

That sounds simple enough, doesn't it? My guess is that you're already "on top" of these suggestions.

There are so many stories out of the life of the late Sir William Ossler that it makes him almost seem bigger than life. One of my favorites is about the time he was making rounds in a children's ward and he saw all the children playing games—in the sandbox—dressing dolls—except one little girl who sat all by herself on the corner of her high, narrow bed, clutching a cheap doll. Dr. Ossler looked at the little forlorn creature and asked the nurse about her.

The nurse said, "Well, we try to get Susan to play but the other children won't have anything to do with her. No one comes to see her. Her mother is dead and her dad has only come once and brought her that doll. The children have a strange code. Visitors mean so much. If a child doesn't have any visitors, they ignore the child."

Sir William Ossler walked over to the child's bed and asked in a voice loud enough for all the other kids to hear, "May I sit down, please, dear?" The little girl's eyes lit up.

Dr. Ossler said, "I can't stay very long on this visit but I wanted to see you so badly."

He even asked about the doll's health and took his stethoscope and put it on the doll's heart.

As he left he said, "Honey, you won't forget our little secret, will you? And don't tell anyone."

As he walked out of the ward he saw all the other children cluster around this lonely child. They were curious and admiring.

What a difference just a little bit of thoughtfulness makes!

There is nothing quite so satisfying as self-satisfaction; nothing feels quite as good as feeling good about yourself.

A fine line exists, however, between self-confidence and cockiness. Feeling good about ourselves should not make others feel miserable in our presence. Feeling good should not come from our reflection in a mirror, but when we are reflected in the lives of those we touch.

Insecurity and a lack of self-assurance can be painful and devastating. We compensate by building defenses and hiding behind them. We become braggers given to grandiosity. Catch a braggart in an unguarded moment, with his defenses down, and you may see an empty and fearful look.

Or we go to the opposite extreme to hide our insecurity by exuding modesty and self-deprecation. By advertising our poor feelings about ourselves, we keep from feeling the pain of those feelings. In a sense, self-deprecation is a way to hedge our bets and shout to the world not to expect too much from us.

Another defense is to associate with helpless and insecure people. What may pass for compassion for the less fortunate may be an attempt to find companions that will make us feel superior.

If we don't hide behind our defenses, what can we do to build a positive self-image and enhance our self-assurance?

For starters, model yourself after self-confident people. In childhood, we grow and develop by imitation; there is no reason to quit as adults. Choose individuals who feel good about themselves and use them as role models.

Next, try to determine what makes you feel good about yourself. Then make a concerted effort to put yourself in that climate as much and as often as possible.

Finally, identify tasks you want to do and accomplish them. You will build today's confidence on the blocks of yesterday's success.

It is right to be contented with what we have, never with what we are," Sir James MacKintosh wrote nearly two centuries ago. Were he to view our modern society, he might find circumstances reversed. We are seldom contented with what we have and all too easily satisfied with mediocrity in our lifestyles.

We may give lip service to humble self-deprecation, but most of us are relatively satisfied with what we are. We have emerged from an era of self-acceptance; we have grabbed onto the belief that "I'm okay." Rarely do we express a desire to be better, only to have more. We think we deserve better than we have; we complain about not receiving our fair share of breaks.

Samuel Johnson wrote, "The fountain of content must spring up in the mind; and he who has so little knowledge of human nature as to seek happiness by changing anything but his own disposition, will waste his life in fruitless efforts, and multiply the griefs which he proposes to remove." He was saying simply that better living depends on our desire to improve our dispositions—our true, inner self.

Our tendency is not to improve, but to envy others, pained by their successes. Jealousy provides a pitiful cover for our failure to improve ourselves. Jealousy tells the world that we feel inferior, that we are discontent with ourselves.

Such discontent with ourselves serves a noble purpose if it provides the catalyst to dedicate ourselves to improvement.

During this season of Thanksgiving, "Count your many blessings...
name them one by one ... and it will surprise you what the Lord hath
done." Nowhere are our many blessings spelled out more eloquently and
more simply than in the words of The Honorable Marietta Tree, former
ambassador to the U.N. Trustee Council:

I am thankful for...

The first ten amendments to the U.S. Constitution, the bulwark
of our democracy.

The friendliness and spontaneous good manners. "Hello,"
"Glad to see you," "Thank you" and "You're welcome." "Have
a good day" from everybody to everybody.

Ice cream.

The co-mingling of races and cultures which breeds tension but
also tolerance, variety and cultural richness.

The fluid society and the feeling of equality. We know that
anyone born here can become president; that a penniless boy
who rode the rails became a great Supreme Court Justice; that an
immigrant can become Secretary of State, or make a billion; and
that we can look any of our neighbors in the eye.

Communications, possibly the most distinguished feature of the
era. In the U.S. we have the best and most varied television, the
best telephone system, the best newspapers and news magazines,
the most efficient and comfortable airlines.

New York City. Living in this dynamo is difficult and dazzling.

Generosity. Last year, Americans gave more away than in
any year in our history.

The overwhelming natural beauty of the U.S. from sea to
shining sea.

Inventiveness. Lately the great breakthroughs in medicine,
space travel.

The sense of humor. Regional jokes, *New Yorker* cartoons,
the legacy of Mark Twain, W. C. Fields, Ed Wynn, the political
humor inherited from Lincoln, Will Rogers, Adlai Stevenson,
John F. Kennedy, the contemporary comments of Art Buchwald
and Russell Baker.

The waning appeal of materialism. Hot dogs and baseball...
the work ethic ... dogwoods.

At Thanksgiving time, let us take a few moments to reflect on our abundant riches and bounty through the eyes of three different authors.

Georgia Sibaugh wrote, "Thanksgiving time! And in my heart a prayer, for all the little, hungry children everywhere. 'Tis by God's grace my table's duly spread. His spirit whispers always, 'share thy daily bread.' Thanksgiving time! And in my heart a sob, for statesmanship that writes agreements without God. For He so loved the world He paid the price, that thankful hearts, redeemed, might share their Christ. Thanksgiving time! And in my heart a wish, that peoples everywhere will know the dawn of peace; that ere long, wandering ones, now forced to roam, will find that warm hearthglow we know as home."

The *American Lutheran* challenged,

> If you were God, and God were you, and He were given a holiday to go to church to praise and pray, and then He feasted and stayed away, without a thought of God or prayer, or thanks for all your loving care; if you were God and God were you, say—what would YOU do?
>
> If you were God and God were you, and a nation set aside a day for prayer, but only one had time to spare, for every hundred that didn't care; would you believe they were sincere, and bless that nation again next year? If you were God and God were you, say—what would YOU do?
>
> If you were God and God were you, and millions professed a faith in you, as giver of all good gifts and true, but never said "thanks" or thought it due. But then, when trouble came their way, expected your help without delay; if you were God and God were you, say—what would YOU do?

Jane Crewdson simply said, "O Thou, Whose bounty fills my cup, with every blessing meet! I give Thee thanks for every drop—the bitter and the sweet. I praise Thee for the desert road. And for the riverside. For all Thy goodness hath bestowed, and all Thy grace denied."

Contemplate the following dimensions—113 feet by 26 feet. Visualize that area; about one-sixth the size of a football field; about the area of a small store or a large home. That limited size—113 feet by 26 feet—represents the dimensions of the *Mayflower* that brought our Pilgrim Fathers to Plymouth in 1620. That tiny ship spent 67 days on the storm-tossed North Atlantic, filled beyond capacity with 120 passengers.

The *Mayflower* remains a striking illustration that size doesn't necessarily mean quality or importance. The *Mayflower* would be dwarfed by the mighty *Queen Elizabeth II*; the Pilgrims' vessel could rest comfortably on the foredeck of the massive oceanliner. And yet, the *QE II* most likely will never carry a passenger list as significant and historically important as that of the *Mayflower*.

The *Mayflower* withstood the rigors and the mercy of the seas, but the real power was the faith of the 120 passengers. That faith brought them not to a wilderness, but to a promised land; a land not to be bought by tradesmen and merchants, but a land for their stewardship.

After the struggle for survival seemed won, it was natural for the Pilgrims to declare a season of Thanksgiving. Even that day was as rugged as their adventure as they gathered for a feast in the crisp autumn air of the Northeast. Around the table loaded with the fruits of their toil, sweat, and tears, they established the precedent for us.

Thanksgiving—a family with hands clasped together around a table in humble prayer.

Thanksgiving—a giving of thanks and the challenge of promises yet to keep.

Thanksgiving—the smell of food baking, children laughing, grown-ups chattering.

Thanksgiving—the open door; open hearts; open hands; open minds.

Thanksgiving—the second part of the word, "giving," is at the heart of the feast.

Thanksgiving—parent to child to parent, neighbor to neighbor, bound by the fraternal spirit and faith that renders us one people under God.

Only 113 feet by 26 feet, a tiny ship, filled not with cargo but with people who believed in God. Throughout history, God has used seemingly simple things of the world to confound the mighty.

The climax of autumn, to me, is the opportunity of celebrating Thanksgiving. I'm not suggesting that we reduce our thanksgiving and contain it within a single day, for giving thanks is an attitude more than a ceremony. To some extent, how high we soar depends a great deal on how deeply we kneel in praise each day.

Have you seen in reruns of "All in the Family" the episode where Archie Bunker came in from work suddenly very anxious to give thanks? At work he came very near being crushed by some falling building supplies. Still shook up by that incident, he gathered with the family for the evening meal:

Archie: "Hold it! Hold it! Nobody eats nothin' here until we say grace."
Gloria: "Daddy, we never say grace."
Archie: "Well, little girl, we're going to say it from now on."
Edith: "I always say grace in my heart."
Archie: "Well, in your mouth you're going to say it tonight. We're gonna give thanks for the food on this table, which comes from Him."
Archie: (Proceeding to pray) "Hello, Lord. A. Bunker here. I wanna give Thou thanks for the food . . . for instance the salad, the meatloaf, some chopped-up green stuff here. And for snatchin' me from the whadda-u-call jaws of death, I'll thank You for that in private."

There certainly are episodes in life that make praise or thanksgiving automatic. Thanksgiving Day is peculiar unto our country but it was not originated by us. Our Jewish friends for centuries have celebrated the holiday of Sukkos, which really is a chance to say, "Thank you, God." The Jewish farmers in those early times wanted to pause and give thanks to God for the beauty and bounty about them and they did this just before they gathered up their autumn harvest, as recorded in the Old Testament.

There is a strong feeling that our Pilgrim Fathers, who were Bible readers, were inspired to celebrate Thanksgiving Day because they felt like the Jews of olden times who had left a land of bondage, wandered over unknown territory, and come upon a land of promise and freedom.

To some degree each of us has made a journey like that, and most of us have so very much for which to be thankful. May we pause today and count our blessings.

Attending the first nine grades of school in Massachusetts probably meant I had more Ralph Waldo Emerson that I might have had in other locations. So many years after he was gone this great American was revered. Well, he is respected by all, but in Massachusetts he was literally revered. Even now when I pull down a book of his essays and read them at a time when I just need a little mental stimulation or emotional support, I find why he was respected in his day and every day since. Let me give you two examples of quotes that are helpful:

He only is rich who owns the day, and no one owns the day who allows it to be invaded with worry, fret, and anxiety. Finish every day and be done with it. You have done what you could. Some blunders and absurdities no doubt crept in; forget them as soon as you can. Tomorrow is a new day, begin it well and serenely and with too high a spirit to be cumbered with your old nonsense. The day is all that is good and fair. It is too dear, with its hopes and invitations, to waste a moment on the yesterdays.

Reading these words brings me face to face with the here and now, so that prepared me for another very brief but pithy statement when this sage of Concord wrote: "We are always getting ready to live but never living." How do we actually live? My basic suggestion would be that good living is dependent upon an attitude of Thanksgiving. That is, today we take our work as a gift. We are grateful for the free time we have after work, the hobbies we might be able to enjoy. We are thankful for our friends and we strengthen the friendship by looking for pleasant, cheerful greetings we can extend to each other. In the midst of a defeat we look for a way to use that defeat as a building block to our next opportunity. Appreciative of our minds, we meet our problems with a decision right now. We feel that the ultimate of gratitude is planning to do something good. Today let's not get ready to live—let's just live.

We place exercise toys in the cribs of infants to strengthen developing muscles. We present problems to be solved to elementary school youngsters to stretch budding intellects. We use obstacle courses to test the stamina and skill of soldiers and athletes.

But we—we have only the hectic, daily rat race to strain and train us!

The rat race, as we have come to call the pressure-packed, gut-wrenching, nerve-racking pace of today's business world, is actually a good-news/bad-news joke on modern man. Life's pressures can line your face and gray your hair and wear you down; pressure can reduce the strong to tears and raise the meek to anger.

But the truth of the matter is, a world without pressure would be boring. The pressures of life fuel our creativity. We simply have to guard against letting the pressure become so great that it smothers us.

1. *In the rat race, we overcome by facing our troubles.* Few men had the problems of Abraham Lincoln, yet he had the ability to reduce problems to their simplest dimensions. Once asked why his two sons were crying, he replied, "They have the problems of the world. I've three walnuts and each wants two." Problems, when reduced, become solvable.

2. *In the rat race, we accept handicaps as compliments.* Golfers are respected for their handicaps; the best race horses carry the greatest handicaps. The thoroughbreds in the rat race are honored by the handicaps they can carry; many can never be given such pressures.

3. *In the rat race, we must retain our humor.* There is balance and toleration of the rat race if you don't become too serious. Accept what you cannot change; seek humor in your blunders. Nothing relieves pressure like a good laugh.

The secret of prayer is not what you do or how you do it, for God knows our needs, even before we ask. Actually, prayer is nothing more than opening up the lines of communication, establishing rapport, and removing the roadblocks between you and God. Here's a favorite story:

When my two older brothers were growing up, they suffered the normal childhood diseases—mumps, measles, chicken pox and "want of an electric train," the worst of all boyhood afflictions. They approached our father, who was somewhat hard-pressed financially, and made their plea. My brothers were told to pray about it, as we were instructed to do concerning all our needs. They prayed and prayed—all to no avail—and went back to Dad in frustration. He told them they would just have to pray harder if they wanted that electric train.

Both boys were puzzled and perplexed by what Dad meant by praying "harder". They put their adolescent heads together and reached a conclusion based on a youngster's perspective. They had watched Dad when he worked hard—"First he takes off his coat, then his collar; he rolls up his sleeves and, sometimes when he works really hard, he wrinkles his forehead and makes those sounds." The pair agreed; they had discovered the secret of praying hard.

That evening when my brothers got down on their knees to pray with the rest of the family, they first removed their jackets, unbuttoned their collars, rolled up their sleeves and wrinkled their foreheads. And, from deep within both of them came grunting sounds never before heard in our family: "O-o-o-o-h-h-h-h God, give us an electric train!" My parents felt a mixture of pride and amusement at the boys' deep sincerity and their youthful interpretation of praying "hard."

Funnier still was what happened the following day. My father received a call from a parishioner. He had had a windfall on a real estate sale and, in addition to his regular contribution to the church, was giving some money specially earmarked for my father to buy his sons something he otherwise could not have afforded. Something like an electric train.

You see, it didn't matter to God if my brothers understood what praying "hard" meant. He knew, before they asked, what they wanted. Their boyish prayers just opened up the lines of communication between themselves and their Heavenly Father.

Every one of us can open up those lines of communication, not by trying to pray eloquently or theologically or even grammatically—but sincerely and honestly before our Lord.

Every age has probably felt that it was the best and, at the same time, the worst. We refer to the "good old days" with near reverence and long to return to those simpler days. At the same time, we have all either been on the preaching end or the receiving end of a statement beginning, "When I was your age..." followed by a time-clouded account of miles to school or how hot it was before air conditioning.

Today is no different. We appreciate the knowledge that mankind has accumulated and the wonders that knowledge brings. We marvel at technological advances undreamed of just a generation ago. At the same time, we suffer hardships unknown to our forebears—the pressures and stress of modern times, the dues paid for life in the fast lane.

Who knows which generation had it worse? In these trying times, I find comfort in the wisdom of oft-quoted phrases:

"When it is dark, we see the stars"—Ralph Waldo Emerson

"All sunshine makes a desert"—Oriental proverb

"Man's extremity is God's opportunity"—author unknown

"We triumph without glory when we conquer without danger"
—Pierre Corneillo

"Trouble creates capacity to handle it"—Oliver Wendell Holmes

Who can lead us out of these perplexing times? The faint-hearted lose their perspective and flee in panic, while over their shoulders they shout some over-simplified answers and second guesses. The aimless martyrs stand unmovable, drawing attention to their sacrifice and revealing a closed mind to what could be done by stooping to help lift another.

We lead ourselves by the vision of an open mind, receiving facts and reflecting the prejudice of misguided friends. The light for our venture of danger and intrigue comes from the Eternal. The darker the times, the brighter appears the light.

A ll of us who have ever felt discouraged or dejected will deeply appreciate the thoughts of Virginia Opal Myers, who wrote "A Creed for the Discouraged":

I believe that God created me to be happy, to enjoy the blessings of life, to be useful to my fellow beings, and an honor to my country. I believe that the trials which beset me today are but the fiery tests by which my character is strengthened, ennobled and made worthy to enjoy the higher things of life, which I believe are in store for me. I believe that my soul is too grand to be crushed by defeat; I will rise above it! I believe that I am the architect of my own fate; therefore, I will be master of circumstances and surroundings, not their slave. I will not yield to discouragements. I will trample them underfoot and make them serve as stepping stones to success. I will conquer my obstacles and turn them into opportunities.

My failures of today will help to guide me on to victory on the morrow. The morrow will bring new strength and new hopes, new opportunities and new beginnings. I will be ready to meet it with a brave heart, a calm mind, and an undaunted spirit. In all things I will do my best and leave the rest to the Infinite. I will not waste my mental energies by useless worry. I will learn to dominate my restless thoughts and look on the bright side of things. I will face the world bravely. I will not be a coward. I will assert my God-given birthright and be a man. For I am immortal and nothing can overcome me.

It is a curious fact that adversity brings out the best in us, like tempering steel in a flame. The Apostle Paul rose to greatness as frustration fanned the embers of his faith and hardship stirred up his courage. Demosthenes rose above his speech defect to become the greatest orator of his day. He filled his mouth with pebbles and shouted above the roar of the waves until he learned to speak without stammering.

Though we face discouragement on all sides, meeting the challenge brings meaning to our lives. Using the gifts of God, we have the ability to triumph over our frustrations. We are not overcome by the adversities we face, but by the impatience with which we suffer them. We can shout, as Edwin Markham did, "I lift my hands to the years ahead and cry, 'Come on, I'm ready for you'."

Making the most out of marriage, like getting the best results from a recipe, requires certain guidelines and rules. Each marriage becomes what the partners decide to make it. The more you are willing to put into your marriage, the more you may derive from it. Why not invest in your marriage and its future happiness by heeding the following commandments?

1. Thou shalt understand the nature of marriage. Marriage is a God-given opportunity for creating a family and building character through a permanent union.
2. Thou shalt accept each other with respect and love. Accept the personality that each brings to the marriage, so that your mate does not lose his or her personality and become merely a rubber stamp.
3. Thou shalt talk things through. Life's problems need to be anticipated and discussed; decisions can then be based on sound judgment rather than on confused emotions when in distress. When there is love and respect, all problems can be solved with fair-minded calm and thorough consideration.
4. Thou shalt trust one another fully. Trust is the necessary cement that bonds and holds a marriage together. Trust always inspires others to do their best.
5. Thou shalt forgive each other. This is a Christian virtue that must be practiced daily. Each partner must learn to accept and give forgiveness.
6. Thou shalt cultivate a sense of humor. Paraphrasing the old adage, "A laugh a day keeps the lawyer away."
7. Thou shalt be loyal to one another. Marriage means leaving father and mother and putting the marriage and home first, above all else. Always be on your partner's side, rooting for them and supporting them as long as you believe they are in the right.
8. Thou shalt make a positive approach to marriage. Constantly look for the best in each other. Express love and appreciation continually. Most nagging and complaining stem from feelings of not being appreciated or of being neglected.
9. Thou shalt continue to cultivate thy romance. The loving-kindness and thoughtful consideration that won your mate is needed in daily doses to keep your mate.
10. Thou shalt make thy marriage Christian. This requires personal devotion, as well as family devotion, and the practice of Christian virtues in daily life. Family Bible reading and prayer bring God's power and truth into your life, giving peace and strength to each member.

A couple of decades ago I was sitting in the lounge on a Lockheed Electra visiting with a young man named Joe Namath and the head coach of the University of Texas, Darrell Royal. They had been to Easley, South Carolina, to address an All-Sports Banquet, while I had been speaking for the Chamber of Commerce of Greenville. The year before had been less than what Darrell Royal had hoped for his team (in those days more than one loss was a disaster at the University of Texas). We were visiting about how to stimulate or motivate people, and it was just like a light bulb went on in his head when he said, "We designed some innovative game plans but we've become careless on basics. Next year we're going back to blocking, tackling, etc." That next year Texas had another championship team.

We banter the word "basics" around so often. We know they're essential and we shouldn't overlook them. It is just difficult to be so disciplined that we keep ourselves charged up over what could be called routine.

It was my privilege to join a group of food industry executives studying some of the current issues facing us in business locally as well as worldwide. One of the speakers chosen to lead our discussion was Jack Shewmaker, former Vice Chairman of Wal-Mart. When you read what is written about Wal-Mart—and most of it is relatively accurate—it would make one look for a secret that is glamorous, unique, and never tried before. Then when you visit with Sam Walton or Jack Shewmaker, you realize they have been able to keep themselves excited about that which is basic. *They continue to do the right things in the right way at the right time.* For instance, Jack Shewmaker "preaches" these twelve points:

- Be an enthusiastic leader
- Learn to ask questions
- Make the customer number one
- Seek out and solve employees' annoyances
- Get your employees involved
- Keep learning
- Monitor your competitors
- Monitor your own business
- Monitor yourself
- Live within your means
- Don't waste time
- Support community activities

It doesn't matter where you're employed, these make sense. We must find a way to keep the routine invigorating.

Last year on CNN, and repeated in *USA Today*, the feature story was telling us that in summer camps, canoes have replaced computers. It seems it was as recent as a couple of years ago that the camps turning away young people were those offering technology and futuristic trends. Now, apparently, camp directors have gone back to their warehouses, dusted off their discarded canoes and repainted the oars because the young people want to learn something about living, not just how to perform a task. Almost every trend line that the demographics identifies speaks well for what we're all about. The point is, we're just down-to-earth solid American citizens going about our business of making a living and sharing with others.

At times one might think morals and ethics are something new, the way they're being hyped. Most of us have never thought philosophically about whether we're doing right or wrong. We're just reacting positively from the fine teaching we had as children.

If you'll allow me to try to put it in words, I believe you would agree that these statements make up your convictions:

1. My faith in God means that I recognize and respect all the people God created, whether they be my relatives, associates at work, customers, or even the people I have difficulty liking.
2. My home and family are the foundation for all other relationships I enjoy.
3. My job is the opportunity to use the talents that have been entrusted to me, so it is not necessary that I be smarter than someone else or stronger, but that I be faithful in the job I have. Economic security depends upon abundance, and abundance is the result of industrious and efficient work, which depends upon my being energetic, willing and eager. I believe "profit" to be a wholesome word.

When I started this page by saying that youngsters in camp want canoes instead of computers, it only reflects the feelings of most of us. Whereas we use technology to make us efficient workers, it is our beliefs that give us an effective lifestyle.

This one thing I do, forgetting those things which are behind, and reaching for those things which are before." This sound advice, offered centuries ago by the Apostle Paul, can be the basis for a good week.

The biggest hurdle you and I face is *last* week. Academically, we can tell ourselves that last week is gone and that we cannot do anything about the past. And yet, we try to. We are great at replaying the ballgame. We let the sunshine of this week be shadowed by the week before. Even the first month of the year is named for the Roman god, Janus, who used eyes in the back of his head as well as the front to look backward as well as forward.

Fortunately, we divided our time by days and weeks, each segment offering a new beginning. We only need to forget about last week to be effective this week:

1. Forget personal offenses. If you were hurt last week by a fellow employee, either forget it or be strong enough to talk it out. You must still work together. You will undermine your own work if your eyes are clouded by a grudge. If it was a customer or client who offended you, put it all behind you. Yesterday's hurts have a way of deflating themselves, unless you keep blowing them up.
2. Forget the past failures. Hindsight is always possessed of clearer vision; it's easy to play Monday-morning quarterback and secondguess yourself. Don't fall into the trap of thinking, "If only . . . If only I had done things differently; if only I hadn't made that decision."
3. Forget family problems. Problems of the family will not disappear, but if you have done all in your power to correct them, then put them behind you. Nothing gnaws at your insides like a family problem. You cannot live your children's lives for them; you cannot always reconcile problems between husband and wife—and you certainly cannot do anything about it while you are working.

As Paul emphasized, it is as important to reach out to this week as it is to forget about last week. The best way to forget yesterday's failure is to accept today's challenge.

Today in this country, we have come to take our religious freedom for granted. Too many among us exercise a freedom *from* religion, rather than a freedom *of* religion.

We forget that many of the first settlers and founders of our country were fleeing from the religious persecution of a state church system. The First Amendment to the United States Constitution reads: "Congress shall make no law respecting an establishment of religion, or prohibiting the free exercise thereof." We reduce this simply to the principle of separation of church and state. It means that, but also much more.

Religious freedom means that each person has an inalienable right to choose or not to choose religious beliefs or practices. The First Amendment means:

1. No religious test can be required of any public official.
2. No religious group may have jurisdiction over any governmental matter.
3. Government may not have jurisdiction over religious matters.
4. No religious group or teaching may be endorsed or officially established by government. Nor may it be given preferential treatment.
5. No religious group or teaching may receive government support or promotion even though such support is offered to all alike.
6. No government funds can be expended to support any religious activity or institution.
7. No person may be required to support any religious group or teaching.
8. Every person shall have the right of religious freedom. Religious faith is a voluntary matter arising from the heart of man and must neither be coerced nor restricted by government in any way.

This precious guarantee should make us value the privilege of worship, not neglect the privilege. The price of religious freedom is not eternal vigilance as much as personal commitment to our choice of faith.

Man has a tendency to talk himself into failure. It seems that for every person I meet who is optimistic and at peace, I meet 10 who feel afraid about tomorrow. Perhaps this imbalance is a reflection of our modern environment.

Rarely do I excuse our faults and failings because of the environment we live in. But have you listened critically to a 30-minute newscast lately? Forget trying to absorb what is happening, and concentrate on the tone of the broadcast. We are bombarded with an overemphasis on losses and limitations, misery and suffering. I even know an individual who has just about given up reading newspapers—he says he cannot afford the depressant. You, too, might feel you have enough problems in your own life without hearing the news.

Perhaps you have seen the lithograph that pictures a large, awkwardly designed rowboat, beached on dry land with the oars resting on the sand. What a hopeless picture of failure! But under the picture is the caption, "The tide always comes back." True to that thought, the tide will come in; the boat will float, and the worn and ugly bottom will be hidden underwater.

We can all take a lesson from this simple thought. Certainly, things may be tough today; your job may be going badly; illness may have invaded your home; debts may be piling up. We have all been beached by these low tides in our lives. But wait; be patient; the tide will come back in; you don't have to abandon ship. The person who fails is the one who gives up and surrenders the ship because the tide is out.

When we are troubled, we tend to think that we are the only ones suffering. Remember, when the tide is out for you, it is out for everyone along the coast. We never suffer long. We have *only* to be patient; we have only to plan mentally and spiritually for the tide's return. Sigmund Freud said, "The chief duty of a human being is to endure life."

It was the late William Henry Belk, founder of the stores bearing his name, whom I first heard say, "The customer may not always be right, but he is always your customer." All of us who deal with the public and who depend on them for our success should listen to our customer:

> You often accuse me of carrying a chip on my shoulder—but I suspect that this is because you do not entirely understand me. Isn't it normal to expect satisfaction for one's money spent?

> Ignore my wants and I simply will cease to exist. Satisfy those wants and I will become increasingly loyal. Add to this satisfaction personal attention and whatever friendly touches you can dream up, and I will become a walking advertisement for your services.

> When I criticize your service, take heed. I am not dreaming up displeasure. The source of it lies in something you have failed to do to make my shopping experience as enjoyable as I had anticipated.

> I am much more sophisticated these days than I was a few years ago. I have grown accustomed to better things, and my needs are more complex. I am perfectly willing to spend more money with you, but I insist on good service from you.

> I am, above all, a human being. I am sensitive—especially when I am spending my money. I can't stand being snubbed, ignored or looked down upon. I am proud. My ego needs the nourishment of a friendly, personal greeting from you. It's important to me that you recognize my importance and appreciate my business.

> Whatever my personal habits might be, you can be sure of this—I am a real nut on the type of service that I receive. If I detect signs of carelessness, ill manners or misconduct, you won't see me again.

> I am your customer now, but you must prove to me again and again that I have made a wise decision. You must provide the incentive for me to do business with you, convince me repeatedly that being your customer is a desirable thing. You must provide something extra in service—something superior enough to beckon me away from other places where I might spend my money.

There is certainly nothing immoral about hard work—so long as it is what you want to do and if it is personally satisfying. But there is something dangerous about being trapped *in* your work and trapped *by* your work.

No child wants a doctor dad who is on call all the time; but each of us wants a doctor we can reach at two o'clock in the morning.

We all feel sorry for the lawyer who brings home a bulging briefcase to pore over all weekend; we all feel sorry for him, that is, all except his client.

When it comes to work, we seem to have one set of values for people who are our neighbors, and another set of values for the people we hire. We don't want a recorded phone response when we call the plumber on Saturday, but we may wonder why he and his wife don't show up at a party Saturday night after he's had an emergency call.

Still there is a valid point. Most of us could work less and accomplish more if trivia could be reduced in our lives—trivia that we initiate or trivia we allow others to impose on us.

It seems the many instruments designed to make our lives efficient, such as computers or electronic word processors, have given us more time to inject more activity into our lives and more rewards in our business. Much of this equipment gives us massive information we never really need.

Perhaps we cannot keep rats from racing, and maybe we cannot resist joining the race, but let's be sure the purpose and price are worth it—and insist on enough time between heats to rest.

Henry Steele Commager, one of our more respected historians, says we Americans are self-assured people who feel good about our own power and success. Our culture is predominantly material: our thinking, quantitative. Our genius is inventive, experimental, and practical. We are also careless, good natured, casual, generous, and extravagant. We cherish individualism, but are also conformists. We believe in order, but distrust authority. And above all, we profess faith in democracy, equality, and liberty. In an exploration of the dominant personal and social values of American society, two sociologists, James Christianson and Choon Yang, rank-ordered American values based on people's expressed preferences. This is how Americans ranked American values:

1. Moral integrity (honesty)
2. Personal freedom
3. Patriotism
4. Work (your job)
5. Being practical and efficient
6. Political democracy
7. Helping others
8. Achievement (getting ahead)
9. National progress
10. Material comfort
11. Leisure (recreation)
12. Equality (racial)
13. Individualism (non-conformity)
14. Equality (sexual)

Other scholars concur that most major dilemmas in our society have some relationship to our value system. Our value system is far from being narrow-gauged. Included in it are activism, hard work, achievement, efficiency, materialism, progress, individualism, quality, morality, humanitarianism, and conformity.

It brings to my mind the late Dr. Charles Steinmetz, accepted by all as one of the world's great scientists. Thus, the press listened when they asked him what he thought would be the ultimate development. He replied, "The greatest discoveries will be made along spiritual lines. Some day people will learn that material things do not bring happiness and are of little use in making men and women creative and powerful. Then the scientists of the world will turn their laboratories to the study of God and prayer. When that day comes, the world will see more advancement in one generation than it has in the last four."

How do we face the tragedies of life? Each of us has our own distinctive way of facing grief—similar to others—yet, we each have to be comfortable in some way to fit into perspective that which at the moment is breaking our hearts. In my neighboring city of Thomasville, North Carolina, Don and Julie Clinard faced the tragedy of losing their seven-month-old daughter, Emily Helen. Mother Julie sat down and framed a letter to her baby daughter, which I find is a great affirmation of faith as well as sustaining grace that comes to us in times of tragedy:

My dearest, sweet daughter Emily,

I don't know where to begin to tell you all the thoughts and feelings that I thought we would have a lifetime to share. You are the most precious treasure in my life. The short time we had you in our lives enriched us. We came to know what pure love is. We were so lucky.

I truly believe you would have been a fine person. You seemed to me to be loving and caring.

I never thought I would be writing a letter such as this to you, but rather leaving one behind for you to read.

I had hoped you and I could have shared a lifetime of things, but I don't feel cheated. To have known your smile, your laugh, your touch for the brief time you were with us was special and meaningful. You added so much to our lives and even though you have left this life, we will continue to grow to love and understand the meaning of your life as time passes.

I feel assured that you are in a special place with loving arms surrounding you.

I always wanted a child to love and nurture and having you, Emily, my special daughter, filled me with such completeness. I thank you for that and I thank God for the time we had together. Daddy and I will never be the same, but we will be better for it!

I started writing this letter to tell you things about life, about nature, about love that I felt you would miss, but I realized while writing this that you are a part of it all: when I see a beautiful sunset, hear the waves, smell spring flowers blooming, feel the warm sun on my face, watch a soft snowfall, that you are with me sharing my thoughts and feelings.

I hope with all my heart that you know the joy you brought us and know how much we love you.

Until we meet again, my daughter, be with us, touch us, and know that you were and always will be our baby girl. I Love You—Mama

Monday. Do you look forward to the start of the workweek with excitement or with a sigh of resignation? Do you think of *enduring* Monday through Friday so you can *enjoy* Saturday and Sunday? If so, your attitude could indicate a denial of your own self-importance, a belittling of your own self-worth. Consider the following story:

While rehearsing one of the world's premier orchestras—right in the middle of the combined voices of the chorus, the thunder of the timpani, the blare of the brass, the clash of the cymbals—Sir Michael Costa suddenly pounded his baton on the stand bringing the symphony to an abrupt halt.

"Where is the piccolo?" questioned the conductor. The instrument had ceased to play. The maestro's ear had missed the tiny sound and, most of all, knew the quality of the performance was diminished. The embarrassed piccolo player had considered his role so insignificant that he had taken an unscheduled break. But Sir Michael Costa knew the distinct tones of the piccolo could not be replaced by any other instrument. Without the piccolo, he knew, there could not be a complete performance.

None of us are unimportant or insignificant; none of our jobs or achievements are small. In the economy of our world, just as in the eyes of God, there are no little people. The president of a giant corporation may be recognized as important, but the job cannot be done without the shelves you stock, the cloth you weave, the wood you finish, the sale you make, the machinery you build, the smile you give the new customer. The company cannot survive without you—even if you at times feel like the piccolo player. Business is a vast and harmonious symphony and, to work properly, it takes all the notes and all the instruments.

In my constant travels, I judge a hotel or motel not by the clerk at the registration desk, not by the size of the room, not by the view, not by the television, not by the food, but by the cleanliness of the room. The person who cleans the room determines whether I will return and whether I will recommend it or just forget it.

You are a very important person. Your name is written in the palms of God's hands. For life to be in harmony, it takes even the piccolo player.

Christmas and Hannukah are so filled with memories. Over the years, the gifts we have received might be forgotten, but not the spirit in which they were given and the love which we have shared. An ancient letter, written by Fra Giovanni in 1515 A.D., offers a timeless expression of the true spirit and meaning of this season:

I salute you. I am your friend, and my love for you goes deep. There is nothing I can give you which you have not got; but there is much, very much, that while I cannot give it, you can take. No heaven can come to us unless our hearts find rest in today. Take heaven. No peace lies in the future which is not hidden in this precious little instant. Take peace. The gloom of the world is but a shadow. Behind it, yet within our reach, is joy. There is radiance and glory in the darkness, could we but see, and to see we have only to look. I beseech you to look. Life is so generous a giver, but we, judging its gifts by their coverings, cast them away as ugly or heavy or hard. Remove the coverings and you will find beneath them a living splendor, woven of love, by wisdom, with power. Welcome it, grasp it, and you touch the angel's hand that brings it to you. Everything we call a trial, a sorrow or a duty, believe me, that angel's hand is there; the gift is there and wonder of an over-shadowing presence. Our joys, too. Be not content with them as joys. They, too, conceal diviner gifts. Life is so full of meaning and purpose, so full of beauty beneath its coverings that you will find earth but cloaks your heaven. Courage then to claim it; that is all. But courage you have, and the knowledge that we are pilgrims together, wending through unknown country our way home. And so at this Christmas time I greet you. Not quite as the world sends greetings, but with profound esteem and with the prayer that for you now and forever the day breaks and the shadows flee away.

Time has not dimmed the sentiment nor diminished the wisdom of the message.

Our great nation, its government and its economy, has been built on initiation, invigoration and innovation. That energy has given rise to a "newer is better" marketplace mentality. To the contrary, we need to emphasize improving the quality and efficiency of existing products, instead of worshiping the new and the novel.

Consumers want verifiable value. We resist being manipulated by slick ad copy, by Madison Avenue shenanigans, by "new and improved" promises.

Business, too, must reevaluate its "newer is better" marketing philosophy. A company cannot be all things to all people. Sales must justify the cost of inventory; stocking a new item or starting a new service can be costly. Before you or your company fall victim to the siren song of "the new," review the following guidelines and suggestions:

1. Something new should be added if—and only if—it expands the company's position to serve. The new product or service may erode the success of what you already have, and you may end up "robbing Peter to pay Paul."
2. Anything new you add to your line of services or products must be of the quality that ensures repeat business.
3. If you begin something new, you must have logistical support or you may find yourself unable to deliver on advertised promises.
4. Don't be quick to change if it means abandoning a proven success. You may only need a new presentation, not a new product.
5. You cannot stand still in a competitive world, but beware of doing something new as a cover-up for poor policy. When the novelty of the new wears off, you will be no better off.

Newer does not necessarily mean better.

Laurels and accolades go not to the person who leads the race, but to the one who finishes. Endurance is the great equalizer.

There is always inequality of talent, but there can be equality of endurance. Talented stars are often defeated by those less talented who possess persistence and endurance. We cannot control the skill of our native talents, ours from birth, but we can adopt and develop endurance. Speed may depend on muscle and body form; endurance stems from desire and dedication. Just how can you develop endurance?

1. Establish the goal you wish to reach. The longer the race, the greater the challenge to allocate your strength and have enough left for a sprint at the finish. Likewise, in all areas of life, the greater the goal, the more endurance it takes to reach it. Shallow individuals constantly need to reach goals to boost their ego, and in fact never adopt a goal that is not within easy grasp. The strong, on the other hand, may be disappointed if they miss a goal, but they will never quit. To the strong, a missed goal is simply an added incentive to try again and again.

2. Spend your time in those activities that properly prepare you to reach your ultimate goals. The runner doesn't just step out on the track and run a championship race. The winning runner trains with dedication, diets wisely and concentrates on a goal. If you want to be a winner at your trade or profession, use today as a warm-up.

3. Doing, not dreaming, develops endurance. Motivation experts will advise you to visualize your goals before you begin. This technique carries the danger of your becoming so enamored of the vision in your mind that you sit down and daydream. Goals are attained by hard work, not dreams.

4. Make sure that you don't adopt goals so challenging that you soon feel discouraged by the enormity of the task. The highest mountain and the smallest hill are both climbed one step at a time—the only difference is endurance. The attitude you use to promptly accomplish the most insignificant task at work today is the same attitude that will someday enable you to reach your highest goals.

English author Owen Feltham wrote, "The greatest results in life are usually attained by simple means and the exercise of ordinary qualities. These may for the most part be summed in these two: common sense and perseverance."

What is it that sets the great individual apart, that makes the outstanding leader stand out? Success is measured, not by the thickness of the pocketbook, but by the traits and characteristics that mark greatness and elicit admiration.

Self-restraint, a characteristic that exists only through moral judgment, is the difference between telling the truth and lying, even when the truth doesn't pay. Self-restraint means the ability to make decisions on positive grounds without reaching for extreme solutions.

An understanding of the qualities that have made this country great is another characteristic of greatness. The single quality most misused is a respect for the freedom of people to work for themselves and their families and their communities, and to do so with a minimum of government interference.

Another quality is an inner calm that allows the leader to cut through crisis and make decisions from a base of mature reflection. It was Napoleon's contention that genius in war belongs to the person who can do the average thing when those around him grow hysterical with emotion and fright.

Experience is another valuable trait. Ambition is fine, but rising to the top too soon can be risky. Experience is an able teacher; a crisis is handled deftly by the person accustomed to crisis. Experience, however, is not to be confused with endurance. Frederick the Great was once asked to promote an officer simply because of his long tenure and faithful service. Pointing to a pack mule, the Prussian king replied, "That mule has carried the pack loyally and effectively for 12 years, but he is still a mule."

Strength of character means leadership and advice result from principle, not expediency. Such a person never runs in the face of adversity or becomes a coward when the going gets tough.

We process the finest hams!"—a comment made to me that just excited me. The employee might be identified as an insignificant member of a large corporation, but he felt responsible about his company. This speaks well for the employee and also the company.

When an employee uses "we" it can sound like he is assigning importance to himself that maybe he doesn't deserve. However, good companies want to hear employees use "we." Each employee is that important to the company. The company feels rewarded when an employee wants to use "we." Such a wholesome attitude doesn't come about automatically nor is it the result of "life service." Companies that give employees a sense of belonging do many of the following things:

1. They clearly announce or inform the employees of policy decisions. They don't judge or reprimand employees on policy that hasn't been clearly stated. Good companies have basic policies as opposed to "hip-pocket" decisions that change constantly.

2. Good companies are listeners. They want to know what their people think about their work. They don't wait for comments. They solicit by questioning employees and asking for suggestions.

3. Good companies take employees into confidence and announce goals as well as new products. The companies want the sales goals and the production people to be related. Any new product is announced to the employees first. Their reaction is good to have and their enthusiasm is necessary for successful production.

4. Admirable companies carefully train new employees, feeling they can only expect what a person is trained to do. If the employee is to be corrected, it is done in private so as not to embarrass. Also, such correction is done while hearing the employee's side as well.

A group of young people was asked what they thought made a mature person. In other words, as they were growing, what did they think they would have to possess if they were to be called mature? Interestingly enough, patience seemed to come out as one of the top characteristics of maturity. Patience they defined in several ways—patience to keep working at a job until it is done; not for short-term benefits but for long-term results. Patience also meant that it is true that it takes "two to tango," meaning when other people were quick to express temper, lose their cool, the mature person patiently seeks to calm the situation or at least change the course from the irritation.

The second characteristic of the mature person is that such a person has a concern for others and has reached a point where he or she is not so wrapped up in themselves that they can overlook the hurts of others. Check the community needs and find how often young people are on the cutting edge of trying to solve the problems. They are out there gathering up the used clothes which will help someone else. They are bringing the coal to the cold. They are volunteering to sit with the elderly and lonely. They may be impetuous but they often stand up with courage while our age becomes somewhat cynical and figures there is nothing that can be done to change the course of human events.

Third, young people also felt that the mature person has enough courage to be different—not to go along with the crowd but to find his or her way to individuality. That does not mean they want to be different for just the sake of difference, even though there is a temptation to do that when we're young. We sometimes felt that to find our own identity we had to stand out in the crowd. Basically, these young people felt they had a responsibility to contribute their unique individuality rather than become faceless and nameless.

That's what young people think, but I feel that what they concluded was not just for youth, but just as true for middle-agers and above—that patience, compassion, and individual responsibility are good traits for young people to learn and adults to practice.

While we of the Christian faith are caught up in Christmas, we should not forget our Jewish friends and neighbors who are celebrating Chanukah around the same time of year. Often, we hear people mistakenly refer to Chanukah as the "Jewish Christmas." Here is the real meaning of Chanukah.

Pronounced with a guttural sound, Chanukah is the Hebrew word for "dedication." This eight-day holiday commemorates the rededication of the Second Temple of Jerusalem 165 years before the birth of Jesus. The temple had been desecrated by the Syrian troops under a monarch named Antiochus, heir to Alexander the Great. He imposed idolatry and unfair taxes on the lands under his rule—only the people of tiny Judea refused to bow before his idols.

Antiochus brought in a huge army to break the Israelites, who in response employed the first effective guerilla warfare. Led by Judas Maccabeus and his four brothers, the Israelites for three years defeated their much larger foe. The victorious Israelites proceeded to cleanse and rededicate the temple. Within the temple they found only enough undefiled oil to burn for one day. According to legend, the one-day supply of oil miraculously burned for eight days.

Chanukah is observed with prayers, family meals, games and songs, and gift-giving. A special prayer calls upon the worshiper in the memory of the Maccabee-led Israelites to now "battle against apathy, ignorance and intolerance which still threaten to extinguish Thy lamps and to destroy Thine altars." Eight candles are burned, beginning with one and adding another each night. A ninth candle, called the *shamus* or servant candle, is used to light the others, symbolizing the Israelites mandate to add light and enlightenment to society.

As we celebrate Christmas, let us remember that, according to the Gospel of John, Jesus celebrated the Festival of Chanukah (Dedication). Let us join with our Jewish friends in the spirit of Chanukah, celebrating a victory in the struggle for freedom of conscience and the light of liberty.

"Christmas is not a day or a season, but a condition of heart and mind. If we love our neighbors as ourselves; if in our riches we are poor in spirit and in our poverty we are rich in grace; if our charity vaunteth not itself, but suffereth long and is kind; if when our brother asks for a loaf, we give ourselves instead; if each day dawns in opportunity and sets in achievement, however small—then every day is Christ's day and Christmas is always near." These beautiful lines were penned by James Wallingford.

During this holiday season, as Christmas draws near, let us remember that it is a holy time of year. Christmas is the time, as Paul Scherer so touchingly expresses it, when "God walked down the stairs of heaven with a Baby in His arms." Let us remember also that Christ was born in the first century, but He belongs to all time. He was born a Jew, but He belongs to all races. He was born in Bethlehem, yet He belongs to all countries.

As beautiful as the cards and wrappings, lights and decorations that appear during this season are the sentiments of various eloquent individuals concerning Christmas. Edgar DeWitt captured his feelings in "If Every Day Were Christmas":

> If the spirit of Christmas were with us every day, some revolutionary events would occur. Selfishness would die a death of starvation. Avarice would be hung higher than Haman. Foolish pride would go down in crushing defeat. Senseless strife and silly bickerings would shame each other to death. The prayer of Jesus for the unity of His followers would be answered. Racial animosities would be drowned in a sea of brotherhood. "Peace on earth" would become a glorious reality.

Without the love that we offer, receive and share at this time of year, Christmas would be a dreary occasion indeed. Expressing this sentiment, Roy L. Smith said, "He who has not Christmas in his heart will never find it under a tree." The true meaning of Christmas is there for all who wish to find it. But then, so is Christ. Our individual and family customs may differ at Christmastime, but the one thing we all have in common is the Christ child.

This Christmas season is a time to celebrate the glory of life, the joy of love, and the spirit of giving. The following stories, each in an unusual and different way, illustrate the essence of the season.

As Christmas approached, a missionary serving in Africa told his native students how Christians express their joy by exchanging gifts on Christ's birthday. On Christmas morning, one of the natives brought the missionary an extraordinarily beautiful seashell. When asked where he had discovered such a gorgeous shell, the native replied that he had walked for many miles to a remote bay, the only site where such shells could be found. The missionary praised and thanked his pupil for traveling so far to obtain such a lovely gift. His eyes sparkling, the native answered, "Long walk part of gift."

The spirit of giving is at its highest when it embraces compassion. An American journalist covering the savage fighting during one battle of the Korean war came upon an advanced medical outpost. Inside, he watched as a nurse prepared a wounded soldier for surgery. The man was bloody and filthy, but the nurse went about her work without hesitation. Fascinated by the bold juxtaposition of the gruesome evidence of man's inhumanity to man and the wonderful proof of human tenderness and compassion, the hard-boiled newspaperman said softly, "Sister, I wouldn't do that for a million dollars." The nurse, without stopping in her work, replied even softer, "Brother, neither would I."

Each of us has a contribution to make to life. We have only to discover what that is and do it with a willing, generous spirit. Henry David Thoreau expressed this idea: "A man is rich in proportion to the things he can do without. Sell your goods and keep your thoughts."

Christmas, with all its planning and shopping and celebrating, has grown far beyond a one-day occasion. So, too, the spirit and true meaning of Christmas can last far beyond that special day. The classic "Keeping Christmas" by Henry Van Dyke can help us keep Christmas in its proper perspective:

> There is a better thing than the observance of Christmas and that is keeping Christmas.
>
> Are you willing to forget what you have done for other people and to remember what other people have done for you?
>
> To ignore what the world owes you and to think of what you owe the world?
>
> To know that the only good reason for your existence is not what you are going to get out of life, but what you are going to give to life?
>
> Are you willing to stoop down and consider the needs and desires of little children?
>
> To remember the weakness and loneliness of people who are growing old?
>
> To stop asking how much your friends like you and ask yourself whether you love them enough?
>
> To try to understand what those who live in the same house with you really want without waiting for them to tell you?
>
> To trim your lamp so it will give more light and less smoke and to carry it in front so that your shadow will fall behind you?
>
> To make a grave for your ugly thoughts and a garden for your kindly feelings with the gate open?
>
> Are you willing to do these things even for a day?
>
> Then you can keep Christmas.
>
> Are you willing to believe that love is the strongest thing in the world . . . stronger than death . . . and that the Blessed Life which began in Bethlehem nineteen hundred years ago is the image and brightness of Eternal Life?
>
> Then you can keep Christmas; and if you keep it for a day, why not always? But you can't keep it alone.

While we are caught up in the excitement of the Christmas season, we cannot let our joy blind our eyes or limit our concern. While we struggle to guess what our loved ones need that they don't already have, there are millions in the world who would gratefully settle for bread.

As we think of Christ at Christmas, let us recall the basic tenet of the prayer He taught His disciples: "Give us this day our daily bread." The prayer's emphasis on bread indicates that God is concerned about our total life. Somehow we think of God in the dramatic, calling upon Him in times of crisis and fear and despair; and yet He is also present for our mundane daily needs as well. Praying for our daily bread also acknowledges our dependence upon God. We often acquire an arrogance in life and must be reminded that life itself is a gift created by God.

If you are old enough to remember the years prior to World War II when unemployment was 14 percent, you know what it was for America literally to pray for bread. Today, thankfully, almost all the people of our nation have something to eat. In other troubled corners of the world, however, people pray for enough bread just to live through the next 24 hours.

During the past five years, more people have starved to death than all the casualties of all the world's wars and revolutions and earthquakes. Thousands of children, each as precious as your own, die of starvation each day.

Does such news tug at our hearts, does it compel us, does it move us to action? Or do we accept the reports of thousands dying? God will not accept such and has placed the solution in our hands. He will guide us, but we must be his instruments.

So during this joyous season, pause and look beyond your own doorstep, beyond your own family. Reach out and let the spirit of Christmas be seen clearly in you.

Where do you begin to help the world? Your world may begin with the family of your community that needs your help—the Salvation Army has a kettle on the street corner. Christmas is giving ... and giving.

Next to the fireplace in our den hangs a handmade bellows to help light the fire. What I like is that the craftsman who made them for me carved his name in the wood. In our trophy case are some delicately crafted birds. They are made from driftwood by the skilled hands of an artist in New Hampshire, and he proudly signed his work. There are a number of other keepsakes whose value is enhanced because the craftsman signed his work.

There was a day when a man's word was his bond and his signature was his contract. Growing up in Massachusetts we heard so often, "Sign your John Hancock." As a lad I wondered why Mr. Day would ask Mr. Richardson to sign his "John Hancock." My mom explained that John Hancock was a signer of the Declaration of Independence, who probably had the most even and legible hand. His writing bespoke identity, pride and quality. Of course, an insurance company used the name to world class success.

Have you seen the TV commercial where everyone signs his work? The garment worker would put his name on the pajamas; the upholsterer would sign the chair; the brickmason would sign the cornerstone; the weaver would sign the cloth; the mechanic would sign the work order.

Signing would give us recognition but, better still, would be assuming responsibility. It would encourage the repairman to fix it right the first time—the clothier to ship the suit with buttons sewn tight—the busy waiter to pick up the food order before it cools in the kitchen—the cleaner to remove the spot before pressing it in permanently—the lawyer moving expediently so the infraction doesn't become a major case—the doctor not abandoning you in the waiting room until your common cold is complicated by the disease you contracted from the contagious patient sitting next to you.

Quality is caring, and such caring, encouraged and exemplified from the top down, becomes a corporate culture.

If your work is once begun,
Never leave it till it's done;
Be the labor great or small,
Do it well or not at all.

Christmas is a day of tradition and legend. We do the same thing each year without apology and actually with gusto. We accept without question these practices, feeling Christmas is only Christmas with them. For instance:

Today the Christmas tree is a center of our festivities. Topped with a star and glittering with lights and ornaments, it is a part of the beauty and meaning of the Christmas season.

How did the Christmas tree come to play such an important part in the observance of Christmas?

There is a legend that comes down to us from the early days of Christianity in England. One of those helping to spread Christianity among the Druids was a monk named Wilfred (later, Saint Wilfred). One day, surrounded by a group of his converts, he struck down a huge oak tree, which, in the Druid religion, was an object of worship.

As it fell to the earth, the oak tree split into four pieces and from its center sprang up a young fir tree. The crowd gazed in amazement.

Wilfred let his axe drop and turned to speak. "This little tree shall be your Holy Tree tonight. It is the wood of peace, for your houses are built of the fir. It is the sign of an endless life, for its leaves are evergreen. See how it points towards the heavens? Let this be called the tree of the Christ Child. Gather about it, not in the wilderness, but in your homes. There it will be surrounded with loving gifts and rites of kindness."

And to this day, that is why the fir tree is one of our loveliest symbols of Christmas.

A bonus of the Christmas tree is the sharing that comes when the family joins in decorating the tree. Here is an evening spent in warm spirits and anticipation.

Dwight Vredenberg, a successful food executive in Iowa, stands out as a reminder that business isn't easy, but success depends upon our philosophy and attitude as much as our work and energy. His definition of what it takes to be a successful grocer could apply to all our businesses:

1. There is no substitute for hard work.

2. We must like people and have an inherent sense of fairness in dealing with them, whether customers or employees.

3. We must give back some of what we earn. That means investing back into our own store or company. I have never seen a successful operator who didn't put some of his profits back into updating and upgrading his operation.

4. We must pay our "civic dues." That doesn't mean big financial contributions to every fund drive. Be selective. But it also means giving of ourselves to worthy causes, such as the Chamber of Commerce, Boy Scouts, church work.

5. Look at the food distribution business as one industry from farm to table, and look at our policies and procedures from the broadest possible viewpoint. Obviously self-interest is essential for survival, but it should be enlightened self-interest. We should realize that anything we do which hurts another segment of the industry may well weaken the whole industry and ourselves.

6. We must live within our financial means and must manage our balance sheet. Growth is important. It provides for the reinvestment of profits. It is a great incentive, a great morale booster for our people. It also gives great personal satisfaction to the proprietors. It is heady stuff. But it is also dangerous stuff if not controlled. When growth is dictated by ego rather than good analytical business judgment, it can lead to dangerous excesses.

7. Keep up with the state of the art, but don't be first in line for every new innovation. Let someone else do the pioneering.

8. We must dedicate ourselves to give the customer honest value. We try to emphasize to our managers that they should price their goods as cheaply as possible, consistent with a decent profit.

How often do you use the phrase, "The best laid plans of mice and men often go astray"? But, do you know the origin of the phrase?

Robert Burns, one of the classic poets of the English language, was the toast of Scotland in his day. In 1785, while plowing a field on his farm, he turned over a mouse's nest. Instead of killing the mouse, he watched the helpless creature dart about wondering what had happened to the nest that had taken so long to build. The sorrow the poet felt for the tiny mouse inspired him to write these lines:

But, mouse, thou art not thyself alone,
In proving foresight may be vain;
The best-laid plans o' mice an' men,
Oft go awry an' leave us not but grief and pain,
For promised joy.

Thankfully, a great many of us are perfectly satisfied with our living. This doesn't mean we are easily satisfied, but that we have been fortunate enough to achieve our basic goals. Others are not as fortunate.

Has this year been a year of dissatisfaction and disappointment for you? Perhaps you felt it was to be a year of success, but your plans went astray—your job didn't work out as planned, you didn't get the promotion you sought, you didn't build that addition onto your store.

If you were disappointed by this year, it may seem too easy and cheap to advise, "Don't give up; keep trying." But the advice holds true. A man I tried to help land three jobs last year, all to no avail, finally found a job that exceeded his greatest expectations. His successful secret is that he was prepared and kept improving his skills. He became more determined with each rejection because he was a man, not a mouse. Each closed door made him even more enthusiastic when the right door did open.

May that same outlook be yours and mine!

Anyone who ever served in the armed forces or was married to a serviceman or, perhaps, has ever watched "From Here To Eternity" or some other military film, is familiar with the term AWOL—either pronounced letter by letter or jargonized as "AY-wall"—Absent Without Leave. And, those who served in the military know the consequences.

Today, however, we joke about playing hooky—whether it's a child from school, a worker at a plant or an executive talking about a floating holiday. We have come to believe and accept the adage, "Don't buy a car built in Detroit on a Monday," meaning that such a car was shoddily thrown together by a skeleton workforce reduced by chronic absenteeism.

Add to industrial absenteeism the perpetual tardiness, abuse of coffee breaks and extended lunch hours. We are only fooling ourselves and fooling away our responsibility—as a result, other countries are outproducing us. America's declining productivity is not a lack of machinery, but a lack of motivation. Let's look at the causes, some justified and some not.

Today's employee lives farther and farther from the work place. With the increase in distance have come increases in traffic volume and driving time, more time committed to work. The employee arrives at work tired and irritated, then dreads the drive home.

Today's life is more complicated and there are more and more errands and commitments to juggle. If your car needs repairs, for instance, you have to take it in during normal working hours since few dealers have night or weekend hours.

Today's affluency allows us to play hard on weekends. When this exercise is added to our emotional frustrations, we may not be in shape to work on Monday.

Today's executive sets a poor example. Employee absenteeism rose 10 percent one year, but manager absenteeism jumped by 25 percent.

We would never rob from another, but what should we call it when we don't show up for work as promised? Let's don't be like the fellow whose manager exclaimed, "Joe, you only averaged four days a week" and Joe explained, "Gee, Boss, I just can't make it on three."

We adults tend to go around asking ourselves and each other what is wrong with America. The very question forces a negative response. Kids, on the other hand, view life with a refreshing innocence and naivete'. Not long ago, a group of youngsters were questioned at random on what they liked about the United States. Here is a sample of the answers:

Jackie, age 9—"We've got more stuff and things in America than anywhere in the world. We have pizza as well and it don't grow any other place on earth except maybe Italy."

Heather, age 5—"America is the best because people in other countries are smaller and they get trodden on easy."

Elliott, age 9—"Everybody wants to live in America because we own the moon. The President bought the moon from God for a million dollars and I saw him send spacemen up on T.V."

Tina, age 6—"America is great because you get the best friends here. The last time I counted, I had a thousand friends—and I don't know anyone with as many friends as me."

David, age 9—"America is great because it's bigger and has more supermarkets. I don't know much about other countries except Russia. I know there's a lot of Russians in Russia."

Jonathan, age 8—"Other countries aren't free like America. They won't let you go to church and if you do, they throw you in prison and whip you."

Sean, age 9—America is great because they have the most plumbers in the world. That's because we've got more tubs. I want to be a plumber like my uncle 'cause he's real rich."

And Lew, age 6, brings us back down to earth. Asked what he liked about America, this youngster replied, "What's America . . .?"

We have done clouds an injustice and a disservice. In our lexicon of common usage, we endow the sun with a meaning of sunshine, brightness, warmth, a good day. At the same time, we identify clouds with rain, darkness, gloom, the undesirable.

In all fairness, haven't we all felt relief on a scorching day when the sun ducked behind the shield of a welcome cloud? And, haven't we all looked longingly at distant clouds during a long dry spell and hoped they would bring rain our way? And which of us as children played with our imaginations, creating images out of the cloud formations chasing each other across the sky? Even in ancient history, the Israelites believed God used a cloud to lead them toward the Promised Land.

Even the darkest, most ominous black cloud will hover for only a short duration. The clouds in our lives can be a challenge if we take them in stride. Life is never free of disappointments; the test is whether we master what may devastate another. Two people at a particular company, for example, might have lost the promotion each expected. One became sour and quit. The other asked his supervisor, "How can I improve myself to become more valuable to our company and entrusted with more responsibility?"

George Handel, the celebrated composer, survived an illness that left him paralyzed for a time, and he also became blind later in life. His creditors were knocking on the door. Instead of succumbing to the dark clouds, he sat down and composed *The Messiah* with its majestic "Hallelujah Chorus." John Bunyan, imprisoned unjustly for 12 years, didn't sit and curse the darkness of his clouds. Instead, he wrote the book many consider second only to the Bible—*Pilgrim's Progress.*

Clouds, if accepted with the right attitude, can break the monotony of a clear blue sky. Like a child looking for images in the clouds, we need to look for opportunity in the cloudy days of our lives, to make positive use of our imaginations. Not only will the clouds pass sooner, but the rainbows will be more colorful.

Who cares about the upperdog? Historically, America has always pulled for the underdog. Coaches have tried to keep their teams the underdog for their advantage. Court decisions in recent years have seemed to favor the underdog at the expense of the majority.

Dr. Miller Upton at Beloit College wrote:

> I have just about reached the end of my tolerance for the way our society now seems to have sympathetic concern only for the misfit, the chronic criminal, the underachiever. It seems to me we have lost touch with reality and have become warped in our attachments.
>
> I feel it is time for someone like me to stand up and say, in short, "I'm for the upperdog."
>
> I'm for the achiever—the one who sets out to do something and does it; the one who recognizes the problems and opportunities at hand, and endeavors to deal with them; the one who is successful at his immediate task because he is not worrying about someone else's failing; the one who doesn't consider it *square* to be constantly looking for more to do, who isn't always rationalizing why he shouldn't be doing what he is doing; the one who, in short, carries the work of his part of the world squarely on his shoulders.
>
> It is important to recognize that the quality of any society is directly related to the quality of the individuals who make it up. Therefore, let us stop referring naively to creating a "great" society. It is enough at this stage of our development to aspire to create a decent society. And to do so, our first task is to help each individual be decent unto himself and in his relationship with other individuals.
>
> We will never create a good society, much less a great one, until individual excellence and achievement are not only respected but also encouraged. That is why I am for the upperdog—the achiever, the succeeder.

Thank you, Dr. Upton. For years I've instructed sales managers not to waste all their time with the unsuccessful salesman. it will pull the average down. Instead, continue emphasis on the winners and it will challenge the others to pull up.

Our interest in the underdog may not be mercy but a superficial feeling of superiority felt by being able to look down on someone while the upperdog may actually make us jealous. Don't be jealous—be challenged.

You've heard of the Australian who bought a new boomerang but couldn't throw the old one away. It kept coming back to hit him. Hate is like a boomerang. It always destroys the sender.

Forgiveness can be man's most serious problem. I chat with people who are being destroyed because they cannot forgive themselves. Others have directed all their energy to gain revenge and, with such a one-way desire, are missing the positive joys of living.

Upon the assassination of Abraham Lincoln, Mrs. Lincoln chided the president's bodyguard for not having kept a more watchful eye. The guard had loved President Lincoln and was deeply repentant for any neglect on his part. His only explanation was that he couldn't believe anyone would destroy the life of someone as good as President Lincoln. He felt all people shared his respect and affection for the president.

Mrs. Lincoln dismissed him, "So now, it's really not you I can't forgive. It is the assassin."

Young Tad Lincoln overheard his mother's confrontation with the guard and said quietly to himself, "If Pa had lived, he would have forgiven the man who shot him. Pa forgave everybody."

Few of us need to be sold on the value of forgiveness. We believe academically in forgiving. Our weakness is practicing what we believe.

Jesus gave us two instructions. When Peter asked if forgiving someone seven times as commanded by Mosaic Code wasn't enough. Jesus said, "No! Seventy times seven!"

The other lesson of Jesus was a parable about a king who found one of his merchant subjects owed the kingdom a vast sum, maybe for uncollected taxes. The king forgave the merchant, but the king was shocked to hear that the merchant grabbed people who owed him small amounts and literally choked the money out of them.

The king ordered the merchant back to the palace and demanded: "You scoundrel! Here I forgave you a tremendous debt just because you asked, but you are unmerciful to your small debtors. Away to torture for you!"

Jesus was suggesting we are to forgive as we are forgiven.

Forgiveness is a heavenly gift, but also a selfish one. Forgiveness given results in inner peace and solace. Better to be like my dad when I asked for forgiveness: "Son, I forgave you when you did the deed, but your request clears the air between us. Now we're together."

NOTES

NOTES

NOTES

NOTES

NOTES

NOTES

NOTES

NOTES

NOTES

NOTES

NOTES

NOTES

NOTES

NOTES